2

TAX POLICY-MAKING
IN THE UNITED KINGDOM

TAX POLICY-MAKING IN THE UNITED KINGDOM

A STUDY OF RATIONALITY, IDEOLOGY AND POLITICS

Ann Robinson
and
Cedric Sandford

Heinemann Educational Books

Heinemann Educational Books Ltd
22 Bedford Square, London WC1B 3HH

LONDON   EDINBURGH   MELBOURNE   AUCKLAND
HONG KONG   SINGAPORE   KUALA LUMPUR   NEW DELHI
IBADAN   NAIROBI   JOHANNESBURG
EXETER (NH)   KINGSTON   PORT OF SPAIN

ISBN 0 435 84784 8 cased
ISBN 0 435 84785 6 paper

Typeset by Inforum Ltd, Portsmouth
Printed in Great Britain by Biddles Ltd, Guildford, Surrey

Contents

Acknowledgements

Our thanks must go first to the many busy people, including ministers, MPs, civil servants, party officials, officers of interest groups and academics, who generously gave up their time for interviews, often spent further time validating a transcript and, in one or two cases, sent us written notes on matters on which we sought information. Without their help the study would not have been possible.

Likewise our gratitude goes to the Social Science Research Council whose contribution in financing the study was no less vital.

We are grateful to the editor of *Accountancy*, for permission to reproduce, in Chapter 6, material (principally Figures 6.9 and 6.10) first published by one of the authors in that journal and to the editors of *British Tax Review* for permission to reproduce, in Chapter 7, material on Green Papers which first appeared in *British Tax Review*.

Professor Richard Rose and Professor Rudolf Klein both made valuable comments on the study in its early stages. Donald Ironside and the late Mrs Dorothy Johnstone gave us their helpful comments on an early draft. We are no less indebted to the considerable number of distinguished people who were kind enough to read and comment upon all or part of the penultimate draft of the manuscript: Anthony Christopher, John King, Michael O'Higgins, Chris Patten MP, Sir Norman Price, Dr Brian Smith, Valerie Strachan and Robert Willis. The book has been much improved as a result of their perceptive remarks. On this occasion even more than most, the authors stress that none of these readers has any responsibility for the errors that remain or the opinions expressed – these can be laid only at the door of the authors.

We wish to thank Vilma Flegmann for assistance with much of the documentary research, and Barbara Hall, ably assisted by Sue Powell, for speedy, accurate and good-natured typing.

Our final word of appreciation must go to Michael Robinson and Evelyn Sandford for their forbearance, especially during the final stages of writing; and to David Hill of Heinemann Educational Books for his understanding at the repeated delays to the manuscript.

Ann Robinson
Cedric Sandford
Centre for Fiscal Studies, University of Bath

Introduction

Taxation is one of the most contentious of political topics and it lies at the very heart of politics. Historically, in Britain and elsewhere, taxation, when deemed arbitrary or oppressive, has been a potent solvent of constitutional change and a cause of revolution. Today, the nature and extent of taxation and of public expenditure (which implies taxation) has profound effects on the economy and society. Yet, curiously, taxation has been little studied as a discrete phenomenon by modern political scientists. A few studies have been made of the tax policy process in the United States (Surrey, 1957, 1973; Sharkansky, 1969; Break and Pechman, 1975; Pechman, 1977), but even there no comprehensive body of knowledge has yet been established. In the United Kingdom even less attention has been paid to tax policy-making. There are many technical descriptions and analyses of individual taxes, there are descriptions of some features of the tax policy-making environment (Brittan, 1971; Johnstone, 1975), but no real attempt to make a systematic and comprehensive survey of the way in which tax policy is formed. Despite its crucial importance, the widespread complaints that taxes commonly generate, and the recognition of defects in the policy process, we have little idea of how our tax system came to be as it is – whether as a result of economic forces, political ideology, bureaucratic power, or other influences.

Perhaps one reason for the neglect of taxation as a discrete element of policy is that it is often thought of simply as a tool of short-term economic management, rather than as an element of policy in its own right. Another reason is that policy-making is generally studied by political scientists, and tax is a highly technical subject little understood except by specialists. Specialists in tax, however, tend to be interested in analysis of its details rather than in discovering how those details came to be as they are. As tax has become more technical and more complex in recent years the problems of studying its development have increased. The skills of an economist specialising in public finance and interested in the political process, would have to be combined with the skills of a political scientist knowledgeable about economics, to unravel the complexities of tax policy-making. We, as political scientist and economist, have tried to provide such an analysis in this book.

Given the complexities of a study of policy-making what would be the best approach to adopt? Policy studies have, so far, consisted of two basic methodological types: those that attempt to relate aggregate changes in political outputs at national or local government level to broad explanatory theories and individual case studies. Each has its advantages and disadvantages.

The 'global' or correlational approach to the study of political outputs suffers from being too broad and too crude. And it can be used only to test existing theories – it can generate no new data of its own. Case studies have their shortcomings too. They are about unique events, specific and circumscribed. Valid generalisations cannot be made from data generated from a single case study. If several case studies presented together have no integrating thread of theory (Heidenheimer, Heclo and Adams, 1976; Coombes *et al.*, 1976), they will amount to little more than useful description – they cannot explain. Moreover, case studies tend to produce pluralistic explanations of the policy-making process. Many factors appear to be significant, but it is difficult to assess the relative importance of any of them. But case studies are particularly useful when a subject – like that of tax policy-making in the United Kingdom – is unexplored territory. Their tendency to produce pluralistic explanations can, to some extent, be overcome by presenting a series of case studies on closely related topics, preferably undertaken by the same researchers using the same broad tools, as the basis for comparative analysis. Comparisons between cases provide some clues as to the relative significance of different factors present in the policy-making process. A group of case studies can also be used to test a large variety of different theories of the policy-making process already developed by political scientists. This is what we have attempted.

Our study is based on eight detailed cases. Six (counting the two forms of corporation tax) are new taxes introduced since 1964: capital gains tax, corporation tax (classical system), selective employment tax, corporation tax (imputation system), value added tax and capital transfer tax. Two are 'taxes'* that passed through the initial stages of policy-making but never reached the statute book (though neither can be regarded as permanently dead): the tax-credit scheme and an annual wealth tax.

In Chapter 1 we examine the objectives that the new taxes were intended to achieve and we consider a variety of different modes of decision-making. The modes of decision-making provide 'theories' of the policy process that we shall test with our cases. In the second chapter we examine briefly the origins of each new tax in turn, describe its original form as introduced, and note subsequent changes. There-

---

* It is convenient to refer to the tax-credit scheme as a 'tax', although the proposed credits were to replace not only tax allowances but also some social security benefits.

after, we compare and contrast the treatment accorded to the various taxes at each stage of the policy-making process – in the political parties, in the government departments and at the various Parliamentary stages. We also examine the process of pre-legislative consultation and the role of interest groups. In the final chapter the wheel comes full circle. We re-examine theories of the policy-making process in the light of our findings on new taxes and try to answer the question 'What determines policy on new taxes?' Our conclusions also help us to assess the shortcomings of the policy-making process and re-evaluate some of the criticisms that have been advanced by politicians and commentators on supposed deficiencies.

An immediate question will spring to the mind of the perceptive reader: 'Why restrict the study to new taxes?' Changes in tax rates may have more social and economic significance than changes in the tax structure. Moreover the creation of new taxes is not the only way of effecting structural change. Unheralded and so-called temporary modifications to the tax structure, such as the measures of stock relief introduced into the United Kingdom in November 1974, can have profound effects. Fundamental changes in the tax structure can also take place simply by default, by a failure to adjust the system to external cirumstances – of which a notable example in the United Kingdom is the way inflation without indexation was allowed to alter quite dramatically the incidence of income tax on families of different sizes and income levels in the period 1974–7, and to change significantly the balance of direct to indirect taxation. All this we admit. Our failure to include such changes in our study (save incidentally) is in part a practical response to the enormous scope of the subject area. The field of study had, of necessity, to be circumscribed and drawing the boundaries in such a way as to include only new taxes had the advantage, *prima facie*, that objectives, origins, motives and processes ought to emerge more clearly. New taxes are the outcome of positive political decisions to make a policy change, rather than the product of inertia or negative decisions. They are the result of 'critical' decisions as opposed to 'routine' decisions (Bauer and Gergen, 1968, p.2). Moreover, there have been an unusual number of such decisions on taxation in the period from 1964, and several Finance Bills have been dominated by new tax legislation and, in subsequent years, by amendments to 'tidy-up'.

Here questions of definition arise. First, what is a tax? This may seem an otiose question, but it can be argued with considerable justification that the national insurance contribution is properly regarded as a tax and that the changes in 1966 involving the addition of an earnings-related element constituted a major structural change. Subsequently the unification of the flat rate and earnings-related components effectively turned the national insurance contribution into a (largely) proportional tax. However, the decisions on the national insurance contribution took place largely outside the usual tax policy-making environment and encompassed many different considerations, and it would have taken us too far afield to have included them. Second, when is a tax new? Two debatable candidates emerge during the period 1964–76. Should the unified income tax be counted in as a new tax and should corporation tax (imputation system) be left out? We have taken the view that a tax should be regarded as new if it embodies a major change of principle. The changes by which Anthony (now Lord) Barber combined income tax and surtax in a new unified income tax structure, effective from 1973, did not seem to us to involve a major change of principle save in matters of administration; it was therefore excluded. On the other hand the change in corporation tax from the classical system (with its complete separation of company tax from income tax) to a system which imputed a credit to income tax payers, did represent a significant change of principle; accordingly corporation tax mark II is treated as a new tax.

Finally, in the case of new taxes different policy-making processes are generally employed from those used to make adjustments to existing taxes. All the taxes that we consider represented attempts to alter the basic structure of taxation and, as such, most of them followed a long process of investigation and consultation. Changes in the structure of existing taxes, however, are often desired for short-term objectives such as demand management, even if in the end the cumulative effect of many such changes is to alter the structure of taxation. Such short-term changes often require speed of response from policymakers and hence a different set of policy processes are appropriate.

It was not possible for us to include all new taxes introduced between 1964 and 1976. This was a period of 'tax reform' that followed closely on the period of economic policy reappraisal of the early 1960s. More new taxes were created in this particular period than before or since. We have included only those taxes that may be regarded as 'mainstream' – taxes likely directly to affect a very large number of persons or firms. Thus we have omitted a number of new taxes during the period (some of them very short-lived): the 'special charge' for 1967–8, licence duty for off-course betting, car tax, development gains tax and development land tax, and petroleum revenue tax.

Two main methods were used in the study – documentary analysis and interviews. Documents consulted included Finance Bills and Acts, debates and statements in Parliament, Green and White Papers, reports of, and evidence presented to, select committees of the House of Commons, election manifestos and other party political literature, reports and pamphlets produced by interest groups, and political commentaries, biographies and autobiographies. Interviews were held with about one hundred people concerned with the various stages of the policy-making process: ministers and MPs, civil servants, officials in the party organisations and representatives of pressure groups. It should be noted that the terms 'official' and 'minister' and 'Member of Parliament' are used, without distinction, for past as well as for present holders of these positions. This procedure protects anonymity by making the individual less readily identifiable and ensures that the description, on this wider definition, is accurate for the reader, for a present minister at the time of writing may have become a past minister at the time of reading. Interviews were semi-structured, the structure being determined by the point occupied by the respondent in the policy process. Interviewees were, without exception, frank and helpful. The evidence of interviewees may, of course, be unreliable either because of faulty memory or because of a desire to present an issue in a particular light. To guard against this danger no interview material is used in this book which is not corroborated by documentary evidence or the testimony of other interviewees, save in the case of opinion recorded as such. In many cases, to ensure the accuracy of the interview transcripts, reference was made back to the interviewees.

Thus, in this book, by use of published data and of the personal testimonies of many of the principal actors, we have sought to chart the course of a series of new taxes from their origins through (when they went that far) to implementation, revealing in the sequence of events, the relative effect of political attitudes, personalities and groups, and of political institutions, both formal and informal, upon the structure of the British tax system.

1 The Tax Policy Environment

Why new taxes?
Between the years 1964 and 1976 an unprecedented number of new taxes were put on the statute book. The period can with justification be described as an era of tax reform. But these manifold and important changes in the structure of taxation cannot be said to be part of an overall plan for an effective tax structure. Of the new taxes, capital gains tax (CGT), corporation tax (CT), selective employment tax (SET), value added tax (VAT), capital transfer tax (CTT), as well as two taxes initiated but not (yet) introduced, tax credits (TC) and an annual wealth tax (WT), are examined in this book. These new taxes did not result from a thorough assessment and study of the entire tax system on the lines of the Canadian Carter Commission of 1966. A Royal Commission on Taxation was indeed appointed in January 1951 and presented its Final Report in June 1955 (Cmd 9474), but its terms of reference were restricted to profits and income and no new taxes were proposed in the Majority Report.* Other reports on taxation from committees set up by Government also appeared during the period, notably the Richardson Report on VAT (Cmnd 2300), but they were restricted to particular aspects of taxation. In no sense has there been, since the Second World War, any government-initiated comprehensive inquiry into the tax system laying the foundations for systematic overhaul. (In fact, the most thorough inquiry into the UK tax system since World War II was privately sponsored, the Meade Committee, set up by the Institute for Fiscal Studies. Its Report, *The Structure and Reform of Direct Taxation*, was published in 1978. Even that, as the title indicates, was restricted to direct taxation.) The new taxes introduced since 1964 have been piecemeal additions to the existing system or have replaced other taxes that tapped more or less the same taxable capacity. Like Topsy, the British tax system 'just growed'.

Of course, the Chancellors who introduced all these new taxes had their reasons. They may have lacked a coherent plan for structural reform based on a comprehensive review but the three Chancellors of the Exchequer† who, during this period, took office at the beginning of

---

* The Minority Report, signed by H.L. Bullock, N. Kaldor and G. Woodcock, did recommend two new taxes and was thus influential in the development of CGT (p. 24) and CT (p. 29).

† Excluding Iain Macleod, who died just a month after taking office.

a new Parliament each announced, in an early Budget speech, plans for major changes in the tax structure. Indeed, Chancellors Callaghan and Barber went so far as to declare their intention to evolve a long-term tax strategy. The initial enthusiasm for comprehensive structural reform tended to wane as the Government's capacity for radical change was eroded by the pressures of day-to-day economic management and congestion in the revenue departments. But, as we have seen, many new taxes were introduced and their introduction prompts the question 'What impelled Chancellors to bring forward so many new taxes between 1964 and 1976?'

Tax policy goals

Many commentators and economic historians have described the period from 1960 as a period of economic policy reappraisal (Brittan, 1971; Stewart, 1977; Keegan and Pennant-Rae, 1979). Until the late 1950s governments were primarily occupied with post-war reconstruction and the re-establishment of normal trade and economic arrangements. Once the war-time structure had been dismantled the public sector of the British economy was relatively small, but by the early 1960s public expenditure had begun to grow and was becoming a crucial variable in the economic equation. At the same time signs were appearing that the underlying economy was not growing rapidly or smoothly. There was a rising concern with the supply side of the economy and with the encouragement of changes in the economic structure. In addition inflation had become a growing cause of anxiety and most politicians were convinced that an incomes policy was necessary for successful economic management. In particular, Governments sought ways of promoting growth by encouraging investment and methods of managing the economy that would not disrupt their own public expenditure plans. For these objectives taxation proved a popular instrument with Chancellors: thus James Callaghan, as Chancellor of the Exchequer, stated in his 1964 Budget Statement:

I must use the taxation system to ensure social justice for those who stand in need . . . a healthy foreign balance, stable prices, and full employment, social justice for the needy, fair play for all tax-payers, sound planning of public expenditure, rewards for the energetic and sustained economic growth.

(HC Debates, 11 November 1964, col. 1025)

That taxation could be used to perform a variety of functions apart from revenue-raising was no new discovery, as the early statements on the objectives of taxation by J.S. Mill, Ricardo, Wicksell and others (quoted in Musgrave and Peacock, 1958) make clear. But in the 1960s and 1970s the use of taxation for purposes other than or additional to revenue-raising reached a peak.

A distinction can be made between short and long-term objectives. Short-term aspects of taxation include the capacity to regulate a given economic structure; long-term aspects include the capacity to re-shape that economic structure itself. Recognising this distinction, Sir Richard Clarke in his article 'The Long-term Planning of Taxation' (Crick and Robson, 1973) suggested that any fundamental structural reform of taxation ought to take account of four aspects:

1. Short-term demand management;
2. Social policy (i.e. the use of taxation to change the distribution of income and other social objectives);
3. Economic policy (i.e. the effect of taxes on incentives for individuals and companies and the implications for economic growth and other economic objectives);
4. The efficient raising of money to pay for public spending – simplicity, cheapness of collection, acceptability and fairness between tax-payers.

Sir Richard pointed out that at different periods these goals will figure in different proportions; writing in 1972 he commented that 'In the last twenty-five years it is probably true to say that considerations of short-term demand management have been predominant' (p. 161). Other commentators (Brittan, 1971) have also noted that the Treasury view of the role of taxation in the economy was essentially a short-term one. This concentration of officials and politicians on 'managing the economy' may help to explain why there was no overall analysis of the structural features of taxation during this period and why, therefore, the approach to reform was piecemeal. Nevertheless the mass of new tax legislation that emerged from 1964 to 1976 reflects some degree of concern with the tax structure in the longer-term even if that concern was intermittent and uncoordinated. Which of the longer-term objectives was in the minds of the Chancellors in introducing the new taxes?

Taxes for revenue-raising
Almost always taxes to some extent fulfil the objective of revenue-raising. One possible answer to the question 'Why new taxes?' is that, from time to time, governments felt the need to find new sources of revenue to finance the burgeoning social services such as education, health and social security.

One possible response to such a need would be hypothecated taxes – taxes specifically related to particular forms of expenditure. The national insurance contribution (NIC) might be regarded as such a tax; but none of the taxes that form the subject of our study are in this category. However, this does not mean that new taxes may not be introduced to make a general contribution to revenue needs. What was the revenue situation?

When plans were laid in the 1950s for the expansion of the public services no serious attempts were made to ensure that future revenue would match the level of expenditure of the programmes when fully developed. Following the Plowden Report (Cmnd 1432, 1961) the Public Expenditure Survey Committee (PESC) was established to remedy this defect. Its task was to examine future public spending plans in the light of 'prospective resources'. Prospective resources, however, were not defined clearly in terms of *both* economic growth and future taxable capacity. Prospective resources were generally taken to mean future expansion of the economy alone. Taxation was largely left out of the reckoning – a point which has been noted by some critics of the PESC system (Brittan, 1971; Else and Marshall, 1979; Robinson and Ysander, 1981; Pliatsky, 1982). By and large it was not reckoned that fundamental adjustments would be required to the tax structure in order to bring in extra revenue. Economic growth alone would be sufficient to permit the enjoyment of the pleasures of public expenditure without the pain of excessive taxation or overly oppressive redistribution of income. Politicians throughout the period 1960–80 continued to reiterate the view that expansion of public services could come from economic growth. Even in the late 1970s Ministers were expressing optimism about the prospects of economic growth. Joel Barnett, Chief Secretary to the Treasury, in his evidence to the General Sub-Committee of the Expenditure Committee (HC 299, 1975/6), when questioned about the apparently high expectations of growth in Treasury forecasts replied that the failure of the economy to grow in the recent past did not mean that it might not be expected to do so in the coming years.

In spite of this optimistic view that economic growth would provide the 'future resources' there was an underlying pressure to find new sources of revenue even before the later 1970s and Aaron Wildavsky could write:

> By 1966 it was clear that the economy was not growing fast enough. The government was hard pressed to meet its large political commitments for social programmes.
>
> (Wildavsky, 1975, p. 372)

If economic growth was not automatically going to provide the additional revenue needed for the growth in public expenditure, the funds would have to come from increases in existing taxes, or from new taxes, or from other means (principally borrowing). In practice all three methods of revenue-raising were used.

Table 1.1 shows total government expenditure, tax revenue and

Table 1.1 Government expenditure and tax revenue, 1964–78

Year	Government expenditure[a] (GE) (£ m)	Gross domestic product[b] (GDP) (£ m)	GE as % of GDP	Tax revenue[c] (£ m)	Tax revenue[c] (% of GDP)	Government borrowing requirement[d] (£ m)	Government borrowing requirement[d] (% of GDP)
1964	12 042	29 200	41.2	9 717	33.3	994	3.4
1965	13 376	31 193	42.9	10 961	35.1	1188	3.8
1966	14 448	33 099	43.7	11 791	35.6	957	2.9
1967	16 672	34 891	47.8	13 168	37.7	1880	5.4
1968	18 289	37 554	48.7	15 253	40.6	1314	3.5
1969	18 984	39 616	47.9	17 138	43.3	−290	−0.7
1970	20 867	43 460	48.0	19 132	44.0	−148	−0.3
1971	23 445	49 428	47.4	20 280	41.0	1314	2.7
1972	26 316	55 147	47.7	21 437	38.9	2114	3.8
1973	30 503	64 154	47.5	24 210	37.7	3679	5.7
1974	39 146	74 073	52.8	29 970	40.5	5630	7.6
1975	51 642	93 502	55.2	38 519	41.2	9974	10.7
1976	58 362	110 268	52.9	44 701	40.5	7889	7.2
1977	61 738	125 211	49.3	50 969	40.7	4652	3.7
1978	71 351	141 999	50.2	56 480	39.8	9030	6.4

Source: National Income Blue Books

Notes: [a] 'Total government expenditure' from general government accounts in National Income Blue Books, comprising central plus local government combined current and capital accounts including expenditure on financial assets. (Alternative measures show different totals but the same pattern of change.)
[b] Measured at factor cost.
[c] Central plus local government including national insurance contributions.
[d] Central plus local government excluding borrowings by local from central government.

borrowing in £ million and as a percentage of gross domestic product (GDP) measured at factor cost (i.e. excluding the effect of indirect taxes and subsidies). The period saw a major increase in government spending, with particular spurts between 1964 and 1968 and between 1973 and 1975, both in real terms and as a percentage of GDP. Tax revenue increased as a proportion of GDP (from 33 to 40 per cent) but not by as much as government spending and there was an increase in borrowing.

Table 1.2 shows the respective contributions of different categories of taxation to government expenditure. Taxes on income and capital, besides rising in real terms, increased as a proportion of expenditure over the period, reaching a peak in 1970 at the end of a six-year period of Labour government; thereafter the new Conservative government cut back on income tax.

Much of this rise in revenue from income taxation was the outcome of inflation without indexation – the effect of so-called 'fiscal drag'. The size of the tax allowances and the width of tax bands were not increased sufficiently to offset the effects of inflation, so that the tax rates became heavier in real terms. Additional revenue therefore accrued to the Exchequer by means of 'taxation without representation' as Milton Friedman has put it.*

National insurance contributions and other revenue (principally borrowing) also showed a significant if fluctuating increase as a proportion of total revenue.

No less important was the marked decline in the proportion of revenue raised by taxes on expenditure; between 1964 and 1976 the yield from these taxes fell from 37 to 28 per cent of revenue (having reached a peak figure of 41 per cent in 1969). Partly this fall was a product of 'negative fiscal drag'. Where taxes on goods and services are not *ad valorem* (proportional to price) but *specific* (determined by some characteristic other than value, e.g. weight), then in times of inflation the real burden of the tax falls unless the rates are regularly adjusted. Over this period Chancellors allowed this reduction in the real rates of excise duties to take place. They may not fully have realised how much these duties were being eroded by inflation. Also they might have hesitated to adjust them fully because this visible effect on the cost of living might have prejudiced attempts to keep down wage increases by incomes policies. Nonetheless the failure of Chancellors to ensure that

---

* In 1977 the Rooker–Wise amendment, so-called after the two Labour MPs who voted in Committee against their Government, required a Chancellor, henceforward, to explain any failure to increase income tax allowances in line with inflation. This amendment did not prevent Chancellors from raising allowances less than the rise in prices nor provide for the indexation of tax bands.

Table 1.2 Finance of government expenditure, 1964–78

Year	Contributions to revenue as percentage of total government expenditure[a]							
	Taxes on income and capital		Taxes on expenditure[a]		NI etc. contributions		Other revenue	
	(£ m)	(%)	(£ m)	(%)	(£ m)	(%)	(£ m)	(%)
1964	3 836	31.9	4 437	36.8	1 444	12.0	2 325	19.3
1965	4 314	32.3	4 962	37.1	1 685	12.6	2 415	18.1
1966	4 881	33.8	5 421	37.5	1 804	12.5	2 342	16.2
1967	5 601	33.6	5 997	36.0	1 909	11.5	3 165	19.0
1968	6 283	34.4	6 809	37.2	2 161	11.8	3 036	16.6
1969	7 114	37.5	7 782	41.0	2 242	11.8	1 899	10.0
1970	8 061	38.6	8 416	40.3	2 655	12.7	1 731	8.3
1971	8 667	37.0	8 787	37.5	2 826	12.1	3 165	13.5
1972	8 869	33.7	9 267	35.2	3 337	12.7	4 843	18.4
1973	10 151	33.3	10 122	33.2	3 937	12.9	6 293	20.6
1974	13 393	34.2	11 469	29.3	5 000	12.8	9 284	23.7
1975	17 511	33.8	14 163	27.5	6 845	13.3	13 123	25.4
1976	19 725	33.7	16 546	28.3	8 430	14.4	13 661	23.4
1977	21 244	34.4	20 230	32.7	9 495	15.3	10 769	17.4
1978	23 219	32.5	23 238	32.5	10 023	14.0	14 871	20.8

Source: National Income Blue Books
Note: [a] Includes local rates

taxes on goods and services at least kept pace with inflation is interesting. Had they done so the pressure to find additional revenue from other sources would have been eased.

But let us look specifically at the contribution of the *new* taxes to revenue. Table 1.3 sets out the basic facts but requires a word of explanation. The figures of total revenue from taxation (TRT) relate only to central government (i.e. they exclude local rates) and also exclude national insurance contributions; consequently the contribution of the new taxes to revenue tends to be overstated when expressed as a percentage of TRT. In other words the figures place the revenue contribution of these taxes in as 'favourable' a light as possible.

Of the five taxes in Table 1.3, only SET was completely new from a revenue point of view in the sense that it was the only one which did not replace an existing tax. CGT comprehended the previous short-term gains tax, but for the first time taxed long-term gains; CT (classical) replaced income tax and profits tax on corporate profits; CT (imputation) replaced CT (classical) and also had the effect of reducing revenue from income tax by providing a credit to be set against income tax on dividends; VAT replaced purchase tax and SET; and CTT replaced estate duty, though CTT provided for the taxation of lifetime gifts, which had escaped estate duty, unless the gifts were made within seven years before death.

Of these new taxes CGT has never yielded much revenue. It took five years for the yield to rise to 1 per cent of central government revenue from taxation and, although in between it rose somewhat higher, that remained its average yield in the last three years shown in our table, 1975/6 to 1977/8. Had CGT been indexed for inflation its yield would have been even lower. However, it should be recognised that the taxation of capital gains made by companies raises the yield of CT, whilst in so far as CGT discourages the holding of assets for growth and encourages investment in income-yielding assets, income tax revenue would increase. In other words the net revenue increase as a result of CGT was somewhat more than the direct yield of the tax. Comparisons of CT (classical) with the previous situation and of CT (imputation) with CT (classical) are confused by the effects on income tax receipts and the changing methods of investment incentives; but the motives behind the CT changes were not revenue (p. 29) and no new taxable capacity was tapped. CTT likewise was not introduced for revenue purposes (pp. 39–40) and, indeed, its contribution to revenue has consistently been less than that of estate duty which it superseded. Although Mr Healey as Chancellor, when introducing CTT, indicated that he expected revenue to fall for a period and then rise as the cumulative provisions of the tax had their effect (p. 42), in fact the reliefs granted by Mr Healey and his successor have ensured that the

Table 1.3 Contribution of new taxes to central government revenue

Financial year	Total revenue from taxation[a] (£m) (TRT)	CGT (£m)	CGT (% of TRT)	CT (£m)	CT (% of TRT)	SET[b] (£m)	SET (% of TRT)	VAT (£m)	VAT (% of TRT)	CTT (£m)	CTT (% of TRT)
1964/65	7 431	—	—	(423)	(5.6)	—	—	—	—	—	—
1965/66	8 324	—	—	(438)	(5.3)	—	—	—	—	—	—
1966/67	9 371	7	0.1	1 034[c]	11.0	258	2.7	—	—	—	—
1967/68	10 031	16	0.2	1 225	12.2	325	3.2	—	—	—	—
1968/69	11 963	47	0.4	1 346	11.2	438	3.7	—	—	—	—
1969/70	13 372	127	0.9	1 687	12.6	527	3.9	—	—	—	—
1970/71	13 829	140	1.0	1 600	11.6	501	3.6	—	—	—	—
1971/72	15 145	160	1.1	1 550	10.2	223	1.5	(PT:1 430)	(9.4)	—	—
1972/73	15 679	210	1.3	1 525	9.7	224	1.4	(PT:1 390)	(8.9)	—	—
1973/74	17 250	320	1.9	2 245[d]	13.0	40	0.2	1 425 (PT: 380)	8.3 (2.2)	(405)	(2.3)
1974/75	22 132	381	1.7	2 850	12.9	—	—	2 497	11.3	(339)	(1.5)
1975/76	26 851	325	1.2	2 125	7.9	—	—	3 275	12.2	150 (165)	0.6 (0.6)
1976/77	32 470	320	1.0	2 650	8.2	—	—	3 750	11.5	260	0.8
1977/78	36 436	340	0.9	3 346	9.2	—	—	4 226	11.6	312 (87)	0.9 (0.2)

Sources: Financial Statements and Financial Statements and Budget Reports.

Notes: Figures in brackets refer to revenue from superseded taxes, which are included for the two years prior to replacement and thereafter as long as they yielded revenue. Note that VAT replaced SET and purchase tax (PT).

[a] Total revenue from taxation excludes national insurance contributions and local rates.

[b] SET receipts are recorded net of repayments except in 1973/74 when only the gross figure was published.

[c] The introduction of CT (classical) coincided with a change from investment allowances (a tax relief) to investment grants (a cash expenditure). Investment grants 1966/67 amounted to £166m. The effect of the change on tax revenue was somewhat lagged.

[d] The introduction of CT (imputation) coincided with a return to a system of investment incentives by way of tax relief – this time taking the form of depreciation allowances. Note also that the imputation system generated a credit against income tax, so there is a revenue offset to the rise in CT.

predicted rise has never taken place and the contribution of CTT has continued to fall (p. 43).

Of the new taxes, only SET was introduced with an immediate revenue purpose (amongst other objectives). At its peak, 1969/70, it was making the modest but significant contribution to revenue of nearly 4 per cent. When VAT was introduced its rates were fixed at that level which would yield approximately the same revenue as purchase tax and SET, which it superseded. In introducing VAT the Conservatives had in mind its potential as a revenue-yielder, with a view to its use not for a net addition to revenue but to change the balance of direct to indirect taxation. However, this potential was not realised until Sir Geoffrey Howe's budget of June 1979.

As to the two taxes initiated but never introduced, the TC scheme, far from raising revenue, on the basis of the illustrative figures of the Green Paper required a net outlay of £1300 m. The WT would have brought in some revenue, but almost certainly an insignificant amount. The Green Paper on *Wealth Tax* (Cmnd 5704, 1974) gave two 'illustrative examples' of scales. Tax A: 1 per cent on wealth of £100,000, rising to $2\frac{1}{2}$ per cent on over £5 m. Tax B: 1 per cent on £100,000, rising to 5 per cent on over £5 m. The Green Paper records that:

If the Wealth Tax had been operating in 1972, subject to the possible offsets in paragraphs 31 and 32, Tax A would have yielded between £200 m and £275 m and Tax B between £350 m and £425 m. The yield will vary from year to year according to changes in the value of the assets held by the wealthy members of the community. (p.1)

How far the yield would fall below these estimates would depend upon the reliefs allowed to special groups such as owners of historic houses, owner-occupiers in agriculture and the owners of private businesses, as well as the form of the exemption or threshold for household goods and any general 'ceiling' provisions. If the introduction of WT was accompanied by reductions in income tax, as the Chancellor hinted in the foreword to the Green Paper, or if the investment income surcharge were allowed as an offset to WT, a possibility suggested in the Green Paper, the net yield would be still further reduced. In addition, sales of assets to meet WT liabilities would have some effect in reducing the yield from CTT (though the realisation of these assets might have increased the revenue from CGT), whilst the abnormally high costs of administering WT would have to be set against the revenue from it.

Even the highest gross estimate of £425 m in 1972/3 would have meant a contribution of less than 3 per cent to central government revenue from taxation (Table 1.3). In fact the Report of the Select Committee (HC 696–1, 1975) made it clear that there was little support for the higher scale (unless accompanied by major reductions in income tax) and strong support for a wide range of reliefs and offsets. It seems unlikely, therefore, that any WT regarded as acceptable would have contributed much more than 1 per cent to central government revenue from taxation, if that. Indeed, this is the pattern of wealth taxes elsewhere in developed countries. Of the ten OECD countries with annual wealth taxes surveyed in a recent report (OECD, 1979) only in the rather special case of Switzerland did the revenue from personal wealth taxes exceed 1 per cent of total revenue from taxation.

It is clear from this analysis that, with the partial exception of SET, the new taxes were not introduced in response to immediate revenue needs. VAT carried the potential for increasing revenue, but its initiators saw it as a way of changing the incidence of taxation rather than providing the basis for an increase in total revenue. The new taxes, therefore, cannot primarily be considered a rational response to the 'public expenditure gap'. Explanation must be sought in other directions.

We have already indicated that there are a number of other possible structural objectives of a tax apart from revenue-raising. Some are primarily economic, others primarily political. The main objectives of the economic class seek to promote particular forms of behaviour by individuals and firms, usually with the purpose of encouraging economic growth. We can call such objectives 'regulatory'. The main structural objectives of the political class are concerned with the promotion of horizontal and vertical equity between groups and classes of tax-payer. These relate to the elusive quality that the politician calls 'fairness', or they may be aimed at a fundamental change in the distribution of income and wealth. Any change affecting the relative contributions of different classes of tax-payer, whether minor or major, alters the distribution of income and wealth and may conveniently be called 'redistributory'. Finally, we can distinguish objectives of an administrative kind, such as an ability to collect taxes more cheaply or a simplification of the tax system.

Economic structural objectives – the regulatory function
We have already mentioned (p. 2) the importance attached by the policy-makers to economic growth during the period of our study. Taxation was used as an instrument of long-term regulation with economic growth as its central objective.

From the early 1960s there was an increasing preoccupation with economic growth, which perhaps arose from the realisation that, although Britain's post-war rate of growth was high by historical standards, it fell considerably short of the rates achieved by our chief trade rivals in continental Europe and elsewhere. The achievement of a high rate of growth was thought to depend on the success of a series of interrelated policies: increasing incentives, especially incentives to invest, to promote higher production and productivity; improving the balance of payments and, in particular, avoiding crises in the balance of payments, which would require a deflationary cut-back in demand; and maintaining a high level of employment without the inflation which would generate a balance of payments deficit.

Whilst much of the tax policy for these purposes took the form of short-term demand management involving changes in tax rates rather than new taxes, an important motivation for the new taxes was an attempt to promote growth by structural change – the regulatory purpose. Thus both the introduction of CT and its change to an imputation system were intended, in rather different ways, to promote investment. SET was seen as a means of improving the balance of payments, in some measure an alternative to devaluation, providing a covert subsidy to manufacturing from which came the bulk of exports. It was also intended to effect a structural change in the economy in favour of manufacturing as against services which was expected both to benefit the balance of payments and improve productivity. VAT had the merit of widening the indirect tax base, so that any short-term policy to reduce demand would have a less damaging effect on particular industries than had changes in purchase tax; it also had the merit that investment attracted no VAT and the mechanism of its collection ensured that there was no spill-over of tax into export prices except for exempt goods (p. 35). Further, the partial switch from income tax to VAT, which was envisaged by the Conservatives in introducing the tax and ultimately carried out in 1979, was expected to improve incentives to work and enterprise. Even CGT had a regulatory function; in so far as the tax discouraged investment in non income-yielding assets, such as pictures and antiques, and led people instead to hold productive assets, it might be expected to promote economic growth.

Political objectives: 'fairness' and 'equality' – redistributive functions

The regulatory economic objectives of the new taxes shade into the political objectives. As we have indicated, an important economic objective was to curb inflation. An incomes policy was one way of trying to do so, and, it was argued, an incomes policy was more likely to stick if taxation was seen to be 'fair'.

The objective of CGT was much less to squeeze the rich than to secure 'fairness', to ensure that those with equal capacity paid the same tax. In general, capital gains were not liable to income tax before 1961, though many economists maintain that such gains are the equivalent of income. Converting taxable income to capital gains had become a favourite avoidance device. The unfairness of the failure to tax capital gains had become particularly apparent in the late 1950s and early 1960s because of the stock market boom (Ilersic, 1962, p.9). Share prices rose rapidly (between 8 October 1959 and 4 January 1960 the Financial Times Index rose from 262.2 to 342.9), and these years saw an extension of share ownership, new forms of share ownership, and the emergence of an information industry to serve the capital market. It became possible for more people to make a living out of buying and selling shares. The share market was dominated by speculative share dealing (Ilersic, 1962). Other sources of capital gain also appeared in this period – especially in land, shops and office property. In 1961 the Conservative Chancellor of the Exchequer, Selwyn Lloyd, introduced a short-term CGT to promote 'fairness'.

This was not going far enough for the Labour Party. They wished to see all capital gains taxed. Foreshadowing the CGT introduced in 1965 James Callaghan said of it:

This measure will bring to an end the state of affairs in which hard work and great energy are fully taxed while the fruits of speculation and passive ownership escape untaxed . . . this is part of fair play as between groups of taxpayers.

(11 November 1964, H.C. Debates, col. 1040)

Introducing the tax in the April 1965 Budget he repeated that fairness was its objective.

The argument for 'fairness' merges almost imperceptibly into that for 'equality' – meaning a change in the distribution of income and wealth to reduce inequalities. CTT and WT were both introduced with the object of promoting 'fairness' in the distribution of burdens as part of a deal with the TUC ('The Social Contract') which would include a measure of incomes restraint. But both were intended to be much more overtly redistributive than CGT.

Interest in the distribution of wealth in Britain had been growing during the 1960s and early 1970s especially as a result of researches by academics (Revell, 1969; Atkinson, 1972) which had suggested that the richest 1 per cent of the population owned about a quarter of the marketable personal wealth in Britain and the richest 10 per cent owned as much as 75 per cent. Although the concentration of wealth in the hands of the richest 1 per cent had declined markedly in recent years, the gainers were largely those in the 2–10 per cent bracket. The effect of estate duty in reducing inequality was only very limited because it could be avoided relatively easily, in particular by gifts, which were tax free if the donor survived seven years. Hence Labour's introduction of CTT, which was intended to remedy this defect and be a more effective engine for reducing inequality. A similar argument was used of WT, although, depending on its form and possible concomitant changes in income tax, a WT could be used to promote horizontal equity (the equal taxation of similar taxable capacity) rather than to reduce inequality of wealth distribution. As a partial substitute for high rates of income tax it could even be part of a policy to stimulate growth, an idea floated by the National Economic Development Council (NEDC, 1963).

Administrative objectives – efficiency and simplicity

Simplifying the tax system was an ambition of Chancellors in this period, especially the Conservative Chancellor, Anthony Barber. Partly in an attempt to make the system fairer by taking into account minor differences of circumstance, partly as a response to the pressures of particular interest groups, partly to try to counteract avoidance and eliminate anomalies, the tax system had over the years become more and more complicated. The increasing complexity of the tax system and its incomprehensibility had been attacked not only by the layman; in the vanguard of the campaign for simplicity were the Law Society and the professional accountancy institutes. Thus the Law Society advised the Chancellor (in a memorandum of October 1967) that 'There are very many examples in the statutes of wording which is unreasonably complicated or antiquated and where the same term is differently defined.' The Institute of Chartered Accountants in England and Wales (whose members might have been expected to profit from the complexity) put the point even more emphatically when, at their annual meeting in 1967, they resolved 'That the simplification of the tax legislation is a matter of the greatest urgency in the interests of the accountancy profession and the community as a whole.'

If these protestations related mainly to the terms in which the taxes were described, there was also evidence on the complications of the tax content. One MP, Sir Gerald Nabarro, made his reputation by exposing the anomalies of purchase tax. Research by Professor C.V. Brown showed how few tax-payers appreciated the intricacies of the earned income allowance as it existed in the income tax before 1973 (Brown, 1968); whilst a study by Dean revealed how few teachers claimed the book allowances to which they were entitled under the income tax (Dean, 1971).

Perhaps even more than in the tax system itself, there was and still is a need for simplification at the frontier between the tax and social security systems (Sandford, Pond and Walker (eds.), 1981). The most blatant example arose from the so-called 'poverty trap' or 'poverty surtax' under which it was possible for a low-income worker to obtain an increase in earnings only to find himself subsequently worse off; the tax and national insurance contributions on the extra income, combined with the loss of means-tested welfare benefits, could in extreme cases exceed the increase in income.

The most notable progress in simplification in this period was in relation to existing taxes – in particular the unification of income tax and surtax, including the replacement of the earned income relief by the more straightforward investment income surcharge. However, a concern for administrative simplicity was evident in the introduction of VAT. VAT replaced two taxes, purchase tax and SET, but this could hardly be called a simplification: the costs of collecting VAT and the compliance costs were much higher than those of the taxes superseded (Sandford *et al.*, 1981). However, having adopted a complex tax, Mr Barber was concerned that it should be 'the simplest VAT in Europe' and endeavoured to keep the rate structure as simple as was compatible with avoiding regressiveness. However, the tax in this period that would have done most to simplify both the tax and social security systems was the TC scheme which was never implemented.

There remains one unique objective for a new tax not covered by the categories we have described. Although it is possible that the Conservatives would have introduced VAT anyway, there can be no doubt that the need to adopt VAT if Britain were to join the EEC pushed them in that direction. Thus there could be said to be a constitutional objective in respect of VAT.

How is tax policy made? – the significance of models

Our main purpose in this book is to describe how tax policy is made in the United Kingdom and to evaluate the effectiveness of that process for achieving the intended policy objectives. But it would be a mistake to assume from the outset that there is only one way in which policy can be made, and to use that single model as our framework for analysis and our yardstick for assessing effectiveness.

It is important for several reasons to appreciate the existence of a range of decision-making models. Firstly, in looking for evidence and data to complete our description of the policy process, the use of more than one model focuses our attention on a greater range of elements in that process. If we confine ourselves to a single model we may omit much that, in fact, proves important in the determination of policy. Graham Allison (1969, 1971) has clearly demonstrated this effect in his study of the Cuban Missile Crisis. Subjecting the one issue to analysis using three different models uncovered a greater variety of data than if he had concentrated on only one. Data revealed by one model, he showed, was not necessarily revealed by the others.

Secondly, if we are to go beyond mere description and are to evaluate the effectiveness of the process, we must recognise that different models yield different criteria of effectiveness. Most previous commentators on the British tax system have fallen into the trap of assuming (often unconsciously) that one model alone – that of rational economic choice (below, p. 18) – is relevant in an understanding and evaluation of tax policy-making. They therefore evaluate the processes of tax policy-making solely in so far as they fall short of the criteria of economic rationality. Few have considered that other criteria – including political rationality or power relationships – might be relevant for assessing the effectiveness of the political machine for processing tax changes. It is easy to understand how commentators have made this error. On the surface there is an obvious lack of 'pure' or 'economic' rationality in the British tax policy-making process, especially in its more visible open stages in Parliament where there is little opportunity for rational consideration of the Government's legislative proposals. And there is substantial evidence that the resulting statutes are increasingly complex and riddled with loopholes. But as Yeziekiel Dror (1968, p. 130ff) has pointed out, the criteria on which to judge the success or failure of policy-making and to identify weaknesses in the process themselves derive from the model of the decision-making process chosen as the basis for analysis.

Finally, different models of the policy-making process may reflect the routes chosen by policy-makers to suit particular circumstances and different policy goals. As G.L. Bach (1971) reminds us at the start of his study of the making of fiscal and monetary policy in the United States, 'Both history and theory suggest that optimal policy-making will depend partly on the goals sought and partly on what specific policies are most likely to achieve those goals' (p. 2). There may be no one single way of doing things that is employed by politicians for every case. To suggest that different models of the decision-making process may reflect the practice in different circumstances is not to deny that there may be an 'issue machine' (Braybrooke, 1974) or a set of institutions through which all policies flow. But they flow through the machine to a greater or lesser extent, some faster and some more slowly, some by-passing sections of the machine at which other policies are held up for a long time. Moreover, the attitudes and behaviour of the actors and the way in which they use the 'issue machine' will vary according to the goals that they are pursuing. Goals or objectives, as well as institutional structures, shape the attitudes of the actors in the policy-making process and determine the paths that policies travel on the road to implementation.

The essential connection between the nature of policy objectives and the means employed to implement them has been noted by many recent students of policy-making processes. They have been influenced by the work of Theodore Lowi (1964) who stressed the importance for policy analysis and evaluation of distinguishing different types of policy according to the impact that each had upon society. The three types that he produced are relevant to most studies of economic policy-making and so it is worth considering them at some length; they are (i) distributive, (ii) regulatory and (iii) redistributive policies. Distributive policies confer direct benefits on individuals or groups. Regulatory policies are specific in their effect, but do not affect such small sections of society as distributive policies. Their impact is on sectors, e.g. sectors of industry. Redistributive policies, unlike the first two categories, involve broad sections of society approaching the size of social classes. The groups affected by redistributive policies can be identified as the 'haves' and the 'have nots' or as the 'rich' and the 'poor'. Because each of these policy types affects different sized sectors and groups in society it generates its own characteristic decision-making mode. Thus we arrive at the whole point of Lowi's classification scheme.

If we can identify the effect that a policy will have (or is intended to have) on society, then we can identify the likely mode of decision-making that will accompany its introduction. Lowi suggests that distributive policies that confer benefits on a wide selection of small groups and individuals can be dispensed bit by bit under a patronage or 'log-rolling' system. Regulatory policies, because they affect larger groups in society, where special interests have something substantial to lose or gain are characteristically introduced under a more conflictual style of decision-making. Redistributive policies, because they involve effects on large groups or classes, which may stand opposed to each other in an adversarial power relationship bound by strong ideologies, are generally carried through in an adversarial conflict-ridden mode. Ideology, absent from the first two categories of policy, plays a significant part in the mode of decision-making where policies are intended to be redistributive in effect.

Lowi's threefold classification of policy types according to the influence they have on society, with its concomitant threefold classification of political decision-making modes, provides a useful addition to the model of economic rational choice to produce a framework for the analysis of tax policy-making. It fits fairly well with the goals and objectives of new taxes as laid out in the earlier pages of this chapter. It is particularly easy to see how taxes fit into the regulatory and redistributive categories. Taxes intended to produce efficiency, stabilisation and growth are often 'regulatory' in their impact where they are aimed at particular sectors of the economy. Those taxes with the objectives of vertical equity and even those aimed at horizontal equity, fall easily into the 'redistributive' category. It is perhaps more difficult immediately to think of taxes as 'distributive' in effect. Taxes usually withdraw money from individuals – they are rarely intended to provide a direct disbursement of benefits to particular groups, though exceptionally they may do so, like the premium to manufacturing industry which was part of SET and aspects of the TC scheme. But much of tax policy in practice does have a distributive effect. Benefits are acquired for small groups of tax-payers during the course of consultation on draft legislation and in the course of the legislative process itself. Particular interest groups are able to obtain concessions that relieve all (or part) of a charge that is generally applicable. Moreover, if the tax is levied to pay for communal benefits, these can then be enjoyed by the concession-aires without their having to make a (full) contribution to the costs. This effect of tax legislation has received increasing attention in recent years following the work of Stanley Surrey (1957). Surrey calls such tax reliefs (e.g. mortgage interest relief for owner-occupiers) 'tax expend-itures' because they have the effect of a positive payment to the beneficiary from the state. The existence of 'tax expenditures' is now fully recognised in the USA where they are listed in the annual Budget, and partially recognised in Britain where in recent years they have been listed in the public expenditure White Papers. Very often distributive policies may appear by accretion rather than by design. They may become a significant feature of taxes that were originally intended to have a regulatory or a redistributive impact. As Surrey has demon-strated (1957), a Government may not have the intention of distributing benefits when it introduces a new tax, but that may be the end result of the influence of groups during the various stages of policy formulation and enactment.

Thus the three categories of policy types with their characteristic political modes of decision-making produce a helpful framework for analysing tax policy because they provide a political addition to the purely economic concept of tax policy and its counterpart model of rational economic choice. The categories of policy types and the models of decision-making that accompany them are not, of course, discrete and exclusive to each individual tax. Any particular tax may demon-strate features of more than one type. A tax may start with features of one type and acquire over time features of another. But it is clear that tax policies do have both economic and political effects upon society and that therefore models of both economic and political choice are relevant as a framework for the description, analysis and evaluation of tax policy-making. We turn now to consider, in more detail, particular models of decision-making.

The models: economic and political rationality

If taxation were merely an economic device designed to raise revenue, to regulate economic activity, and to promote economic growth, then a natural starting point, with an obvious intuitive appeal when trying to answer the question 'How are tax policies made?', would be to consider tax policy as the outcome of rational economic choice. The model of economic rationality assumes that there is an objective – a perceived need to act; that alternative strategies to attain the objective can be identified; that the policy-maker takes account of the constraints, assesses the costs and benefits of the alternatives with their probable outcomes: and that he then chooses the optimum alternative, which will enable the goal to be attained at least cost in resources. The economic rationality model also implies a consistent policy review, so that the results of decisions can be compared with predictions and an assessment made of the degree of success in achieving the objectives. It is entirely a model of the rationality of *means* – we shall consider the question of the choice of rational ends below.

If tax policy were entirely concerned with economic objectives then the kinds of question that a study of tax policy-making might pose would be: 'Do the tax policy-makers have goals which are sufficiently clearly defined? 'Have they adequate information to know all the alternative means of attaining the objective(s)?' 'Can they fully weigh up the consequences of choosing one means rather than another?' 'Are there any behavioural or political impediments to the operation of rational choice?'

The limits to this sort of formal rationality have been well-documented in many studies of political and bureaucratic behaviour and have given rise to a variety of 'alternative' models of decision-making, most of them variants of the basic or pure model of rational choice. These studies cast grave doubts upon the actual existence of pure rational choice in any field of political activity. Firstly, even with the many modern aids to computation and rational evaluation of alternatives, there appears to be a limit to man's intellectual capacity to assess and to predict economic and social events and effects. Secondly, there are constraints of time and cost, which prevent a thorough evaluation of alternatives. Thirdly, human behaviour in practice, with its preference for easy answers and its urge to maintain good relations between working colleagues, further erodes the capacity of the political machine to be perfectly rational. It appears from studies of decision-making in political and bureaucratic organisations that there are both institutional and psychological forces at work conditioning the behaviour of political actors.

Actors within the political institutions of government are often less than purely rational in their general approach to decision-making. Personal and institutional forces draw them away from the requirements of pure rationality. They prefer to 'satisfice' (i.e. to take the first satisfactory solution which offers) rather than optimise when making policy decisions (Simon, 1957; Cyert and March, 1964; Downs, 1967). Issues are rarely examined from their foundations upwards, but rather each decision is taken sequentially in relation to existing situations. The requirements of pure rationality are too stringent to fit with the needs of good relations in small political communities (Heclo and Wildavsky, 1975). Although various techniques such as planning programme budgeting systems, cost-benefit analysis, zero-based budgeting and 'sunset' legislation have been introduced by Governments to strengthen their capacity for rational choice, the 'satisficing' mode remains dominant. Politicians and bureaucrats find the new aids to rationality hard to use (Robinson and Ysander, 1981).

The overall effect of the limits to rational choice is to produce a pattern of policy-making by 'incrementalism' (Lindblom, 1959). Decision is built upon decision in a layer effect to create policy, and hard 'root rational' choices are avoided. Deep, underlying forces act as restraints, limits or blinders on policy choice. Policy-makers may become fixed in their attitudes and unable to see another point of view (Brittan, 1971; Moseley, 1981). Thus policy can become set into a 'hard path' (Lindberg, 1977) from which major deviations are unlikely, or achieved only under extraordinary circumstances. This hard path appears to exist in many policy areas not excluding taxation. Thus G. Clayton and R.W. Houghton writing of the British tax system state that:

It has never been fundamentally revised but has been patched up and modified whenever demands for change have become so insistent that the natural conservatism and aversion to change of those charged with its administration has been overcome.

(1973, p.88)

G.L. Bach comes to a similar conclusion about US monetary and fiscal policy-making which he describes as

Commonly the result of a kind of 'disjointed incrementalism' . . . usually only major crises or disruptions, like the great depression or a war, bring about quick, radical changes in major policy.

(1971, pp. 37–8)

Ira Sharkansky agrees with Bach that incrementalism is a good description of the way in which tax policy is made in the USA (1969, pp. 51–2). However, limits on rational choice do not come only from limited time and intellectual capacity and the effects of institutional forces and psychological drives. There are also political constraints on rational choice. Politicians are not always particularly interested in rational evaluation and calculation of the effects of their desired policy innovations. This is particularly true where they are pursuing 'political' rather than economic objectives. Political ideology or even prejudice may guide choice and determine the appropriate means. Where there are pressing political constraints on the choice of means, policy-makers may turn to what Dror called the 'extra rational model' of choice (1968). Sir Geoffrey Vickers (1965) has referred to this method of making decisions as 'the art of judgement'; in this model intuition or judgement or even 'hunches' give the politician the preferred solution.

The existence of political constraints is recognised in the model of political bargaining and exchange (Lindblom, 1955; Riker, 1962; Curry and Wade, 1968). This model is based upon the idea that politicians do try to make rational choices but that these are mainly concerned with their need to satisfy their own goals or needs such as re-election or promotion to office. Some variants of this model admit the possibility of altruism in which the political actor also seeks to maximise benefits for his party, for the pressure groups that he represents and for the electorate (Downs, 1957). Because all politicians seek to maximise benefits all will be unable to achieve everything that they desire and so they will engage in a process of bargaining to divide the costs and benefits between them. Policy thus emerges as the result of the bargains struck in the process of give and take and mutual adjustment between competing political actors.

There is, in the bargaining model, a hint of the concept of political power, for some actors have greater resources than others. Pure power models, however, popular in the 1930s (Lasswell, 1936 reprinted 1951), have been less in evidence in recent years as the framework for the empirical analysis of decision-making, partly perhaps because of the great difficulty of devising suitable indicators for power and influence. But power, of course, is about the achievement of goals. All the models of policy-making that we have surveyed so far have been models of individual choice, developments of the model of rational economic choice, and entirely about the way in which choices are made about the *means* of attaining policy goals. They say nothing about how those goals, objectives or ends, are determined, except in so far as some of them hint that the externally set goals of politicians might be subverted by the practical and behavioural constraints of the political machine. But in any study of policy-making we need also to consider the way in which goals are determined and refined. The word rational, so often applied to the way in which goals are attained in fact has two meanings. Max Weber noted this distinction and labelled the process of discovering rational means to given ends *Zweckrational* and the process of finding rational ends *Wertrational* (Weber, trans. by Henderson and Parsons, 1947). What models are there of the process of determining ends or objectives? Ends may be determined through the intellectual activities of 'reason' or 'judgement'; they may be derived from a system of belief handed down by God (in a theocratic state for example); they may be passed on through a political movement as part of an ideology; or they may be set by a dictator.

Although it is possible to make an analytical distinction between ends and means in policy-making, in practice such a clear distinction rarely exists. Often politicians have only vaguely articulated objectives in mind when they start on the process of creating new policies; sometimes the objectives are refined and adjusted as the means of attaining them are examined. Some commentators would argue (Lindblom, for example) that any attempt to distinguish ends and means is (i) impossible and (ii) probably undesirable for it enhances the likelihood of conflict. Others, however, suggest that one reason for the poor performance of many policy-makers is their incapacity to produce clearly defined goals (Schultze, 1968). Although in practice ends and means are often closely intertwined there is no doubt that in the case of tax policy-making there are objectives, and that these are both political and economic in nature. It is therefore essential to ask some questions about the way in which goals are set, defined and refined by the politicians who introduce new taxes.

Furthermore, in a study of tax policy-making it is possible to go on to ask questions such as, 'What kind of relationship is maintained between the desired goals and the means of attaining them?' 'Do politicians follow the most suitable decision mode for the attainment of their goals?' 'Can goals or objectives be eroded or lost either through failure to clarify them at the start or through the effects of their progress through the institutions of government?' 'Is it possible that a power structure or relationship exists that inhibits the realisation of some types of policy goal?' Such questions our framework permits us to answer.

When looking for models to use as our framework for analysis we have emphasised the relevance of those that are primarily concerned with decisions of individuals, small groups and organisations – pure rationality, satisficing, incrementalism and bargaining. But, finally, we should mention that there are some models of the policy-making process that purport to explain the patterns of decision-making in a society and to explain how a whole society makes its decisions. What do they suggest? Are the policies that a society adopts the result of adding together all the individual decisions made by voters, politicians and bureaucrats? (Buchanan and Tullock, 1962; Breton, 1974). Are they, as the 'pluralists' suggest, the result of the interplay and bargaining between the groups that compose society? (Bentley, 1949 first edition 1908; Truman, 1951; Dahl, 1971). Is there a corporate state in which three great power groups, government, industry and unions, among them determine policy outcomes? Do small elites determine policy outcomes? (Mills, 1956; Polsby, 1960; Bachrach and Baratz, 1962); or perhaps just a few 'great men'? Or are the policies that a modern western capitalist society adopts simply the result of the power exercised by a ruling class? (Miliband, 1969; O'Connor, 1973). Although in the following chapters we shall hope to shed some light on the relevance of the different individual and group models of decision-making, and to answer some questions about the relationship of objectives and means in the development of tax policy, we may only be able to hint at explanations of these broader patterns of policy-making. Questions on whether the decisions that emerge are the result of demands from the masses or an outcome from an elite or a measure in the interests of the ruling class are beset with too many methodological problems, especially when the data are derived from a limited number of case studies, to enable us to do more than offer occasional relevant comments.

2   The New Taxes – Origins, Objectives and Outlines

Introduction

The main object of this chapter is to provide the reader with a convenient reference source. For those taxes in our study that have become law we present a concise summary of origins, the main features at the time of enactment and a brief account of subsequent amendments. For the TC scheme and WT we outline the proposals and the ensuing events, giving the state of play at the time of writing.

The chapter is set out tax by tax with headings and sub-headings in a form designed to make it easy for reference and to allow readers to skip sections with which they may be familiar. The section 'Background and Origins' briefly summarises the main arguments for and against each tax. A fuller account of these arguments as they unfolded over time appears in the description of the debates in Parliament in Chapter 5. Table 2.1, at the beginning of this chapter, summarises some of the basic features of the new taxes, whilst Table 2.4, at the end, encapsulates the conclusions on origins and objectives.

Capital gains tax

Background and origins

Arguments for the taxation of capital gains were advanced in the nineteenth century, generally for 'windfall' or 'exceptional' profits. Such a tax was defended by Wagner, Wicksell and both Mills (Musgrave and Peacock, 1958). An attempt to devise a tax on gains occurring during the First World War was made by a select committee (HC 102) in 1920 but it was unable to produce an agreed scheme. In the same year the Royal Commission on the Income Tax (Cmd 615) recommended taxing gains where these 'constitute a regular source of profit'. A CGT (as part of the income tax code) has existed in the USA since 1913 and may have served as an example. The more immediate inspiration for the adoption of a CGT as part of the Labour Party programme arose from the recommendation of the Minority Report of the Royal Commission on Taxation, 1955 (Cmd 9474) written by Nicholas (now Professor Lord) Kaldor. There was also a Conservative precedent of sorts in a short-term gains tax, introduced by Mr Selwyn Lloyd as Chancellor in 1962, aimed at speculative gains, which taxed as income gains made on

Table 2.1 Mainstream new taxes since 1964

Tax	Year of implementation	Tax replaced (if any)	Party introducing or proposing (Chancellor of Exchequer)	Department(s) responsible for administration	Revenue (£m) in first full year [a]
Capital gains tax (CGT)	1965	(Incorporated, with changes, short term CGT)	Labour (Callaghan)	Inland Revenue	7
Corporation tax (CT) ('classical system')	1965	Profits tax	Labour (Callaghan)	Inland Revenue	1034
Selective employment tax (SET)	1966 (repealed 1973)	—	Labour (Callaghan)	Treasury, Ministries of Labour, Agriculture and Social Security	325[b]
Corporation tax (CT) (imputation system)	1973	CT (classical)	Conservative (Barber)	Inland Revenue	2245
Value added tax (VAT)	1973	Purchase tax and SET	Conservative (Barber)	Customs and Excise	2497
Capital transfer tax (CTT)	1974/5	Estate duty	Labour (Healey)	Inland Revenue	150[c]
Tax credit (TC)	—	—	Conservative (Barber)	Inland Revenue	—
Wealth tax (WT)	—	—	Labour (Healey)	Inland Revenue	—

Notes: [a] The figure given is that for the financial year following the year in which the tax was introduced, drawn from the annual *Financial Statement or Financial Statement and Budget Report*. For some comments on the significance of the revenue yield see pp. 8–11.
[b] Net of refunds, premium payment, etc.
[c] Estate duty still yielding £165 m.

shares and securities held for less than six months and gains on land held for less than three years.

The goals sought for the 1965 tax were both redistributive and regulatory. Its main purpose was horizontal equity. Capital gains constituted spending power which conferred taxable capacity and to leave such gains untaxed was unfair between tax-payers, especially when some were in a position to convert taxable income into untaxed capital gains. Also, as capital gains could only occur to those with property, taxing gains might be expected to promote vertical equity, i.e. to reduce inequality in wealth distribution. The regulatory arguments were that a CGT would reduce investment distortion (the transfer of funds to low or nil income-yielding assets to avoid income tax) and aid the acceptance of an incomes policy.

The contrary arguments were that a CGT involved high administrative and compliance costs for little revenue – especially in its earlier years; that it reduced the mobility of capital by encouraging owners to cling to assets with accrued gains; and that it might discourage enterprise, the reward for which often came in the form of capital gains. As inflation accelerated the argument grew that that CGT was unfair because it taxed money gains when there was no 'real' gain or even a real loss. In his 1982 Budget, the Chancellor ended this argument by providing for indexation against future price rises.

Features of CGT, 1965

The CGT introduced by Mr Callaghan in 1965 was much more comprehensive than Selwyn Lloyd's tax which it superseded. It comprised both a short-term gains tax by which taxable assets acquired and realised within twelve months were assessed to income tax; and a long-term tax on assets held over one year, which were charged at 30 per cent (or alternatively half of the first £5000 of the net gain and all the remainder was taxed as income if this was to the advantage of the tax-payer).

The 1965 tax applied to the total gains realised in the tax year on all assets save those exempted. The most important exempt assets were a principal private residence, saving certificates, premium bonds, life insurance policies and chattels less than £1000 in value. Capital receipts not derived from assets, e.g. gambling winnings, were exempt. Charities and approved superannuation funds were also relieved from liability. The tax-payer was allowed to offset capital losses against capital gains so that only the net gains were chargeable. Any net losses in one year could be carried forward against future gains. Capital gains of companies were treated as part of the income of the company and charged to corporation tax.

Major changes since introduction

Almost every Finance Act since the introduction of CGT has contained some amendments to it. The following amendments probably have the most general application and importance.

1. In 1969 all securities issued or guaranteed by the British government were exempted from CGT if held for more than one year.

2. In 1971 the short-term CGT was completely abolished, gains realised within a year henceforward being subject to the provisions of the long-term gains tax.

3. In 1971 the Conservatives abolished the provision, in the original act, by which death was treated as a 'deemed realisation' so that CGT was no longer levied on the gains which had accrued on an individual's assets at the time of his death. The value at death became the acquisition value for the inheritor.

4. After CTT replaced estate duty (p. 40) the somewhat anomalous situation existed that lifetime gifts might be liable to both CGT and CTT but gifts at death were liable only to CTT. In 1980 this situation was changed; a roll-over relief was introduced for lifetime gifts between individuals which meant that no CGT was paid at the time of the gift but the beneficiary from the gift carried forward the donor's acquisition value against any subsequent disposal of the asset. If CGT liability did arise in the future any CTT paid at the time of the gift could be offset against the gain.

5. The most numerous changes have taken place in relation to exemption limits and form, and reduced rates of CGT. In 1968 a general exemption provision was introduced by which individuals were exempted if their chargeable gains in any year were less than £50. In 1971 the form of the exemption was changed: no gains tax was payable where the proceeds from the total disposal of chargeable assets did not exceed £500 – a sum raised to £1000 in 1976. In 1978, the exemption limit for individual chattels was raised from £1000 to £2000. In the same year individuals were exempted on the first £1000 of taxable gains with new provisions for a reduced rate (replacing the previous provisions) for gains up to £9500. In 1980 this provision in turn was swept away and replaced by a straight exemption for the first £3000 of gains to individuals and the first £1500 for most trusts. The measures of 1978 and 1980 were offered as a concession in recognition of the effects of inflation on CGT (p. 26). Both Mr Healey and Sir Geoffrey Howe considered this question, but rejected the logical treatment – indexation of the acquisition price – on the grounds that it would be complicated and

that to index CGT would be unfair to owners of other forms of assets (e.g. savings bank deposits) for the government could not contemplate a full indexation of all assets and taxes. However, in his 1982 Budget, Sir Geoffrey Howe up-rated the exemptions from £3000 to £5000 and from £1500 to £2500 and provided for indexation for price rises after 1982 for assets held for more than a year.

Corporation tax

Introduction
Although we have designated CT (classical system) and CT (imputation system) as two separate taxes because of the different principles they embody (p. x) it is convenient in this chapter to treat them together in the same section and to modify somewhat the standardised format of the chapter. The background is to a large extent common and the arguments against the classical system are essentially the arguments in favour of the imputation system.

Background: taxing corporate profits before 1966
In order to understand the arguments for the CT of 1966 we need to review the system it superseded. In 1937 corporate profits had been made subject to a national defence contribution. In the following years this was largely superseded by a tax aimed at war profits – excess profits tax. The system was re-formed as profits tax in 1947 and from then until 1958 it applied only to distributed profits. From 1958 it was applied to undistributed profits as well. Thus, in 1965 undistributed profits were charged to income tax at the standard rate, 41.25 per cent, and profits tax at 15 per cent. Distributed profits (dividends) also bore profits tax at 15 per cent and income tax was deducted from them at the standard rate, but the income tax deduction was simply a convenient administrative device for collection at source; the effective rate depended on the tax-payer's personal circumstances. If the tax-payer was not liable to income tax, he reclaimed the excess tax taken from him; if he was liable to surtax, he subsequently paid the excess. The logic behind the links with income tax was that a company was simply a convenient device by means of which a number of persons (shareholders) jointly pursued a business enterprise and that, in principle, the profits of the company whether distributed or not ought to be taxed as income of the shareholders. With dividends this could be achieved simply; with undistributed profits the situation was more difficult, because shareholders paid different rates of income tax according to their personal circumstances. The rough solution adopted was to charge undistributed profits at the standard rate. A comparatively low profits tax additional to income tax was a convenient device for raising some extra revenue,

which some justified (somewhat illogically) as a payment for the benefit of limited liability enjoyed by companies.

Origins of CT, 1966

The classical system of CT, like CGT, owes its origin to the Minority Report of the Royal Commission on Income and Profits; by 1964 it had been accepted as Labour party policy but not without some opposition (p. 59).

A CT separate from income tax offered more flexibility than the previous system – income tax changes would not automatically involve a change in tax on the undistributed profits of companies. The classical system of CT was advocated primarily for regulatory reasons – to promote economic growth by encouraging the reinvestment of profits. It might also make an incomes policy more palatable to the trade unions because it hit property owners by discriminating against dividends. The parallel introduction of CGT meant that, in so far as increased retention of profits generated share appreciation, a proportion of the capital gain would ultimately accrue to the Exchequer. CT was also held to reduce avoidance opportunities.

Features of CT, 1966–73

The new CT severed the link with income tax which had characterised the previous system for taxing corporate profits. Both distributed and undistributed profits were charged to CT (at a rate of 40 per cent as originally introduced). Undistributed profits paid no further tax. Dividends were taxed to income tax at the rate appropriate to the individual shareholders, but, as before, as a device to secure collection at source, income tax at the standard rate was deducted by the company with the individual shareholders reclaiming tax or paying surtax as appropriate. Special provisions related to closely-owned companies.

The main changes in the tax until its replacement by the Conservative government were in the rates, which were increased by Labour governments to a maximum of 45 per cent in 1968, and subsequently reduced by the Conservatives.

Origins of CT, 1973

The Conservatives were not opposed to the principle of a separate CT; they had themselves been toying with the possibility in the early 1960s (p. 116). Their opposition was to the form it took. Their advocacy of a CT which did *not* discriminate against dividends arose out of their parliamentary opposition to the 1966 tax.

They argued that the discrimination against dividends distorted the workings of the market system and led to a misallocation of resources; rapid growth firms, which necessarily needed to go to the market for part of their funds, were starved of capital. Firms encouraged to retain profits might not reinvest them in the business, but, if they did, would often do so in investment with low return. It was further held that the classical system discriminated against overseas investment. In short the Conservatives, like the Labour Party, advocated a particular form of CT primarily for regulatory purposes – to promote growth, but had different views on the means of its attainment. (For an assessment of the arguments, see p. 225).

In his first Budget Anthony Barber indicated his intention to alter the system but left open the precise form as between a split rate system (by which the rate of CT would be lower on dividends, which also bore income tax, than on undistributed profits) or an imputation system (p. 119). The government leaned to the former, but accepted the recommendation of the Select Committee in favour of the imputation system.

Features of CT, and subsequent changes

The Conservatives introduced the new system of CT to become effective in 1973. It retained the 1966 principle of separating the taxation of corporate profits from income tax but removed the discrimination against dividends by allowing (imputing) a credit against income tax for part of the CT related to dividends. On the introduction of the imputation system the rate of CT was set at 50 per cent. CT imputed to the tax-payer on dividends was equivalent to the basic rate of income tax (30 per cent in 1973) which counted as a tax credit in his hands. If he was a basic rate tax-payer, no income tax was required of him; if he was in the higher rate bracket he paid additionally; if his income was below the tax threshold he could claim payment of his credit as cash.

In practice CT under the imputation system is paid in two stages. On payment of a dividend the company is required to make an advance payment of corporation tax (ACT) equivalent to the shareholders' tax credit. (Assuming a 30 per cent basic rate of income tax, ACT is at the rate of three-sevenths of the dividend paid to shareholders.) ACT can then be set off against 'mainstream' corporation tax which is paid on all profits, distributed and undistributed, at the end of the accounting period.

Under the 1973 CT small companies were taxed at a lower rate if profits were under £25,000 – figure which has been increased by successive governments.

Apart from changes in the rates of CT itself and changes in ACT necessitated by alterations in the basic rate of income tax, the amendments to CT have mainly been of a technical nature. Mention should, however, be made of a measure introduced in November 1974 to provide relief for stock appreciation in conditions of rapid inflation.

Subject to certain limitations, companies were allowed to reduce the closing value of their stocks and work in progress for the accounting period concerned by the amount of their increase in book value during the year – thus reducing the taxable profit for the period. The measure was intended to be temporary and to constitute simply a deferral of tax pending an agreement on the best method of inflation accounting; but it has continued and the Chancellor has set a limit on the amount of back payments which will be demanded. In 1981 new arrangements were adopted.

Selective employment tax

Background and origins
SET is the one tax of the eight we are studying which received no previous consideration in either of the party organisations. There was something of a precedent for the form of the tax in an abortive proposal in 1961 for a national insurance surcharge (p. 99). That apart, the tax derived from the ingenuity of Nicholas Kaldor to meet the exigencies of government. The complex interrelationship of political objectives, economic needs, Kaldor's economic theories and administrative practicalities is set out in detail in Chapter 4. Here we might note that SET was intended as a new revenue source and also advocated for regulatory reasons. The Chancellor saw a capitation tax on labour employed, which was repaid with a premium to manufacturing industry, as improving the 'fiscal balance' by taxing services, as a means of economising in manpower and of encouraging manufacturing and therefore exports.

Opponents found these arguments unconvincing. The 'fiscal balance' argument was valid only for personal services (such as hairdressing); SET applied to many services, like retailing, which were part of the provision of goods, many of which carried high rates of purchase tax or excise duty. If economy of labour in service industries was encouraged, the reverse was true of manufacturing. Some big foreign currency earners, such as invisible exports, were hit by SET whilst import-savers, such as agriculture, failed to benefit. Also the tax had positive disadvantages: anomalies arising from the 'establishment' basis (see below) led to artificial rearrangement of the labour force; and the exemption of the self-employed, encouraged sub-contracting especially in the building industry. It tended to favour the employment of the higher paid compared with low-paid workers. It cut across regional policy, which had a high proportion of service labour. Further, the Opposition claimed that it would raise the price of essentials and it probably was slightly regressive in its distributional effects.

In assessing the pros and cons of SET it is worth noting that research evidence gave some credence to the Chancellor's claim that SET raised prices less than if the same revenue had been raised by the more conventional taxes on expenditure. Professor Reddaway, in two reports (1970, 1973), concluded that SET had caused less rise in prices than if the tax had been passed on in full; and that it was likely that SET had caused some rise in productivity. The strongest evidence came from retailing.

Reddaway's conclusions must be viewed with caution. Because SET applied at a low rate over a wide range of economic activity its effects were not very pronounced and therefore the more difficult to establish. Further, the effects of the abolition of retail price maintenance were very difficult to disentangle from the effects of SET. Finally some consequences of SET might create a spurious productivity increase; for example, if a supermarket reduced employees at the check-out points, a rise in labour productivity (sales per worker) might be offset by a decline in the quality of service as customers had longer to queue. Reddaway's findings are of particular interest because Professor Kaldor argued that the tax would raise productivity in retailing (p. 98); but the case cannot be regarded as proved beyond doubt.

Features of SET, 1966

SET was introduced by Mr Callaghan, as Labour Chancellor of the Exchequer, in 1966. Every employer liable to a national insurance contribution in respect of an employee was required to pay an additional weekly sum to the Ministry of Social Security at the rates (as originally introduced) of 25s. (£1.25) for a man, 12s.6d. (62½p) for a woman or boy under 18 and 8s. (40p) for a girl. No payments were made by the self-employed. Employers in manufacturing activities subsequently received a refund of payments plus a premium, at the rates of 7s. 6d. (37½p), 3s. 9d. (18½p) and 2s. 6d. (12½p) respectively. A second group of industries consisting mainly of agriculture, transport, mining, quarrying and fishing received a refund but no premium. The third group, comprising construction, distribution and service industries, received no refund; it was therefore on this latter group that the impact of the tax was primarily felt.

A number of government departments, but neither of the traditional revenue departments, were concerned with the administration of SET. The Treasury directed the operation. Tax was collected by the Ministry of Social Security through the national insurance stamps. Premiums and refunds were normally paid by the Ministry of Labour through its local offices, but sometimes a different department was responsible; for example, refunds to agriculture, horticulture and forestry were paid by the Ministry of Agriculture (or the Secretary of State for Scotland).

For administrative reasons net payment of SET related to an 'establishment' – broadly speaking a work-place having a single address. If more than half the employees in an establishment were eligible for a refund (premium), it was paid in respect of all the employees; if less than half were so entitled, it was paid for none.

Major changes in SET, 1966–73

SET was subject to a variety of changes during its six years of life. Apart from alterations to the category in which particular economic activities were placed, there were changes of more general application.

1. In 1967 employers were allowed to reclaim half their SET payments on behalf of part-time workers (8–12 hours) who had previously counted under the tax as though they had been full-time.

2. In 1967 a regional employment premium (REP) was grafted onto SET to promote employment in development areas. Employers in manufacturing industry in development areas received a premium per worker, in addition to the current SET premium. The REP was to last for a minimum of seven years and then to be tapered off if it were decided to end the scheme.

3. In April 1968, following Britain's devaluation of the previous November, the premium to manufacturing industry was abolished. Initially the abolition did not apply to the development areas, but it was subsequently applied to them, from April 1970, although the REP remained.

4. SET rates were increased in 1968, but the increase did not apply to part-time workers, and it was also determined that full-time workers over 65 should be treated as part-time for refund purposes. A further increase in 1969 brought the rates to a peak: £2.40 for a man with lower rates for other categories of worker.

5. The Conservatives retured to power in 1970 pledged to repeal SET. In his first Budget Mr Anthony Barber halved the rates and he finally abolished SET with the introduction of VAT on 1 April 1973. The Conservatives also gave notice of the termination of REP at the end of the requisite seven-year period. Under Labour a major change in the structure of REP took place in July 1976 when rates for men and women were equalised at £2. It eventually ended, February 1977, except in Northern Ireland.

Recommendations by Reddaway that SET should be applied to the self-employed, and its basis changed to a percentage of payroll, were never implemented because of the change of government and the replacement of SET by VAT.

Value added tax

Background and origins

Interest in VAT developed in the early 1960s from several quarters and for several reasons. Much of the initial emphasis was on the alleged merits of VAT as a stimulus to exports, reflecting the obsession of post-war Britain with the balance of payments. This aspect figures prominently in the parliamentary comments on the tax in the early 1960s (p. 112) and as part of the case for examining VAT as a tax favourable to growth, presented by the National Economic Development Council (NEDC, 1963). Foreign example was influential; the French TVA was frequently cited and, after the recommendations of the Neumark Committee (1963) for the adoption of VAT as a harmonised sales tax throughout the European Economic Community, VAT had to be viewed in the context of the possible entry of Britain into the EEC.

Mr Maudling, Conservative Chancellor in 1963, showed little enthusiasm for the tax, but set up the Richardson Committee on turnover taxation, which considered VAT as a possible replacement for purchase tax and/or profits tax (p. 112). The Committee opposed both changes (Cmnd 2300, 1964), thus reinforcing Maudling's view; on the other hand the Chancellor did acknowledge that the basis of indirect taxation might need to be widened in the future.

It was antipathy to SET (Mr Callaghan's method of widening the scope of indirect taxes) which helped to crystallise opinion in favour of VAT. Because purchase tax was levied at the wholesale stage it could not be applied to services. If the scope of indirect taxes was to be widened and goods and services taxed on the same basis, then the choice effectively narrowed to VAT or a retail sales tax.

Interest in VAT grew within the Conservative Party especially after the commitment to abolish SET (p. 74) and the need, in view of its increasing contribution to revenue (p. 9), to find a substantial revenue source to replace it. Considerable work was undertaken on VAT in the party, but the Conservative manifesto was conditional (p. 74), stressing that a 'new tax of this kind . . . would need detailed consultation with the civil service'. The Liberal Party, with a strong commitment to Europe and without the responsibilities of power, had adopted VAT as Liberal policy in 1967.

In the meantime another official report, *Value Added Tax* (NEDO, 1969, 2nd edn. 1971) had been considerably more favourable towards VAT than the Richardson Report.

In March 1971 came the Conservative Government's announcement of its intention to legislate the following year for a VAT to replace purchase tax and SET to come into effect from 1 April 1973. A Green Paper accompanied the announcement.

The advantages claimed for VAT as originally introduced were of a regulatory nature – to improve the efficiency of resource use in the economy. VAT was intended to reduce distortion by widening the tax base, by taxing services on exactly the same basis as goods and by introducing a single rate, apart from zero-rate. The wider tax base would also make VAT a better instrument for managing the economy than purchase tax, where changes in rates intended to alter aggregate demand had fallen disproportionately on a small range of goods. Further, the multi-stage taxation of VAT and the zero-rating of exports meant that tax could be excluded from export costs. VAT could therefore be expected to improve the balance of payments (Cmnd 4621, p. 5).

The Conservatives also favoured VAT because of its revenue potential which could make possible a switch from direct to indirect taxation. An essential background factor was membership of the EEC, which after 1967 required the adoption of VAT.

The big disadvantage of VAT was high operating costs, both administrative costs to the revenue authorities and compliance costs to firms. Purchase tax was collected only from some 60,000–70,000 wholesalers. By contrast there are now about one and a third million registered VAT traders. By choosing to go for a single standard rate of 10 per cent with no higher rate or reduced rate (other than zero-rating) Mr Barber sought to give Britain 'the simplest VAT in Europe'. But, even at that, the administrative and especially the compliance costs of VAT would much exceed the costs of the taxes it superseded.

The other argument, much used by the Labour Opposition (p. 114), was that VAT would raise living costs and be regressive.

In the light of experience how valid were these arguments? As introduced VAT was almost certainly more neutral than the taxes it superseded, but the existence of zero-rating and exemptions limited its neutral effects; when an additional higher rate was introduced lack of neutrality was accentuated. VAT did benefit the balance of payments, but the effect was very small; moreover, despite the claims, not all exports were wholly freed of VAT; e.g. exports of exempt goods or services, or exports of products serviced by exempt suppliers who had paid input tax. VAT did carry the revenue-potential for a switch to indirect taxes but, probably because of the likely effect on wage claims, no Chancellor took advantage of the possibility until Sir Geoffrey Howe in 1979. In the first few years after its introduction VAT raised 11–12 per cent of central government revenue from taxation (excluding national insurance contributions). In 1980/1 it raised nearly 19 per cent.

VAT undoubtedly imposed heavy collection costs on small firms (Sandford *et al.*, 1981). On the other hand the allegation that VAT was regressive proved unfounded because of the extensive range of zero-rated goods which comprised a larger percentage of the expenditure of the poor than of the better-off. An advantage of the tax, which subsequently became apparent as high rates of price increase became common, was that as an *ad valorem* tax it did not need continual adjustment for inflation.

Features of VAT, 1973

In essence VAT is a tax on final goods and services consumed in the home market, but it is collected at every stage of production and distribution. Value added is the difference between the prices (net of tax) at which a firm sells its products and the costs of the materials and services (such as electricity and transport) that it has bought in. Under the 'invoicing system' of VAT, which applied in the UK and throughout the EEC, a business charges VAT on the output it sells, pays tax on the materials and services it buys and hands over to Customs and Excise the difference between output tax and input tax in each accounting period. Imports become liable to VAT on entry into the country.

As introduced, VAT had a standard rate of 10 per cent on all goods and services except those which were zero-rated or exempt, or were sold by exempted traders.

When a product is zero-rated no output tax is paid and the supplier of a zero-rated product can recover any input tax paid either by setting it off against VAT due to Customs and Excise on standard-rated products or by claiming a repayment. Foodstuffs, books and newspapers, fuel and power, new building and transport, as well as exports, were all zero-rated in 1973; also, very much at the last minute, children's clothing and footwear and a limited range of foodstuffs (including confectionery, ice-cream and potato crisps), which had previously been liable to purchase tax, were added to the list of zero-rated goods.

Exempt activities in 1973 included the renting of land and buildings, insurance, postal services (where provided by the Post Office) financial services, education, medical services, burials and cremations. Traders with a turnover of under £5000 per annum were also exempt.

The difference between zero-rating and exemption is important and perhaps needs explanation. A trader selling zero-rated goods is normally a 'registered' trader, part of the VAT system, recovering from Customs and Excise the whole of the input tax paid on his purchases. An exempt trader (whether by virtue of the products in which he deals or because his turnover is below the limit) is outside the system; he is not a registered trader. If his purchases are subject to VAT he will have to pay tax on them and cannot recover it from Customs and Excise, though he is at liberty to raise his prices to recoup the rise in his costs. Whilst it is generally an advantage to be zero-rated, it is not necessarily an advantage to be exempt rather than standard-rated. A trader selling almost entirely to the general public will usually gain by being exempt, but a trader may find exemption a disadvantage if he is selling to registered traders as they will prefer to buy from other registered traders. A registered trader who buys from another registered trader can offset input tax against output tax; but a registered trader buying from an exempt trader cannot offset any input tax, even though the price of his inputs may be higher to allow for the VAT paid by the exempt trader. For this reason the provision exists for a trader to seek voluntary registration if his turnover is below the exemption limit.

When VAT was introduced certain other tax adjustments were made. A large proportion of the revenue from purchase tax had come from cars, which had borne considerably more tax than they would pay with a 10 per cent VAT. Because the Chancellor did not wish to forgo this revenue he introduced a special car tax of 10 per cent, levied at the wholesale stage. On the other hand Customs and Excise duties on tobacco and alcoholic drinks were reduced on the introduction of VAT, to keep the overall tax revenue from them much as before.

Major changes since introduction
No major changes were made during the remaining life of the Heath government, but under the Chancellorships of Mr Denis Healey and Sir Geoffrey Howe some important alterations were made. They can be summarised as follows:

April 1974	Some changes in VAT ratings: petrol, diesel, road fuel and confectionery were standard-rated; aids for the disabled and protective clothing were zero-rated.
July 1974	Standard rate cut to 8 per cent.
November 1974	New higher rate of VAT, of 25 per cent, applied to petrol.
May 1975	Coverage of higher rate extended to most domestic electrical goods (excluding cookers, space heaters) and to cameras, furs, jewellery, pleasure-boats, light aircraft and most caravans.
April 1976	Higher rate reduced from 25 to 12½ per cent.
April 1978	Various administrative simplifications effected.
June 1979	Higher rate of VAT abolished and standard rate increased from 8 to 15 per cent.

In addition the minimum turnover for compulsory registration has been raised in a series of stages more or less in line with inflation. After the 1982 Budget it stood at £17,000.

Capital transfer tax

Background and origins
Two interconnecting threads merge to explain the origin of the CTT: on the one hand the administrative deficiencies of the estate duty which CTT replaced and on the other the desire of the Labour Party for a more effective attack on inequality in the distribution of wealth. But each thread is variegated and the pattern woven is complex.

During the 1960s, and indeed earlier, there was widespread agreement that estate duty was not working well. Broadly speaking, estate duty was a tax levied on the total value of property passing at death or within a specified period before death. It was the first consistently progressive tax to be introduced in the United Kingdom (1894), and it remained very progressive with a top rate of 80 per cent of the total estate (before amendment in 1972). But, whilst nominally heavy, it was widely known as 'the voluntary tax' because of the ease with which it could be avoided. The simplest way to escape tax was by lifetime gift; if the donor survived for the requisite period no tax was payable. For the more sophisticated there were various artificial devices for avoiding duty of which perhaps the most important was the discretionary trust. Whilst these were the deficiencies of estate duty which made most impression on egalitarians, other criticisms of the tax were not lacking and were summarised in the Green Paper issued by the Conservatives, *Taxation of Capital on Death: A Possible Inheritance Tax in Place of Estate Duty* (Cmnd 4930, 1972).

The principal deficiency of estate duty could not really be rectified without a change of structure. The gifts *inter vivos* period, as it was called, i.e. the period before death during which any gifts would be chargeable to estate duty, had been extended in stages, from the one year specified in the 1894 Finance Act to the seven years set by Mr Roy Jenkins, as Chancellor, in 1968. The logical outcome of this process was for Britain to follow the example of almost every other country and introduce a regular gifts tax to supplement estate duty. The avoidance loophole of discretionary trusts also needed more comprehensive treatment. An attempt by Mr Jenkins in 1969 to deal with the trust loophole was generally held not to have been particularly successful.

At the same time another discussion amongst both tax theorists and policy-makers was under way about the best form of death duty (and allied gift tax); should it be an estate type or an inheritance type? The estate tax charged the donor on what he gave and on his total estate at death; the inheritance tax levied the charge on what was received by the beneficiary in gifts and legacies regardless of the size of estate from which it came. In this controversy it was held that estate tax was easier to administer and the better revenue yielder; advocates of the inheritance tax claimed that to tax the beneficiary accorded more closely with ideas of ability to pay; that the inheritance tax could be more readily adjusted to the circumstances of the heir (e.g. preferential scales for the immediate family); and that it was a better medium for reducing inequality of wealth because tax was geared to the size of receipt and it was large receipts, not large estates as such, that perpetuated inequality.*

Academics were to be found on both sides of the divide. Wheatcroft (1965) and Prest (1967) favoured the estate duty form whilst Meade (1964), Stutchbury (1968) and Sandford, Willis and Ironside (1973) preferred the inheritance tax form.

Among the parties, the Liberals had many years earlier come down in favour of inheritance tax as party policy, and reiterated the proposal for a legacy and gift tax in their 1964 election manifesto. The latter-day Conservative Party† had debated the issue less than Liberals or Labour, but Anthony Barber as Chancellor was responsible for the Green Paper in 1972 which raised the possibility of an inheritance tax, but left the Government uncommitted. From the later 1960s the Labour Party Conference and the NEC were calling for 'strong measures' to deal with large gifts and, with the party in Opposition in the early 1970s, the emphasis on policy-making grew. However, the party seemed to have difficulties in deciding between a donor or a donee-based tax (p. 13). The 1974 manifesto simply referred to a 'new' tax on major transfers of personal wealth . When it came it was donor based.

Whatever its form, the fire of Labour's enthusiasm for a new transfer tax was fuelled by private research which indicated the continuing extent of inequality (p. 13). When Labour achieved office in 1974 it is notable that the Government set up a Royal Commission, under the chairmanship of Lord Diamond, on the Distribution of Income and Wealth. Its remit was to undertake a 'thorough and comprehensive inquiry' into the existing distribution of income and wealth, to study past trends and to make regular assessment of subsequent changes.

*Not all these claims would be accepted without dispute. For a convenient statement of the issues see *The Taxation of Net Wealth, Capital Transfers and Capital Gains of Individuals*, OECD, 1979, pp. 60–2.

†When estate duty was introduced in 1894 the Conservatives in the Commons, led by Balfour, argued the case for an inheritance tax very persuasively (Sandford, 1971).

Superficially this procedure might appear to accord with the rationality model of policy-making: first find out all the facts, then let the facts guide policy. Sadly, however, Mr Healey committed the government to both CTT and a wealth tax before the Commission was even set up; and CTT was enacted and the Wealth Tax Select Committee had completed its evidence before the publication of the first Report of the Diamond Commission (Sandford 1979).

Thus, the main purpose of CTT was redistributive. As Mr Healey put it, it was part of 'a determined attack on the maldistribution of wealth in Britain'. CTT was to close the loopholes that had reduced the effectiveness of estate duty.

The arguments against CTT reflected two very different approaches. The Conservative Opposition generally attacked it for its severity and particularly alleged that the tax would have detrimental effects on private business, including agriculture. Indeed, Mrs Thatcher, as the Opposition spokesman on the Bill, roundly declared that the Conservatives would repeal the tax. Opposition from other quarters, including the Liberal Party and some academics, attacked the Government for choosing an inappropriate form of tax for reducing inequality of wealth: a cumulative tax on the donee, they maintained, would have been much more effective.

Features of CTT, 1974

In his first budget in March 1974, within a few weeks of Labour taking office, Mr Denis Healey, announced the introduction of a lifetime gifts tax to, as he put it, 'mesh in' with estate duty. A White Paper in August 1974 gave further details and the new capital transfer tax was enacted by a special Finance Bill in the autumn of 1974. The tax came into force for lifetime transfers from 26 March 1974, the day of its announcement; it replaced estate duty on transfers at death from 13 March 1975.

The main distinguishing characteristics of CTT as compared with estate duty were that the charge extended to gifts, whereas estate duty had only applied to gifts within seven years before death, and it was cumulative – the rate of tax on any gift or on the estate left at death was determined by the amount of taxable transfers previously made. It thus struck at avoidance by means of gifts, which had characterised estate duty; also by providing for a periodic charge to be levied on discretionary trusts, it rendered unattractive another favoured method of avoidance.

The nominal rates of CTT for transfers at death were somewhat lower than those of estate duty. At the time of its abolition estate duty rates rose from a marginal rate of 25 per cent on estates over £15,000 to a maximum marginal rate of 75 per cent on estates over £½ m; by contrast, as first introduced, CTT on transfers at death started at 10 per cent on estates over £15,000, carried a 65 per cent rate at £½–1 m and only achieved the maximum rate of 75 per cent on estates over £2 m. But, of course, CTT included lifetime transfers and was cumulative. The White Paper and the Finance Bill had proposed that the rates of CTT should be the same for lifetime gifts as for transfers at death. However, during the passage of the Bill, the Chancellor conceded a lower scale of rates for gifts up to £300,000. One very important relief within the CTT, which had not applied to estate duty, was that transfers between husband and wife, whether during lifetime or at death, were tax exempt.

On inception CTT carried an annual exemption for the first £100 of gifts to any one recipient, and over and above that, the exemption of £1000 per donor per annum. Gifts made out of income that formed part of expenditure and wedding gifts (subject to certain limits) were also exempted. Because the first £15,000 of transfers carried a nil rate, there was, in effect, in addition to the annual exemptions, a lifetime exemption of £15,000. The original Act provided for a concession to agricultural property, but, unlike the former estate duty relief, it only applied to 'full-time working farmers'.

Major changes since introduction
Since 1973 CTT has been the subject of major modifications both under the Labour government and the Conservatives (from 1979), who reneged on Mrs Thatcher's pledge to abolish the tax but instead sought to ease its burden. The main changes can be summarised as follows:

April 1976	The form of relief for 'full-time working farmers' contained in the act imposing CTT had been based on a rental formula. In 1976 this was changed to a 50 per cent reduction in the valuation of land and farm buildings for CTT purposes.
	A relief was also introduced for private businesses, by which a transfer of business assets by a sole proprietor or partner or a controlling shareholder in an unquoted company would only be taxed at 70 per cent of its value.
	The annual exemption for gifts was raised from £1000 to £2000.
October 1977	CTT threshold was raised from £15,000 to £25,000. Business relief (above) was increased (henceforward the relieved assets

	would be taxed at 50 per cent of their value) and a new 20 per cent relief was introduced for minority shareholdings in unquoted companies (all subject to a cumulative limit of £500,000).
March 1980	CTT threshold was raised to £50,000.
	Small gifts exemption was raised to £250.
March 1981	A new rate schedule was introduced for lifetime transfers, with a maximum rate of 50 per cent (as compared with 75 per cent on transfers at death and, hitherto, on lifetime transfers).
	The cumulation period was reduced to ten years. (Thus a married couple would be able to give away £100,000 of property every ten years entirely tax free.)
	The annual exemption for lifetime transfers was raised to £3000.
	A new relief was introduced to benefit agricultural landlords. Transfers of let agricultural land would be subject to a 20 per cent reduction in their valuation for CTT purposes.
March 1982	The Chancellor proposed to raise the exemption limit to £55,000, to widen the bands for both transfers at death and during life and henceforward to index the bands. A new regime for trusts was promised in the Finance Bill.

The cumulative effect of the alterations to CTT from the principles set out in the original White Paper has been to change its nature almost completely. Far from being the great attack on the inequality in wealth distribution which Mr Healey had announced at its inauguration, it is even less effective than estate duty.

Mr Healey had expected CTT to yield less revenue than estate duty initially, but subsequently to yield more than estate duty would have done. The lower scale of CTT and the free transfers between husband and wife would cause a falling off in revenue until such time as the taxation of gifts and the cumulative provisions began to bite. However, the reliefs introduced subsequently by Mr Healey himself, followed by the changes made by Sir Geoffrey Howe, have rendered very remote the possibility that CTT will ever yield more than estate duty in real terms. Because of the lag in payment of death duties, which for some property can be spread over eight years, there is no neat dividing line between the end of revenue from estate duty and the beginning of revenue from CTT. Nonetheless the message of Table 2.2 is very clear. Despite inflation, in 1981 the yield of death and gift taxes was less in money terms than estate duty yielded in 1972. Expressed as a percentage of GDP, which, though imperfect, is probably the best basis for comparison, CTT in 1981 was contributing barely one-third of what the maligned estate duty produced in 1972 – and that before the Budget reliefs of 1981, with their scope for avoidance by gifts, have had the chance to take effect. The sole method by which an estate duty or donor-based tax (unlike an inheritance tax) reduces inequality in wealth-holding is by transferring property from private wealth holders to the state. The figures in Table 2.2 therefore indicate how very far CTT has fallen short of the objective proclaimed by Mr Healey, a shortfall apparent even before Sir Geoffrey Howe's deliberate change of direction.

Table 2.2 Yield of death and gift taxes, UK 1972–81

	£ m	Per cent of government revenue from taxation[a]	Per cent of GDP at factor cost
1972	482	2.24	0.87
1974	379	1.26	0.51
1976	359	0.80	0.32
1978	348	0.62	0.24
1979	393	0.58	0.23
1980	433	0.52	0.22
1981	451	0.47	0.21

Source: National Income and Expenditure, 1982.
Note: [a] Includes national insurance contributions and local rates.

Tax credit scheme

Background and origins
Despite their very different fields, there is a distinct parallel in background between CTT and the tax credit scheme. In both cases feedback from the administrative machine, not to mention external commentators, made it clear that existing procedures were not working well; and in both cases there was a fairly long standing broad-based academic debate centred round a search for the optimum solution.

The failure of existing machinery was revealed by the so-called 'poverty trap' or 'poverty surtax'. Over a period of time, as part of the social security system, a series of means-tested benefits had come into existence in the UK. By the early 1970s they numbered over forty, of which the principal ones were rent and rate rebates, free school meals and milk, and family income supplement (FIS), a benefit for low-paid married wage-earners with at least one child. Because of an overlap between the social security and tax systems it was possible for a family actually to be made worse off by getting a wage increase. On the one hand the increase would be subject to income tax and to a deduction for national insurance contributions; on the other hand the rise in income would reduce eligibility for benefit. Although not all the reduction in benefits would come into effect immediately, the net result could be that, in extreme cases, the combined tax and loss of benefit would exceed the wage increase; in many more cases the net addition to income would be only a small fraction of the wage increase. Thus, the poor could not drag themselves out of poverty.

Whilst the poverty trap was an immediate concern in the 1960s and 1970s, of longer standing was a search in both the UK and the USA for a system linking welfare payments with income tax and effecting in the process a major simplification.

In the United Kingdom Lady Juliet Rhys Williams (1943) was the first to propose a social dividend. Under her scheme a weekly dividend would be paid to all, at adequate rates of support; national insurance contributions, income tax and surtax would be abolished and a proportional tax levied on all income except the social dividend. Lady Rhys Williams gave evidence to the Royal Commission on the Taxation of Profits and Income (1955), but the Royal Commission thought there were practical difficulties in the scheme (p. 11). Sir Brandon Rhys Williams, Lady Juliet's son and a Conservative MP, has continued to elaborate on the social dividend principle and press the advantages of such schemes (e.g. Rhys Williams, 1967). A less ambitious proposal for a negative income tax was put forward by Professor Dennis Lees (1967) and a more comprehensive scheme by Professor James Meade (1972).*

An eminent American advocate has been Professor Milton Friedman (1962). In the USA there has been not only extensive debate but some experimentation (Brown and Jackson, 1978); in the early 1970s Presidential candidate Senator George McGovern advocated a 'demo-grant' financed by a 33.5 per cent tax rate.

All the political parties in the UK showed interest in some simplification and integration of income tax and social security provisions (see

---

*For a recent comprehensive survey of the family of social dividend and negative income tax schemes, see D. Collard, 'Social Dividend and Negative Income Tax', Sandford, Pond and Walker (eds.) (1981).

Chapter 3). The Liberals welcomed Lady Rhys Williams's proposals and have consistently pressed for some kind of negative income tax. Labour showed interest (p. 65) and eventually emerged with the child benefit scheme (p. 48) but nothing more comprehensive. It was the Conservative Party who undertook most work in this field, under the leadership of Brendon Sewill, Director of the Conservative Research Department 1965–70, and for whom it was a personal interest (p. 74). However, no definite scheme had emerged from the Conservative Party deliberations by 1970. The form which the TC scheme ultimately took was rather different from the lines along which the Conservative Research Department had been working. The architect of the TC proposals was Anthony Barber's special adviser, Mr Arthur (now Lord) Cockfield (p. 95), who became a Treasury Minister in 1979.

The tax credit proposals

In his budget speech in March 1972, Mr Anthony Barber indicated the possibility of a tax credit scheme and promised a Green Paper, which appeared in October 1972; the Government suggested that the scheme should be examined by a select committee of the House of Commons, which was duly set up.

At the time of the Green Paper the Government was not irrevocably committed to a TC scheme but it 'commended the proposals'. Although fairly precise in its administrative details, some important issues were left open in the Green Paper, notably whether child credits should be paid to the father by employers or to the mother through the Post Office.

The TC scheme involved a partial merger of the tax and social security systems, to be brought about through the introduction of a new form of credit which would replace (i) the main personal allowances granted under income tax, i.e. the single, married persons and child allowances; (ii) the family allowance (FAM), paid through the Post Office to the mother in respect of second and subsequent children; and (iii) family income supplement (FIS).

Credits were to be paid through their employer to those in work and on occupational pension schemes; through the Department of Health and Social Security to people drawing national insurance benefits such as sickness or retirement benefits; and through the Department of Employment to those temporarily unemployed.

Each individual in the scheme would receive a notification of credit entitlement which he would give to the paying authority, which would deduct tax at the basic rate (then 30 per cent) from all his income, setting the credit against tax. If tax exceeded credit, the individual paid the net figure in tax; if credit exceeded tax, then the difference was paid to the individual.

The Green Paper used the following illustrative figures for the credits: £4 for a single person, £6 for a married man or the parent of a one-parent family, and £2 for a child. Table 2.3 describes the working of the scheme.

Table 2.3   Illustration of the operation of the tax credit proposals

Family size	Weekly pay (£)	Less tax at 30% (£)	Plus credit (£)	Pay after tax and credit (£)
Single persons	10	3	4	11
	25	7.50	4	21.50
	50	15	4	39
Married couple with two children	10	3	10	17
	25	7.50	10	27.50
	50	15	10	45

To achieve the simplification of taxing all income at basic rate, existing tax allowances either had to be eliminated or paid as year-end adjustments. Thus the tax allowances on insurance premiums and on mortgage interest for home-owners were to be replaced by lower rates of premiums or interest, with the Government providing the difference directly to the insurance companies and building societies. After reviewing the alternatives, the Green Paper proposed that the tax allowance for working wives should remain at its current level and be paid as a tax allowance against the wife's earnings. For higher rate tax-payers, the main personal allowances would continue to be given against higher rate tax; regular tax deductions would continue, but on a non-cumulative PAYE basis with end-year adjustments.

The TC scheme was intended to cover most employed persons, the main national insurance beneficiaries, both short and long-term (including all on state retirement pensions) and most occupational pensioners. The principal groups excluded were the self-employed (who paid tax in arrears) and those with earnings of under £8 per week (who would need more extensive help than the credit would provide). The Green Paper expressed the hope that it might be possible to incorporate these groups into the scheme at a later date.

The objectives as set out in the Green Paper were 'to improve the system of income support for poor people', and 'to simplify and reform the whole system of personal tax collection'. The replacement of tax allowances by tax credits gave help to many people whose income was too low for them to pay tax and these people also gained from some of the compensating changes resulting from the proposed abolition of tax reliefs, such as that on insurance premiums. The system of relief by means of tax credits had the big advantages of being automatic and stigma-free with a high take-up. On the tax side, the abolition of coding and of cumulation under PAYE would effect economies in tax administration and in the compliance costs of firms. An incidental advantage was that the TC scheme would also make it easier to tax sickness and unemployment benefits, which was widely accepted as desirable but administratively difficult under the existing scheme.

The main criticisms of the scheme came from academics (notably Professors Atkinson and Kaldor) and poverty lobbies such as the Child Poverty Action Group who presented evidence to the Select Committee and whose views are reflected in the Minority Reports (p. 170). The critics pointed to the limited coverage and to the large number of means-tested benefits that would remain. They condemned the failure of the Green Paper to explain satisfactorily the source of the extra £1300 million needed to finance the scheme – a crucial omission because this determined the net effect of the income distribution; on a 'revenue-neutral' basis the value of the benefits would be some 17–18 per cent lower and a number of poor would finish up worse off (Atkinson, 1973). Conversely, they argued that, on the basis of the illustrative figures, the majority of the expenditure benefited those not in poverty; if £1300 million were available for relief of poverty, it could be much more effective if differently applied. Moreover, the critics feared that the scheme would make it more difficult to introduce steady progression into the income tax scale, because it would increase the advantages and convenience of taxing a wide band of income at a single marginal rate; in the same vein, they considered the scheme insufficiently flexible to ensure that help could be directed to those most in need.

Developments since the Green Paper

The Select Committee approved the TC scheme, but not unanimously, and there were two Minority Reports.

The Committee's recommendations included the proposal that all the child credit should be paid through the Post Office to the mother; but before their report was issued, the Chancellor had realised the strength of feeling and given the assurance that the Government would 'not adopt any arrangement which leaves mothers being paid less than they are at present' (HC Debates, 6 March 1973, col. 242).

The Conservatives held up the computerisation programme for PAYE pending the consideration of the scheme. After the Select Committee had reported, they committed themselves to introduce tax credits in 1977 if they won the 1974 election.

The Labour victors in 1974 shelved the TC scheme. In his first Budget speech Mr Healey stressed its 'serious drawbacks', but added: 'We have not taken any decision against the principle of negative income tax' (26 March 1974, col. 312). The Labour Government introduced the child benefit scheme – a cash payment in respect of all children, payable to mothers via the Post Office – in place of family allowances and child tax allowances, and they have also changed the system of tax relief for insurance premiums. Both these measures could be regarded as the application of part of the TC scheme; but beyond that Labour has shown no further interest in the proposals.

The Conservatives in Opposition attempted some further work on the subject. Their 1979 election manifesto made it clear that the TC scheme was still on the agenda, but not for immediate implementation, both for reasons of cost and technical reasons arising from the switch to computers.

Wealth tax

Background and origins

A wealth tax (WT) or, to give it its more accurate and comprehensive title, an annual, personal, net wealth tax,* is a charge on the aggregate net value (assets minus liabilities) of a person's possessions, including stocks and shares, bank balances, unincorporated business assets, houses, land and personal possessions like a car, boat, furniture and jewellery. The charge extends to all assets save those specifically exempted and to persons whose aggregate wealth exceeds some specified threshold.

The idea of a WT for the United Kingdom developed very much within the Labour Party, with particular encouragement from the left wing of the party and the TUC. The party's interest can, perhaps, be dated from 1956 (p. 69), but the idea only took hold from the early 1960s. In Labour Party literature a WT was seen very much as an instrument for reducing inequality in the distribution of wealth (p. 13). Whilst European precedents for an annual WT are mentioned in Labour publications (p. 61), unlike the Labour Party proposals, the continental WTs were aimed primarily at horizontal rather than vertical equity. They are properly regarded as an alternative to the United Kingdom practice of taxing investment income more heavily than earned income (Sandford, Willis and Ironside, 1975).

*A 'once and for all' tax on wealth, or a capital levy, was widely canvassed after the First World War (Dalton, 1923); also Sir Stafford Cripps in 1948 and Mr Roy Jenkins in 1968 introduced 'once and for all' charges based on investment income.

A WT rather more on continental lines was considered by the Conservatives as part of a package to abolish the differential taxation on investment income and reduce estate duty; but the flirtation was brief (pp. 72–3).

The Conservatives may have been impressed not only by the appeal of a WT to those seeking horizontal equity but also by the possibility that, as part of a reform package, it could help to stimulate growth. This idea had been floated by the NEDC: 'The introduction of a wealth tax here would be a controversial step but it may have a useful role in any major review of taxation related to a programme for growth' (NEDC, 1963). Academics referred to all three possible objectives in their consideration of the subject (e.g. Sandford, 1971).

However, it was not growth which was in mind when the proposal for a WT eventually gained Labour Party manifesto status in 1974.

The wealth tax proposals

In his first budget, three weeks after the election of February 1974, Mr Healey stated the Government's intention to introduce a WT. However, as such a tax was new to the United Kingdom, he proposed to publish a Green Paper to promote a full discussion of the possibilities and suggested that a House of Commons select committee might take evidence from a wide range of sources. The Green Paper (Cmnd 5704) appeared in August 1974 and the Select Committee was set up at the end of 1974 and reported in November 1975 (HC 696).

The Green Paper was notable for the range of options which it nominally left open. A careful reading reveals only two completely 'hard' commitments – that there would be a WT and that the value of pensions rights would not count as wealth for purposes of the tax. But the threshold, the rates, whether the introduction of a WT would be accompanied by income tax reductions, whether a 'ceiling provision' (restricting the proportion of income that could be taken in income tax and wealth tax combined) should be included – all these and many other features were nominally left open, though with some possibilities being indicated. Nonetheless from the 'illustrative' figures, the general tenor of the document and the subsequent memoranda from the Inland Revenue to the Select Committee, it is clear that a WT was envisaged with a threshold of around £100,000, with rates rising to a maximum of anywhere from $2\frac{1}{2}$ to 5 per cent, with little, if any, reduction in income tax at the time of its introduction and with minimal concessions to agriculture, private industry and heritage objects. It was also envisaged that it would be administered from new regional offices and linked with CTT rather than with income tax as was normal with continental WTs. It would be operated on a self-assessment basis.

In announcing to Parliament his intention to introduce a WT, Mr

Healey presented it squarely as part of his 'determined attack on the maldistribution of wealth in Britain' (p. 121). In his Foreword to the Green Paper, however, the Chancellor drew on the horizontal equity argument: 'Income by itself is not an adequate measure of taxable capacity. The ownership of wealth, whether it produces income or not, adds to the economic resources of a taxpayer so that the person who has wealth as well as income of a given size necessarily has a greater taxable capacity than one who has only income of that size.' Both objectives, vertical and horizontal equity, place Labour's WT proposals firmly in the redistributive category.

However, there were also hints in the debates in Parliament (p. 122) that a WT might be acceptable to Conservatives and others who would not otherwise approve it, if it were part of a wider tax package, increasing incentives and promoting growth (a regulatory function). These views were to find expression in the various reports of the Select Committee.

The arguments against a WT were most fully set out in the evidence presented to, and the reports produced by, the Select Committee (p. 186). The main arguments were that a WT is administratively cumbersome and with a high ratio of cost to yield; that, in practice, because of administrative problems, notably valuation difficulties, inequities arise; and that a heavy WT might seriously harm the economy through its effect on saving and investment, especially in private industry and agriculture, where expansion would become more difficult and fragmentation might result. Further, it was pointed out that a WT with a threshold as high as £100,000 would do little to promote horizontal equity; to meet this objective would, logically, require a threshold low enough to enable WT to replace the investment income surcharge (around £30,000 at the time).

Developments since the Green Paper
The Select Committee never achieved a majority report; instead it published five minority drafts. Of these, all but one expressed the view that horizontal equity should be the prime purpose of the tax with a threshold below that of the Green Paper. The one exception to this view was the report receiving the least support.

Thereafter it appeared that the Government was seeking quietly to bury the WT, perhaps because it was impressed (especially in the depressed state of the economy) with the possible economic detriments and the high ratio of administrative cost to yield. The month after the Select Committee reported the Chancellor announced that because the Committee had taken longer than expected he did not feel able to introduce a WT in that session, but that the Inland Revenue would continue preparatory work and that he might publish draft clauses for discussion during 1976. No such clauses were published. Towards the end of 1976 the Chancellor further announced that he was not proposing to introduce a WT in that Parliament.

The TUC reacted to this statement by pressing Ministers to agree to the setting up of a working party, under the auspices of the TUC/Labour Party Liaison Committee (pp. 207–8), with the object of finding practical ways of bringing in a WT. The outcome, in December 1977, was a commitment of the Liaison Committee, with the Prime Minister present, to a WT with a threshold of £100,000, with rates rising progressively from 1 to 5 per cent on fortunes over £5 million. The form of WT envisaged was that aiming at vertical rather than horizontal equity.

In the 1979 general election the Conservatives specifically repudiated a WT. Labour, on the other hand, pledged itself in the next Parliament to introduce WT with a threshold of £150,000 (p. 65). Thus, a WT remains very much on Labour's agenda.

Summary and conclusions
Table 2.4 tabulates the objectives of the taxes and lists significant influences. The main conclusions may be summarised as follows:

Objectives
1. Only in the case of SET was revenue-raising an immediate objective, but one of the reasons VAT was attractive to the Conservatives was its revenue potential for a switch from direct to indirect taxation.

2. Of the five Labour taxes, redistribution was a predominant motive in three and a subsidiary motive in a fourth.

3. In a variety of ways regulatory objectives were sought: the efficient use of resources, economic growth, rendering incomes policies more acceptable. In two of the three Conservative taxes, CT (imputation) and VAT, regulatory goals predominated, whilst regulatory goals figured prominently with the Labour Party's CT (classical) and SET.

4. In two cases, CTT and TC, the deficiencies of the existing system exercised a potent influence on change. In addition objections to SET stimulated consideration of VAT.

Origins and influences
1. The influence of foreign example is very difficult to assess; but it may have played some (very limited) part with CGT and WT and must have been an important underlying factor with VAT once the EEC had chosen VAT as its sales tax.

2. The influence of individuals is clearly important; most notably Nicholas Kaldor on the Labour side and, to a lesser extent, Arthur Cockfield on the Conservative side.

3. Clearly, party ideology is a dominating influence. Labour's concern is with equality, and hence redistribution, and even its regulatory taxes have a hint of an anti-wealthy bias about them, i.e. CT (classical) and SET (which was regarded in some quarters as anti-City). The Conservative ideology is reflected in the concern for promoting private enterprise, giving incentives and removing distortions. These objectives enter into CT (imputation) and into VAT which, apart from its 'neutrality', represented a means by which direct taxes might be reduced. Also, Conservatives have been more concerned with simplifying the tax system.

Thus parties play a vital role in the origins of at least some new taxes. We now turn to a more detailed consideration of the forces within the political parties that determine the adoption of policies on new taxes.

Table 2.4 *Summary of objectives and origins*

Year of implementation (or proposal)	Tax and party	Objectives	Significant influences on introduction
1965	CGT (Labour)	*Redistributive:* Horizontal equity; vertical equity *Regulatory:* Counteract investment distortion; promote acceptance of incomes policy	Minority Report of Royal Commission (Nicholas Kaldor) Foreign example – USA Short-term CGT
1966	CT (classical) (Labour)	*Regulatory:* Promote growth by retention and reinvestment of profits; promote acceptance of incomes policy *Redistributive:* Heavier tax on dividends	Minority Report of Royal Commission (Nicholas Kaldor)
1966	SET (Labour)	*Revenue:* Significant net revenue yield *Regulatory:* Improving 'fiscal balance' by taxing services; encouraging manpower savings in service industries; favouring manufacturing and indirectly exports	Brain child of Nicholas Kaldor in context of revenue needs and unfavourable trade balance
1973	CT (imputation) (Conservative)	*Regulatory:* Promote growth by ending discrimination against dividends; encourage reinvestment through the market	Opposition to CT (classical)

Table 2.4 (contd.)

Year of implementation (or proposal)	Tax and party	Objectives	Significant influence on introduction
1973	VAT (Conservative)	*Regulatory*: More neutral indirect tax system; less distortion; benefit to balance of payments *Revenue*: Potential from wider base; possible switch from direct taxation	Opposition to, and disadvantages of, SET Foreign influence – first French example, then EEC harmonisation
1974	CTT (Labour)	*Redistributive*: Vertical equity; an instrument for correcting the maldistribution of wealth	Ease by which estate duty could be avoided General debate on most suitable form of death and gift taxes
(1973)	Tax credit (Conservative)	*Simplification*: Improved form of relief of poverty and tax simplification *Redistributive*: To limited extent	Recognised deficiencies of overlapping tax and social security provisions General debate on negative income tax Brain child of Arthur Cockfield
(1974)	WT (Labour)	*Redistributive*: Vertical equity; horizontal equity	Pressure of left wing of Labour Party and TUC Imperfectly understood foreign examples

3 The Political Parties

The role of the party

The 'adversary' nature of British politics and the ever present thread of ideological thought in the origins of most of the new taxes might lead one to expect that the main political parties have paid particular attention to the development of well-shaped policies on tax. Where a tax has a clearly ideological objective then it is reasonable to expect that the party proposing it has both clarified the objective and worked out in some detail the means to achieve it.

How far does this happen? To what extent are the parties in fact suited to act as instruments for devising new policies prior to attaining office? What machinery do they have and how far is it effective? Is it effective in so crystallising political and ideological objectives that they can be sustained through the long drawn-out processes of departmental and parliamentary consideration? How far are they equipped to choose the best means of attaining their objectives? Do they plan new 'ideological' taxes without sufficient regard to the economic and administrative effects? How far within a party are the two types of objective (economic and political) reconciled before a new policy is formally adopted and placed before the electorate in a manifesto? Are there rash commitments?

The making of party policy has now become a subject of central political concern for all parties, but particularly the Labour Party; even more than the clash of personalities that hit the headlines in 1981, it is at the heart of Labour's current internal difficulties. Is a political party a collection of middle-of-the-roaders who wish to attract the greatest number of electors in order to win an election, or is it a machine for the carrying forward of a great ideology? A party machine that is designed to win elections by appealing to the great mass of voters in the centre is likely to have a very different approach to the development of policy than is a party that has as its main objective the promotion of a particular point of view.

Such questions are central to any estimation of the effectiveness of party machinery for policy-making.

Of the eight taxes that form the basis of this study all but one, SET, were the subject of prior party aspiration and/or commitment when in opposition; and SET, though its *introduction* was in no way foreshadowed in party thinking or literature, was the subject of a firm party commitment to abolish.

The seven taxes that shared a party parenthood, however, differed in many important respects. They did not all enter the party consciousness or party machine by the same route; they differed in the amount of preparatory work undertaken in the party, in the precision or vagueness of the proposals as they emerged from the party machine, and in the degree of commitment in the party programme. They were subject to different influences within the party machine. Moreover the process of policy preparation in the Labour Party differs considerably from that in the Conservative Party.

The Labour Party

The policy-making machinery
In Labour's formal constitution the annual conference is the authoritative body. A two-thirds majority for a particular policy at the Conference makes it official Labour Party policy. Conference also elects the National Executive Committee (NEC), which acts as the ruling authority of the Party between annual conferences. Policies may be adopted at Conference *before* any detailed work has been done on them. Resolutions proposed by any delegates obtaining sufficient support become party policy. The NEC works through a series of sub-committees which can be expected, with the aid of the Research Department, to give substance to the policies passed by Conference. A standing Home Policy Sub-committee meets whether Labour is in Government or Opposition. A sub-committee of the home Policy Sub-committee, on Finance and Economic Affairs, which deals with taxation, may or may not meet when Labour is in Government. Particular working parties on taxation may also be set up.

Counterpoised to, and in an ambiguous relationship with, Conference is the Parliamentary Labour Party (PLP). Its Leader and Deputy are *ex officio* members of the NEC. Other PLP members may be elected to the NEC but the scope is restricted by the method of election.* The PLP has an Economics and Finance Group which meets occasionally, but has no constitutional function in relation to new taxes.

The NEC confers with the PLP at the beginning of each parliamentary session and at other times at the request of either side. Any item for inclusion in the manifesto has to be agreed between the NEC and the PLP (though there have been attempts to change this duality to give the NEC the sole voice in determining the contents of the manifesto). It is laid down as part of the constitution that, when Labour is in Opposition, the Shadow spokesmen are on the relevant NEC sub-committees.

*For details of the Labour Party constitution, see, for example, Reg Underhill, *How the Labour Party Works* (published by the Labour Party).

The membership, besides NEC members, includes a number of co-opted MPs and co-opted experts, the invitations being subject to the approval of the NEC. (As one knowledgeable witness put it: 'People get on the committees if they are strongly supported or if they have no enemies.') The composition of study groups or working parties is not closely examined by the NEC and is, in practice, likely to be determined by the Research Secretary who is Head of the Research Department.

Research and secretarial support for policy-making
Much of the responsibility for working out policy development and the details of policy lies with the Research Department under its Head. The Research Secretary produces the draft of Labour Party programmes. He is *ex officio* on all the policy-making committees of the NEC. He may, and generally does, take the initiative in setting up study groups. He nominates the co-opted members of the committees and the members of the study groups for NEC approval. The General Secretary of the Party nominates the National Executive members of these committees, attempting to reflect the political balance of the parent committee. In some cases the study groups of working parties report to the Research Secretary who reports to the NEC personally; in other cases the group reports to the NEC.

In the 1960s besides its Head, the Labour Party Research Department had around fourteen research assistants, eight clerical workers and eight in the Department's Library (Barker and Rush, 1970). In 1977 there were about twelve research assistants with clerical support, but by then a small information unit had been set up, separately from the Research Department, which took the load off the Research Department in dealing with enquiries on those matters where policy was already determined.

In relation to policy-making the Department processes the flow of resolutions to the Annual Conference. It services the sub-committees of the NEC. But the Research Department engages in a good deal of publicity and propaganda work – publications, press releases and the like. 'The routine jobs take up most of the Department's time leaving a fairly small proportion – perhaps less than one-fifth – for research of a broader and longer-term nature. This proportion is obviously unsatisfactory for an office called a "Research Department".' (Mackintosh, 1968).

Have PLP members any alternative sources of research assistance that may be relevant to tax policy-making? In fact trade union sponsored Labour MPs (almost two-fifths of elected Labour members) may have other sources of research assistance available, but Barker and Rush (1970) hold that the research departments of trade unions have little direct contact with individual MPs and offer only rather particular briefs concerned with fairly narrow trade union matters.

Cooperative MPs* fare better. They receive party and Cooperative Union publications together with various private reports prepared by the Research Department, e.g. a digest of forthcoming legislation with a consumer or cooperative interest. One MP in the Barker and Rush survey said he generally received 'more information from the Co-operative Party than from the Labour Party'; and there was general praise for the quality of information (p. 277). The group had eighteen MPs in 1967. The information may be very relevant to tax policy-making. In the case of SET, as one respondent to the Barker and Rush survey put it, 'The Party "operated a healthy pressure on the Government and subsequently claimed some success" ' (p. 275).

It might be noted at this point that in recent years leading Opposition MPs have received some support from research assistants paid for by the Rowntree Trust – the so-called 'chocolate soldiers'. Also in 1973 a trust fund was established by Sir Sigismund Sternberg, a London metal dealer with Labour sympathies, to provide about £40,000 a year to recruit special advisers for the Labour Shadow Cabinet. (This was a separate fund from that financed by a group of wealthy businessmen to run Sir Harold Wilson's political office during his years in Opposition, 1970–4). Four young advisers were recruited using the Sternberg trust money and placed in offices in the Strand. Sir Harold Wilson planned to link the Rowntree and Sternberg advisers with the Labour Party's own Research Department at Transport House, with Mr Terry Pitt the Research Secretary coordinating all three. Mr Pitt is reported as saying: 'It was a marvellous opportunity to bring together all the researchers working for the Labour Party, but unfortunately Mr Ronald Hayward, the General Secretary, vetoed the whole idea of any cooperation with anyone who was not employed on his own staff' (*The Times*, 19 February 1977).

On Labour's return to Government, Mr Short and Sir Harold Wilson took the initiative in pressing for financial assistance to be given to political parties from public funds. Since 1975 such funds have been available to Opposition parties for research and clerical assistance, though the scale is small.

The sequence of tax policy-making

According to Richard Rose (1974), 'In the five years prior to the 1964 General Election policy-making was more concerned with the politics of opposition than with plans for governing.' Partly because of these internal disputes the party's approach, enunciated by the General

*A group of Labour MPs sponsored by the Cooperative Movement.

Secretary, Morgan Philips, was to concentrate on the errors of the Government, enunciate and agree party values and goals, and avoid drafting policy in detail. The 1961 Annual Conference endorsed this viewpoint when it accepted *Signposts for the Sixties*. After Gaitskell's unexpected death in January 1963 the new leader, Harold Wilson, continued with the same approach, whilst the increasing difficulties of the Conservative Party played into his hands.

Little detailed work seems to have been done within the party on tax policies, although Anthony Crosland, in his influential book *The Future of Socialism* (1956, revised edn. 1964) had considered at length the need for tax reform to promote Socialist ideals. However, the blueprint for CGT and CT (classical style) existed in the Minority Report to the Royal Commission and despite some doughty opposition (from Hugh Dalton on CGT and Harold Lever on CT) by 1964, when the Labour Party Conference Report indicated that the Finance and Economic Policy Sub-committee had been 'mainly concerned with a review of tax policies', both had become accepted as party policy.

The possibility of a WT had also been raised in official party circles before 1964. The 1963 Labour Party Conference passed a composite resolution in favour of a WT (Table 3.1) and in the same year, Mr Callaghan, as Shadow Chancellor, referred to the possibility in a party political broadcast.

Table 3.1   Labour Party annual conferences – references to taxation

| Year | Resolutions | | References in debates |
	Lost	Carried	
1963		WT	WT, CGT,
1964	—		—
1965			CT, CGT
1966	SET		SET
1967	G		SET, CT, CGT, G
1968	G		G
1969	SET		CGT, SET
1970	G		G
1971	—		G
1972		VAT, WT	WT, CTT, VAT
1973		WT, TC	WT, G, TC
1974		G	G

Source: Labour Party annual conference reports
Note: G = tax system generally

However, the view was widely held that tax pledges helped to lose Labour the 1959 general election; as Butler and Rose (1960) put it:

In retrospect the two tax pledges appeared as the turning point of the campaign itself . . . in so far as the income tax and purchase tax pledges lost votes, it was because they tended to bring to the surface latent doubts about the Party's financial capabilities (pp. 61–2).

Consequently the party was wary of giving tax pledges and, of the three new taxes favoured, only one was specifically mentioned in the 1964 manifesto: 'We shall tax capital gains.' However, the manifesto also called for a 'major overhaul of the tax system'. There was also the promise to 'reconstruct' the social security system, but without reference to the possibility of linking it with income tax.

After the election victory on 15 October 1964, in an autumn Budget less than a month later (11 November), the Chancellor announced his intention to introduce a CT and a full CGT the following April. This early announcement, after very little time for careful consideration in office, was intended as a sweetener for Labour Party members in the face of the increase in income tax and petrol tax which the Government had felt obliged to make in view of the balance of payments crisis. The CT and CGT were enacted according to timetable, but the Chancellor subsequently announced, in reply to a parliamentary question, that he was shelving a WT. At the annual conference in 1965 the Chancellor claimed CGT and CT as the 'greatest measure of modernisation of our tax structure'.

The 1966 election manifesto, whilst promising a general betting levy and a levy on the development value of land, contained no reference to other new taxes except that, under social security, it was stated that, 'in the interests of greater equity we shall seek ways of integrating more fully the two quite different systems of social payment – tax allowances and cash benefits under national insurance.'

On 1 March 1966, the day after Mr Wilson announced that the election would be held on 31 March, Mr Callaghan (with the intention of forestalling the charge that Labour were trying to get re-elected before taking harsh and unpopular measures) made a pre-Budget statement, delcaring that he did 'not foresee the need for severe increases in taxation'.

On 3 May 1966 came the Budget containing SET (pp. 127–9). Far from being party policy, SET, conceived from within the Government machine and presented as a *fait accompli*, received a somewhat hostile reception from the annual conference and was particularly opposed by the Cooperative members. A resolution critical of SET was moved, but lost, at the 1966 annual conference; however, further criticisms of SET were voiced at the annual conferences of 1967 and 1969.

Whilst Labour was in Government, from 1964 to 1970, the Finance and Economic Sub-committee never met, but this did not prevent a growing pressure from the NEC and the annual conference for additional taxation of capital, a theme echoed from 1968 onwards in the TUC's annual *Economic Reviews*.

In 1968 the annual conference report indicated that work on the distribution of income and wealth was under way. The 1969 Conference was presented with a statement by the NEC, *Agenda for a Generation*, which recorded: 'Serious consideration must be given to an annual wealth tax, and to strong measures dealing with large gifts made for the purpose of evading (sic) death duties.' A further document, *Into the Seventies*, recommended a wealth tax on 1–5 per cent with a possible exemption limit of £50,000 and a gifts tax. The most specific proposals were contained in *Labour's Economic Strategy* (August 1969) where a wealth tax was recommended 'with a starting point of £50,000 and with progressive rates of 1 per cent through to 5 per cent on wealth above £400,000'. The document added:

A tax of this kind has already been successfully levied in a large number of countries including the whole of Scandinavia, Germany, Luxembourg, Holland and Switzerland, and should present little difficulty here once the nettle has been grasped.

The Chancellor, now Mr Roy Jenkins, showed sympathy with the demand for increased capital taxation in his 1968 Budget speech but professed his inability to act because of congestion in the Inland Revenue (p. 121). However, he did indulge in a 'once and for all' special charge on investment income. The following year he referred to the same overstrain in the Inland Revenue, and added that a gifts tax or a wealth tax would involve 'great administrative tasks . . . for little revenue . . . or little demand effect' (p. 121). An indication of the different views of a WT within the party is given by the intention of Terry Pitt to send out a questionnaire to all party branches in 1970 with the hidden purpose of bringing further pressure on Mr Jenkins to introduce a WT – but the June election intervened (Hatfield, 1978). Nonetheless the note of caution which can be discerned in Mr Jenkins's statement about both the desirability and practicability of gifts tax and WT seems to have prevailed in the minds of those drafting the 1970 election manifesto. Richard Crossman records that enthusiasm in the Cabinet for a WT was muted. 'Roy lectured us saying that we have gone beyond the limits of taxation, and it is true' (Crossman, vol. 3. 1977, p. 629). According to Crossman the WT idea was knocked out of the 1970 manifesto by Roy Jenkins. However this may be, there was no explicit commitment to new taxes in the manifesto and, indeed, no specific section of it devoted to tax. But, under the heading 'Social Equality', besides listing the measures Labour had introduced to tax those living off capital gains and land profits, there followed the general statement:

There is much more to do to achieve a fairer distribution of wealth in our community. A Labour Government will continue its work to create a fairer tax system: we shall ensure that tax burdens are progressively eased from those least able to bear them and that there is a greater contribution to the National Revenue from the rich.

The manifesto also contained an attack on VAT, which, it was said, the Tories would introduce at 4s. in the pound on 'a wide range of essential goods and services so far exempt from tax'. On 'Family Poverty' the party promised to 'review the present system of family allowances and income tax child allowances'.

With Labour in opposition after the 1970 general election a change in the nature and an increase in the tempo of policy-making in the party took place, but not as soon as might have been anticipated. The election had been called unexpectedly early in June and major Government bills had fallen. Following the shock defeat there was a lack of coherent policy, and the party leader was concentrating on writing his memoirs. By early 1972, however, the party had set up a series of study groups and in 1972–3, Mr Terry Pitt maintains, there were over 800 parliamentarians, trade unionists and academics as members of committees and study groups concerned with policy-making.

Immediately after the general election, on the tax and financial affairs side, policy-making centred on Mr Roy Jenkins, former Chancellor, now Shadow Chancellor, and a member of the NEC as Deputy Leader. Jenkins was averse to policy-making by the NEC, preferring a less circumscribed framework. As Hatfield records:

He firmly believed that economic policy-making should be left to him in consultation with his shadow cabinet colleagues. He had already formed his own groups of financial and economic advisers, an indication of his disdain at the quality and expertise to be found in the party organisation.

(1978, p. 57)

However, the Finance and Economic Affairs Sub-committee was re-formed in 1971 with Jenkins as Chairman.* According to the Conference Report for 1971 its work was to result in a new statement of party policy. Its NEC members, besides the Chairman, were recorded in the Report as Mrs R. Short and Mrs S. Williams and Messrs T. Bradley, I. Mikardo, F. Mulley and W. Simpson. Co-opted members were Professors Balogh and Kaldor, Lord Diamond, Harold Lever and Dick Taverne (former Treasury Ministers), together with Messrs J. Barnett, E. Dell, D. Houghton, D. Lea, D. Marquand, R. Opie, J.

*In 1970 a small study group of NEC members had been set up consisting of F. Allaun, T.G. Bradley, J. Callaghan, J. Chalmers, F. Chapple, D. Lea and D. Mills. It does not appear to have achieved anything of significance and the Conference Report for 1971 records that it was wound up and work was transferred to the newly formed Finance and Economic Affairs Sub-committee.

Roper and N. Willis. Professor Robert Neild joined the Committee after his return from an overseas appointment later in the year.

The Finance and Economic Affairs Sub-committee met infrequently under Mr Jenkins's chairmanship. When the split in the party occurred over the EEC, Jenkins resigned as Deputy Leader and so lost his *ex officio* seat on the NEC. However, he remained Shadow Chancellor and hence retained the Chairmanship of the Sub-committee until April 1972, when Mr Healey took over as Shadow Chancellor. Mr Jenkins then ceased to be a Committee member and Mr Healey became Chairman.

Mr Healey had two advantages as Shadow Chancellor and Chairman of the Finance and Economic Affairs Sub-committee. He was a member of the NEC in his own right by election; he also had the assistance of a research assistant, Adrian Ham, paid for by the Rowntree Social Service Trust Ltd (p. 58). Under his chairmanship the Finance and Economic Affairs Sub-committee met regularly and he used it as something of a sounding board to equip himself for the jobs of Shadow Chancellor and Chancellor.

The 1972 Annual Conference produced a large crop of resolutions on taxation, stimulated by the Conservative Government's tax changes. Resolutions passed included the promise that a future Labour Government would repeal VAT and introduce a WT and stringent death duties. Mr Healey, in his first Conference speech as Shadow Chancellor, pledged himself to reverse the tax concessions to the wealthy. The Finance and Economic Affairs Sub-committee produced studies on WT and gifts tax, with further studies on capital taxation and other areas of taxation to follow. A joint working party on negative income tax was set up by the Finance and Economic Affairs Sub-committee and the Social Policy Sub-committee to prepare the Labour Party response to the Conservative Green Paper on tax credit. In Autumn 1972 a Capital Tax Working Party was formed. It met about five times between then and March 1973. The membership, as reported to the 1973 Labour Party Conference, was Mr D. Healey, Chairman, Professors A. Atkinson and N. Kaldor, J. Gilbert, J. Hughes, O. Stutchbury and P. Wyatt.*

'Labour's Programme for Britain', first published in *Labour Weekly*, 8 June 1973, and subsequently published as a booklet, *Labour's Programme 1973*, was a document prepared by the Research Secretary, Mr Terry Pitt, and issued in time to be a basis for resolutions at the Annual Conference of 1973. In a section on 'The Reform of Taxation', the document declared:

*Oliver Stutchbury, *Too Much Government?* (1977, p. 66), records that Mr Joel Barnett was also a member.

We shall abolish estate duty as such, replacing it by a progressive donor tax on capital transfers with lifetime accumulation, thereby extending the principle of breaking up concentrations of wealth by taxing transfers irrespective of their distribution. We shall also introduce a progressive capital receipts tax levied on beneficiaries of transfers and with lifetime accumulation, to encourage the wider distribution of wealth . . .

We shall introduce a wealth tax, consisting of an annual levy on the largest concentrations of private wealth . . . The tax will be progressive on net personal wealth holdings in excess of £50,000 at present values.

The document also contained an attack on VAT, which had come into effect the previous April, but recognised that if Britain remained in the EEC a VAT of some sort would be necessary. If the renegotiation was unsuccessful, then Labour would return to a system 'which discriminated . . . in favour of essential goods and services . . .' In any event 'Labour would prevent harmonisation on a basis which would lead to taxing of basic necessities and the all-round shift towards higher indirect taxes.' Further, Labour would 'reverse the change made by the Tories in the system of corporation tax' and go back to a system favouring retention of profits for reinvestment. Judgement was held in abeyance on the TC scheme then being considered by the Select Committee; but the Programme promised to raise tax thresholds to help the poor and to introduce the child benefit scheme.

Labour's 1973 Conference repeated the call for a WT and for changing the Conservative TC proposals to provide more money for the less well-off. (By now the Select Committee had reported and Labour members had presented minority reports (p. 178)). Mr Healey promised to close tax loopholes, introduce a WT, increase income tax on the better-off and raise taxes on luxuries. He also promised to raise tax thresholds and introduce reduced rates for those at the bottom of the income tax scale.

In the manifesto for the February 1974 general election the party promised to 'Introduce an annual wealth tax on the rich; bring in a new tax on major transfers of personal wealth . . .' The manifesto stressed that 'No harmonisation of VAT would require us to tax necessities.' A new system of child cash allowances to help the low-paid was promised.

After Labour's victory in February 1974 Mr Healey lost no time in introducing CTT (to be effective on gifts from March 1974) and stating his intention to introduce WT. The October 1974 manifesto confirmed the commitment to a WT and made it more specific: 'The next Labour Government will introduce an annual tax on wealth above £100,000.' An account of the subsequent developments in WT is given elsewhere (p. 50–51). It was the TUC rather than the NEC which was primarily responsible for holding the Government to its commitment but no WT reached the statute book.

The October manifesto also reiterated the party's pledge to a new system of child benefit which was in essence the child credit of the TC scheme. After much wrangling, mainly about the 'wallet' to 'handbag' transfer at a time of wage restraint, the new child benefit was introduced. Mr Healey sought to implement his pledge to raise taxes on luxuries by the introduction of the somewhat ill-fated 'higher rate' of VAT (p. 37).

As to Labour's policy-making processes, after Labour became the Government, Mr Healey did not want the Finance and Economic Affairs Sub-committee to meet. It had not done so during Labour's period of government 1964–70. The papers prepared by Mr Andy Thompson, the officer of the Research Department specialising in tax and fiscal affairs, went straight to the Home Policy Sub-committee. At the end of 1975, however, the Finance and Economic Affairs Sub-committee was re-convened, with Mrs Judith Hart as Chairman and dominated by Tribunites.* In common with other NEC sub-committees and the NEC itself, it proved an embarrassment to Ministers. It did not, however, produce any new tax policies.

In the 1979 election manifesto the pledge to a WT reappeared, but with a higher threshold: 'In the next Parliament we shall introduce an annual wealth tax on the small minority of rich people whose total net personal wealth exceeds £150,000.'

The effectiveness of the machinery
As previously described (p. 59), the blueprint for CGT and CT (classical style) was the Minority Report of the Royal Commission. SET was never considered within the party before its enactment. CTT and WT therefore offer the best test of the effectiveness and appropriateness of party policy-making procedures, and we have reviewed in some detail the sequence of events leading to their acceptance by a Labour Government. On the face of things, both seem to have had an extended party airing and examination. Gifts tax and WT had been 'on the road' for something like a decade before 1974. They had been considered in the Finance and Economic Affairs Sub-committee and had been the subject of a special working party. Yet it would appear that some of the most fundamental issues had never been resolved at the party stage. Thus whether the new death and gifts tax would be donor-based like estate duty or donee-based (or consist of both!) had not been finally determined, for one member of the Capital Tax Working Party, Oliver Stutchbury, 'was dismayed to discover that it was proposed to assess the tax on the *donor* rather than the *donee*' and was inclined to blame the

*Members of the Tribune Group, an intra-party organisation named after the left-wing newspaper, *Tribune*.

Inland Revenue (Stutchbury, 1977, p. 66). Again, the abrupt change of principle in CTT during the passage of the Finance Bill, by which a lower scale was introduced for lifetime transfers as compared with transfers at death, does not suggest a scheme well thought out in principle, let alone detail; the same is true of the major reliefs for farmers and private businesses introduced by Mr Healey in the following years (p. 41). As for WT, the Green Paper could hardly have been more vague (p. 197) and the party pledge to introduce a WT was never implemented in the lifetime of the 1974–9 Labour Government.

In reality the depth of consideration given to these taxes was much less than the number of committee meetings or the references in party literature might suggest. There is universal agreement that the meetings of NEC sub-committees are badly attended, often less than half the members being present. The numbers perk up when there is some imminent prospect of the party moving from Opposition to Government, but the circumstances act against effective committee work. Some members are there simply because they are on the NEC, although they have little knowledge of taxation. Meetings are often held in a committee room of the House of Commons. At short notice the time may be changed because of some business of the House; then, when the meeting does take place, MPs often come in briefly only to disappear again. Frequently the level of discussion is low, new taxes being discussed on ideological grounds, hardly at all in terms of administrative detail. One Labour Minister summed up the procedure as 'very informal, very haphazard and very superficial'.

Another Labour Minister maintained that 'The Labour Party isn't interested in tax', by which he meant that few party members, and especially few MPs, were interested or qualified in the details and the practicalities of taxation, even though they might be strong advocates of new taxes on ideological grounds. The smaller working parties (like that on capital taxation and on tax credits) are probably less open to most of these criticisms than the Finance and Economic Affairs Sub-committee. But they are still deficient; and the Capital Taxation Working Party did not meet often enough to get down to significant detail on a WT. Thus they were not sufficiently well prepared to meet the barrage of sniping on detail from the Opposition and interest groups during the WT Select Committee.

Where does the real power lie?
In the process of tax policy-making within the Labour Party where does the real power lie? There is, of course, no single locus of power, nor is the position static; it is affected as much by persons as by the constitution or conventions of the constitution. However, whilst no neat,

precise answer can be given to this question, some relevant observations can be made.

Although constitutionally the Annual Conference is *the* policy-making body, in practice it is circumscribed by its own nature, by the nature of tax policy and by the constitution.

An annual conference is far too large and amorphous a body to do anything but accept, reject, or occasionally amend pre-packaged proposals of a fairly general kind or put forward unconsidered proposals of its own. Proposals cannot be the subject of lengthy debate for there is so much ground to be covered at each conference. Moreover, perhaps more than most subjects, the effect of a tax depends crucially on its details. Thus, with a wealth transfer tax, the vital issues are whether it is donee or donor-based, the threshold, rates, relative treatment of lifetime transfers and transfers at death, cumulation provisions, reliefs, treatment of transfers between husband and wife, provisions on trusts and many other features, which it is quite impossible for a large assembly to decide. Even on its own level of generality, however, the annual conference is circumscribed, in that only a selection from the party programme it has agreed appears in the manifesto. Thus some parts of that programme may be left to wither.

In between conferences the NEC acts on behalf of the conference. The selection of manifesto items is the joint responsibility of the NEC and the PLP. What does this mean in practice? According to Sir Harold Wilson in a letter to *The Times* (2 September 1978) the PLP means 'In modern times the Cabinet or Shadow Cabinet'; and Sir Harold goes on to claim that the PLP can 'veto' any NEC proposal. The logic of this is not hard to see; it is the PLP who have to face the electorate and fight on the platform of the manifesto. The NEC, like the annual conference, is likely to be well to the left of the PLP as represented by Cabinet or Shadow Cabinet. Items favoured by the left but not by the centre or right of the party may be quietly dropped by the PLP and circumstantial evidence supports the hints of witnesses that a WT was treated in this way before 1974. A WT was the subject of party resolutions from the early 1960s but only achieved manifesto status in 1974. In a number of ways the PLP showed a lack of interest in the Select Committee on a Wealth Tax (pp. 177–8); and, although there may have been many explanations, including the weakness of Labour in Parliament, a WT was not in fact enacted during the 1974–9 Labour Government. It is clear that, in practice, in the past, the party leader and his senior colleagues have exercised a considerable degree of control over what *effectively* became party policy.

The circumstances of the postponement of WT during Mr Healey's Chancellorship highlight another weakness of the NEC. Although almost half the membership of the NEC consists of trade unionists elected by trade unionists, the TUC has preferred a more direct approach in its dealings with the Labour Party since 1974 through the TUC Labour Party Liaison Committee (p. 207). One reason is that the trade unionists on the NEC tend to be second-rankers because, by tradition, trade unionists on the NEC resign their membership if they are elected to the TUC General Council (Stutchbury, 1977, p.45). The trade unionists on the NEC are therefore not the big guns of the movement. It was one of the latter, Mr Jack Jones, who, after Mr Healey had announced the postponement of a WT for the life of that Parliament, got the matter put back on the agenda by means of a working party set up by the TUC Labour Party Liaison Committee (p. 208).

In considering the detail of taxation, which is so important, the NEC superficially appear to exercise control. NEC members themselves serve on the sub-committees, which attempt to flesh out policy decisions, and the NEC approves the co-opted members. Yet, as we have described, the consideration which the Finance and Economic Affairs Sub-committee gives to new taxes is 'very informal, very haphazard and very superficial'.

Where attendance at committee meetings is poor and the composition of the membership fluctuates, considerable influence, if not power, may rest in the hands of the one stable element, the officer of the Research Department who acts as secretary. One remarkable example of the power of the 'desk officer' occurs in relation to the choice of a donor or donee-based transfer tax. Whilst not ruling out the importance of Inland Revenue views on that decision (p. 66), there is strong evidence to support the view that a powerful memorandum from the Secretary of the Capital Tax Working Party exercised an appreciable influence in favour of a donor-based tax. If individual desk officers can so affect particular policies it follows that, where policy-making sub-committees all suffer from similar deficiencies, a strong Head of the Research Department may exercise considerable influence over policy-making as a whole. He drafts policy statements and nominates sub-committees.

It also follows that, in such a situation, it becomes possible for a single able individual with clear objectives, who can obtain the ear of the Chairman, to exercise a high degree of personal influence on tax policy-making. This partly accounts for the extraordinary influence of Nicholas Kaldor. Not everyone, even in his own party, regards that influence as beneficent;* but few would challenge the fact of Kaldor's

---

*See, for example, Oliver Stutchbury (1977) who writes of Kaldor (p. 53): 'As their adviser on taxation matters he was a disaster', because he created a log jam in the Inland Revenue which prevented more significant tax reforms.

pre-eminence. Seldom, if ever, can one man, who was neither politician nor permanent civil servant, have exercised so much influence on a particular aspect of policy-making over so long a period. Kaldor played a significant and generally pre-eminent role in all the new mainstream taxes for which Labour Governments were responsible, of which all but SET were adopted as party policy. Kaldor's opposition to the Conservatives' tax measures was also significant.

Kaldor served his tax apprenticeship in the Royal Commission of 1951–5. At the time the Royal Commission was being set up he had just returned from the United Nations for whom he had written a report on full employment. Between Kaldor and Gaitskell, then Chancellor of the Exchequer, there existed a strong bond of mutual respect and it was at Gaitskell's direct intervention that Kaldor was invited to serve on the Royal Commission as a second economist (J.R. Hicks being the other). Until that time Kaldor had not been a student of taxation; his tutors now became the Inland Revenue officials who produced for the Royal Commission dozens of memoranda on all aspects of the tax system.

The taxation of capital gains was only included within the terms of reference of the Royal Commission as a result of a ruling by Mr Gaitskell as Chancellor. As a result, the Minority Report of the Royal Commission, written by Kaldor and signed by the two trade unionists, George Woodcock and H.L. Bullock, was able to air the case for a CGT as well as the classical system of CT. With Gaitskell's support and despite some opposition from Dalton, who was not enamoured of a tax on capital gains (Dalton, 1955), a CGT became official party policy and subsequently the classical system of CT was also so adopted. On WT and CTT Kaldor's influence was probably less; but long before prominent politicians in the Labour Party were talking seriously about a WT for Britain, he had advised the Governments of India and Ceylon to adopt one (Kaldor, 1956). He had also long been a proponent of death duty reform (e.g. Kaldor, 1958). He had advocated a gifts tax to support the death duties and a switch to the inheritance tax principle as a more effective way than estate duty of reducing inequalities in the distribution of wealth; he was converted to the donor-based CTT because of the greater revenue potentialities he saw in it. Whilst special adviser to Mr Callaghan he conceived SET.

In a negative way Kaldor's influence was also important. His antipathy to VAT coloured Labour's attitude; more significantly, he presented a strong case against the TC scheme to the Select Committee, and influenced the Labour Party to reject the scheme (p. 170).

However, even Kaldor's influence was not unlimited. He never succeeded in getting the Labour Party to espouse his favourite scheme for an expenditure tax (Kaldor, 1955).

There remains one other consideration – the influence on tax policy-

making of fringe or party-related organisations. Two deserve mention –
the Fabian Society and Labour Economic, Finance and Taxation
Association (LEFTA), the former of long-standing, the latter of recent
vintage. The Fabian Society has never been particularly concerned
with tax though it has held an occasional conference and published an
occasional tract on the subject, most notably, in our chosen field, Oliver
Stutchbury, *The Case for Capital Taxes* (1968). Probably its views have
little direct effect on tax policy, but someone who writes a persuasive
Fabian pamphlet may find himself invited onto a policy-making committee. LEFTA is a group of moderate, democratic socialists with
professional expertise. It has no direct input into the party machine and
has not played any part in the taxes with which we are concerned. But,
because of its potential for remedying one of the deficiencies of Labour
Party policy-making, it could well become important in the future.

The Conservative Party

The policy-making machinery
Unlike the Labour Party, the constitution of the Conservative Party
gives almost unlimited power to the party leader. However, in practice
the Leader necessarily works in close consultation with senior colleagues in the Cabinet and Shadow Cabinet and must take account of
the views of the parliamentary party, and of the party outside Parliament.

The policy-making groups are more *ad hoc* than in the Labour Party.
There is no formal structure of committees concerned with particular
areas of policy-making; rather, policy groups are set up as and when the
Leader considers they are necessary.

Like the Labour Party, the parliamentary party has its own Parliamentary Finance Committee without executive responsibility. It meets
to discuss and occasionally to hear a visiting speaker. In Opposition,
however, it is chaired by the Shadow Chancellor who meets regularly
with its elected officers to discuss tactics. Those discussions are
primarily concerned with immediate parliamentary and legislative
issues, not longer-term planning. When the Conservatives are in Office
the Parliamentary Finance Committee may alert the Chancellor to any
widespread misgivings among backbenchers on aspects of his tax legislation. The party at large is represented through the annual conference.
The Conservative Party annual conference does not have the same
constitutional authority as the Labour Party conference. However, a
strongly reiterated view from the conference floor cannot be ignored by
the leading party members.

One body has been specifically set up (since 1949), to advise the
Leader on policy: the Advisory Committee on Policy. The Chairman

and Vice-Chairman are appointed by the Leader and it reports directly to the Leader. It consists of upwards of twenty members covering the parliamentary party (including the Lords), the National Union (the Conservative Party in the country, grouped in provincial regions) and a range of *ex officio* members (e.g. the Director of the Research Department) and co-opted members (e.g. the Chairman of the Federation of Conservative Students). The Advisory Committee on Policy meets about once per month when Parliament is sitting and discusses some aspect of policy often prepared by one of the party's policy groups; the subject is usually introduced by a Shadow Minister or (if the party is in Government) a Minister. The Advisory Committee may suggest amendments to the party's policy documents including election manifestos. In the words of Chris Patten (1980): 'It acts as a sounding board on policy for the Party leadership.' Anthony King (1972) writes of it: 'The Advisory Committee on Policy has no formal policy-making status; but it does have a traditional claim to be consulted, to advise, and to warn.'

Research and secretarial support for policy-making

The other body specifically set up with a policy-making role is the Conservative Research Department. The Department was established some half a century ago, independent of Central Office and in a separate building in Old Queen Street.* It is usually chaired by a senior politician. Patten (1980), a former Director of the Research Department, ascribes four functions to it: (i) to act as the Secretariat for the Shadow Cabinet with individual members of the Department acting as research assistants to Front Bench spokesmen; (ii) to service the Advisory Committee on Policy and the policy-making groups; (iii) to provide briefs for the parliamentary party as a whole and act as secretaries to Backbench Committees; (iv) to prepare a series of information publications, for the whole party and a wider audience, e.g. *Politics Today* (fortnightly) and campaign guides for the general election.

The Director of the Research Department is an *ex officio* member of all the policy groups, can suggest who might serve on these groups, usually takes the minutes at meetings of the Shadow Cabinet and may play a dominant role in drafting major policy statements, including election manifestos. The Conservative Research Department has usually employed up to thirty-five graduates when the Conservatives are in Opposition, but rather less when in Government. It has a supporting staff of about thirty.

*In 1979 it was brought within the confines of Central Office, at Smith Square, though it was said that its independence would not be materially altered by the change of location.

The sequence of tax policy-making

Policy-making by the Conservative Party has been very much policy-making in Opposition (Patten, 1980). In the period before 1964 there is therefore little to be said relevant to the taxes with which we are concerned. In the year or so before the 1964 election, when the party was in Government, there was a tax policy group within the Research Department which engaged in budget-making exercises around January and sent a statement of their conclusions to the Chancellor. It is unclear how much influence it had on policy; Ramsden (1980) records, however, that 'On tax policy, the Department enjoyed good relations with both Selwyn Lloyd and Reginald Maudling, so that their advice on budgetary policy may well have carried more weight than usual.' (p. 221).

In the 1964 election, besides indicating that a review of the rating system was under way and that the Conservatives recognised the need to reform rates, the manifesto simply stated:

We shall continue to reform the tax system, both on companies and on individuals, to make it less complicated and fairer in its incidence.

Election defeat in 1964 ended a period of thirteen years of Conservative Office; there was no need for a fundamental change in the attitudes of the party, as in 1945, but it was widely accepted that there was a need for detailed policy-making in preparation for the next period in Government. Shortly after the 1964 election, therefore, the party leader, Sir Alec Douglas-Home, asked Mr Heath as Chairman of the Advisory Committee on Policy to set in motion a wide-ranging policy review. A series of policy study groups were set up which at one stage numbered over thirty. Each member of the policy groups was appointed by the Chairman of the Advisory Committee on Policy with the approval of the party leader. Typically a policy group consisted of a Chairman, who was usually the appropriate Shadow Minister, several backbench MPs, and several experts from outside the parliamentary party, including representatives from the national union, serviced by the appropriate Research Department officer.

The first work on taxation, in the period from October 1964 to 1965, was undertaken by the Economic Policy Group of which a sub-group was responsible for taxation. This Tax Policy Group produced a package of reforms. They included the introduction of a more logical income tax scale, with a basic rate of 30 per cent and a maximum rate of 65 per cent. The differential between earned and unearned income was to be abolished and estate duty reduced, but a gifts tax and a modest WT would be introduced. A split-rate corporation tax and a payroll tax in relation to the health and national insurance systems were also proposed.

Mr Heath as Shadow Chancellor chaired this group, but was not very active in it and much of the work was done by the research officer, John Cope, a young accountant who subsequently entered Parliament. The report of the Committee was never published, as some of the proposals, particularly that on WT were very controversial. The proposal for a WT was eventually dropped following opposition from the agricultural interest within the party and from those who feared that any (modest) WT the Conservatives might introduce could become, in the hands of a subsequent Labour Government, a devastating weapon against wealth-holders (Fisher, 1973 pp. 263–5); but the reform package showed the direction of the Conservatives' thinking. They sought to simplify and reduce direct taxation, to encourage the acquisition of capital and, in removing the tax differential against investment income, to benefit retired people heavily hit by inflation. The Report held that:

Too much has been taken and the dice have been too heavily loaded against initiative and enterprise. The proposals we put forward are designed to produce a fundamental change and to recreate in our economy the conditions in which growth will flourish.

(quoted in Fisher, 1973, p. 264)

In July 1965 Sir Alec Douglas-Home resigned as leader of the party and Mr Heath, helped by the popularity he had gained from his effective leadership in the attack on the 1965 Finance Bill won the ensuing leadership election. The new leader appointed Iain Macleod as Shadow Chancellor at the beginning of August. Although Mr Heath continued to chair the Economic Policy Group for a while, partly because of rivalry between the Shadow Chancellor (Macleod) and former Chancellor (Maudling), both that and the Tax Policy Group were increasingly taken over by Macleod.

With agreement lacking for the tax package which included a WT the 1966 manifesto included only generalities on the subject of taxation: a promise to cut taxes 'to encourage hard work and enterprise' and 'to use tax incentives to encourage individual men and women to earn and save more for themselves and their families'.

After the disagreements over the WT proposals, which came to a head in December 1965 (Ramsden, 1980), the Economic Policy Group did not meet again for almost a year. When it did, after the 1966 election, there had been some recasting of its membership and that of the Tax Policy Group. The Conservative Party does not publish the names of the members of its policy groups, but Nigel Fisher (1973) records that they include Terence Higgins, Patrick Jenkin and Arthur Cockfield. Anthony Barber was not a member, but he was on the working group which orchestrated opposition to the 1965 Finance Bill and he had been particularly responsible for the opposition to CT.

Professor Wheatcroft was invited to later meetings of the Tax Policy Group, particularly to advise on VAT. The basis of a new package, without a WT, was worked out by mid-1968 and ready for presentation to the Advisory Committee on Policy and the party leader for their approval (Ramsden, 1980).

As previously indicated (p. 29) the Conservative concern with a revised form of CT arose out of their opposition to the classical system introduced by Labour. To an important extent their leaning to VAT arose from the same source. They committed themselves to abolish SET, and if they were to reduce direct taxes, had put something in its place, especially as the revenue from SET grew (p. 10). At the same time their European commitment was hardening. The idea of a payroll tax (as in the first reform package proposed by the Tax Policy Committee) was dropped, partly because it was feared it might have adverse effects on exports but also because it would look contradictory to abolish SET only to replace it by a general employment tax. Hence hopes became centred on VAT and much detailed work was done on it, including calculations of the revenue and distributional effects, carried out by Brian Reading of the Research Department. Even so, the 1970 manifesto commitment to VAT, whilst detailed, was also conditional:

We will abolish Selective Employment Tax, as part of a wider reform of indirect taxation possibly involving the replacement of purchase tax by a value-added tax.

The value-added tax, already widely adopted in Western Europe and Scandinavia, is in effect a general sales tax, operated in a way which allows for desirable exemptions – for example, exports. It could help to make our system of taxes on spending more broadly based, less discriminatory, and fairer in its impact on different types of industry and service.

It would not apply to food, except for those few items already subject to purchase tax. It would not apply to normal farming activities, nor to very small businesses; and special arrangements would be made for housing. No Opposition could commit itself finally in advance of an election to a major new tax of this kind which would need detailed consultation with the civil service.

Some form of negative income tax was a personal interest of Brendon Sewill, the then Director of the Conservative Research Department. He sought to develop a distinctive Conservative policy on the whole question of financing the social services. He wrote in *Crossbow* on the subject and was responsible for a pamphlet, published by the Conservative Political Centre (1966) which argued for putting all Inland Revenue taxes and social security payments on one computer system. At his instigation another member of the Research Department, Barney Hayhoe, carried out work in the same field and produced and published a proposal for family allowances payable only to people below the income tax threshold (1968). This early work on tax credits indicates the direction of Conservative thinking. Both this thinking and the limited progress so far made found expression in the Conservative 1970 manifesto:

We will tackle the problem of family poverty and ensure that adequate family allowances go to those families that need them. A scheme based upon negative income tax would allow benefits to be related to family need; other families would benefit by reduced taxation. The Government has exaggerated the administrative problems involved, and we will make a real effort to find a practical solution. If this can be done, it will increase incentive for those at work, and bring much needed help to children living in poverty.

In the event the TC scheme took rather a different form from that of the earlier work, and Arthur Cockfield (p. 95), the architect of the scheme, had no part in this line of enquiry before 1970.

During this period, the party conferences were largely occasions when the members encouraged the leaders in the direction that they were taking and Macleod, in particular, enthused the conference with descriptions of the detailed work accomplished and visions of the promised land in which effort would be rewarded and property-owning encouraged. In 1965 a debate on taxation took place on a resolution approving the Opposition's efforts in amending the Finance Bill and urging the use of the tax system to encourage enterprise and initiative. Resolutions with the themes of tax reform, tax simplification, tax reduction, the creation of incentives, encouragement to saving and a switch from direct to indirect taxation, were debated at every annual conference to 1970 (Table 3.2). In 1967 Macleod pledged the conference that the Conservatives would abolish SET – 'the silliest tax since the tax on windows'. The following year he repeated the pledge,

Table 3.2 Conservative Party annual conference – references to taxation

Year	Resolutions	References in debates
1963	—	G
1964	No conference	—
1965	G	VAT, CGT, G
1966	SET	CGT, estate duty, VAT, SET, CT
1967	SET	CT, SET, CGT, WT
1968	CGT, CT	CGT, WT, CT
1969	G	VAT, WT, G
1970	G	CT, G, VAT, negative income tax
1971	G	CGT, VAT, CT, estate duty, G
1972	VAT	VAT, WT. SET
1973	—	Estate duty, VAT, TC
1974	No conference	—

Source: Conservative Party annual conference reports
Note: G = tax system generally

indicated that he expected purchase tax also to go and, whilst not yet firmly committed to the tax, announced the readiness of the party to commence talks with industry and other interested bodies on the possibilities of VAT. In 1969 he was able to report to conference that talks on VAT with the CBI, the Associated Chamber of Commerce and the National Chamber of Trade had taken place, that during the summer he had held a conference of experts on VAT, including Professor Carl Shoup (Columbia University), 'the father, as he has been called, of the value-added tax'; that Professor Wheatcroft had been invited to prepare a draft of a possible VAT for this country and that this work was far advanced. This 'intensive study' of VAT was to meet the need for a 'broadly based tax on consumption as the complement to our plans for major reductions in personal direct taxation and the encouragement of saving'.

The cautious and conditional commitments to VAT and a negative income tax scheme in the 1970 election manifesto have already been indicated. In addition the manifesto included more general promises to 'reduce and reform taxation' and 'simplify the tax system' and, in particular, make 'progressive and substantial reductions in income tax and surtax'.

During the period of Conservative Government 1970–74 no policy-making groups existed. On tax reform the Conservatives proceeded to implement their promises and conference generally applauded. Not only did the Conservative Government introduce CT (imputation) and VAT, they simplified income tax with a new unified system which combined income tax and surtax, and generated a debate both on tax credits and death duties. Their period of office was particularly notable for more open government on tax policy-making, primarily by the use of Green Papers and select committees.

The February 1974 election manifesto, apart from its statement of tax pledges fulfilled, was primarily concerned with the TC scheme:

We shall continue our programme of tax reform with the tax credit scheme. We shall introduce legislation in the next Parliament in order to implement the Scheme as soon as the economic situation allows.

Five further paragraphs in the manifesto were taken up with a description of the operation and the benefits of the scheme.

In the aftermath of the February 1974 general election only a few policy-making groups were set up and the Tax Policy Group was not one of them. The main concern of the Conservatives was to establish their credibility to govern; it was clear that another general election could not be long delayed.

The manifesto for the October 1974 election reiterated the promise to bring in the TC scheme 'in stages, as economic circumstances permit', starting with a system of child credits. That apart, the main thrust of the taxation section was a response to Labour's CTT and promised WT. The manifesto recorded:

It is wrong to reform capital taxation in a piecemeal way without full consideration of the effects. We will examine the whole system of taxation on capital with the aim of making the system more fair, less a matter in its application of chance or skill in avoidance, and less damaging to thrift, saving and investment on which our future depends.

The manifesto stressed particularly the need to shield small firms from capital taxation and promised free transfers between husband and wife under estate duty and a widening of relief so that relations sharing a family home were not forced to sell in order to meet death duties on the death of parents, brothers or sisters.

After the October defeat it was clear that the Conservatives were in for a longer period of Opposition. With the change of leadership, early in 1975, the new party leader, Mrs Thatcher, appointed Sir Keith Joseph as Chairman of the Advisory Committee on Policy with overall responsibility for policy work, and Mr Angus Maude became Chairman of the Research Department. Various policy groups were established, with a tendency for them to contain more MPs and fewer non-Parliamentary members than in 1964–70. A new Tax Policy Group was formed in May 1975 initially with Mr David Howell, Opposition Spokesman on Treasury and Economic Affairs, as Chairman.

The approach to tax reform was, however, different from that of 1964–70. Tax reform was not to be a major preoccupation of the party when next in office. It was considered that the party had introduced its major tax reforms and a time of recuperation was needed.

As Opposition spokesman on Finance just before she became leader, Mrs Thatcher, in opposing the special Finance Bill which introduced CTT, having listed the iniquities of the tax, roundly declared 'We shall therefore repeal this tax.' Subsequently the approach adopted by her Treasury Shadows was more cautious. They talked instead of 'drawing the teeth' of CTT and taking a long and unhurried look at the future of capital taxation as a whole. The Conservatives, indeed, planned to produce an Opposition Green Paper on the subject, to generate a wider consideration and discussion; but it never got beyond the draft stage; differences within the party could not be resolved and no Green Paper appeared. The 1979 manifesto repeated the general formulae on capital taxes, without being specific:

We reject Labour's plan for a Wealth Tax. We shall deal with the most damaging features of the Capital Transfer and Capital Gains Taxes and propose a simpler and less oppressive system of capital taxation in the longer term.

When the Conservatives regained office in 1979 Sir Geoffrey Howe, as Chancellor of the Exchequer, asked Arthur Cockfield, by then Lord Cockfield and a Minister of State at the Treasury, to undertake a review of capital taxation. It was agreed that, within the confines of a very tight timetable, individuals and organisations could submit evidence to Lord Cockfield, but no Green Paper was issued; there was no attempt to generate a wide-ranging discussion and the review was carried out very much in secret. The outcome has been apparent from the changes in CGT and especially in CTT in Sir Geoffrey's successive budgets (pp. 27–8 and 42–3). One other point on capital taxation is notable. Ever since Mr Barber's Green Paper on *A Possible Inheritance Tax* (Cmnd 4930) a distinct possibility existed that the Conservatives would switch from a donor to a donee-based death duty (p. 39). Speaking at the Centenary Conference of the Institute of Chartered Accountants, in May 1980, the Chancellor announced that the decision had been taken not to make such a switch.

Some interesting work was undertaken on VAT by the Conservatives in Opposition. A 'Task Force', including experienced practitioners, was set up to seek ways of simplifying the tax. The report was published (1977) and (with the permission of Labour Ministers) discussed with Customs and Excise. The main recommendation was a proposal that businesses with a turnover of up to £1 m should be given the option to calculate VAT liability from annual financial accounts. Neither the Labour Government nor the Conservatives, since their return to office, have been willing to implement this recommendation up to the time of writing; but some future move in this direction cannot be ruled out. The 1979 manifesto promised: 'to simplify taxes – like VAT'.

The Conservatives in Opposition after 1974 appear to have given some further thought to the TC scheme, but without any very positive results. The 1979 manifesto repeated the long-term intention to 'move towards the fulfilment of our original tax credit objectives as and when resources are available' but recognised that progress would be difficult in the next few years both on grounds of cost and because of technical problems involved in the switch to computers.

One further comment on the Conservatives in Opposition should be made. In a brilliant speech to the Addington Society, 16 February 1977, subsequently published in the *British Tax Review* (1977), Sir Geoffrey Howe, the Shadow Chancellor, outlined the 'need of a radical reform of our machinery for tax legislation' and made 'practical proposals' to meet that need. These proposals are discussed in subsequent chapters, especially Chapter 5. Regrettably, little attempt has yet been made (end 1981) to implement them.

The effectiveness of the machinery
Patten writes of the period 1964–70: 'The results of all this policy work

were uneven. Some groups had relatively little to show for their efforts. Others produced reforms like the restructuring of the taxation system, which was by any standards a considerable achievement' (1980, p. 16). Similarly, Ramsden writes: 'The Economic Policy Group did much useful work on the tax package, in quite remarkable levels of detail.' (1980, p. 273). Although both comments derive from Conservative sources, our own analysis endorses their general validity. The Conservatives took office in 1970 with a very clear idea of the objectives which they wished to implement in the case of CT and the TC scheme and with much detailed work behind them on perhaps the most complicated of the new taxes, VAT. Iain Macleod appears to have called the Tax Policy Group together frequently until he had got from it all that he required. There was considerable justification for Macleod's boast on tax reform to the party conference of 1969 that:

Our plans are carefully thought out and we shall invite full comment on them. No party in opposition has ever done so much as we under Mr Heath have done to prepare for Government.

It is a tribute to the tax policy-making process within the Conservative Party in this period that, although it centred very much on Macleod, the tax reforms did not die with him. Although the Tax Policy Group was relatively informal, minutes were taken and a detailed record was made of the proposals. Thus Anthony Barber taking over as Chancellor after Macleod's tragic death, although never a member of the Tax Policy Group, could lead a team which implemented all the tax reforms Macleod envisaged.

The period of Opposition from 1974 was less fruitful in tax reform. No clear conclusions seem to have been reached on capital taxation by the time the Conservatives took office in 1979 and no further progress was made on the costly TC scheme, effectively ruled out by economic recession.

Where does the real power lie?
As with the Labour Party, we cannot indicate a single locus of power. According to the constitution of the Conservative Party power over policy-making lies with the leader, but, as Patten (1980) puts it:

The whole structure in practice provides for a constant process of consultation and two-way flow of ideas within its rank and file . . . But the really effective policy-making college is the Shadow Cabinet and within that body the views of those who have been irrelevantly called 'the big beasts in the jungle' – the senior political figures – obviously matter most. (p. 23)

In the Conservative policy-making process personalities matter rather more than formal institutions. Macleod had a very free hand in developing tax reform policies. This may have been partly because, in the period 1964–70, policy-making tended to be more eclectic than in the previous or subsequent period of Conservative Opposition. But Macleod was a very 'big beast' in the party and his views on taxation were broadly in line with those of his leader. In the period of Opposition after 1975, when in any case tax reform was not a major concern of the party, the relationship between Shadow Chancellor and Leader was somewhat different.

As with the Labour Party, the desk officers of the Research Department may play an influential if not a powerful role in policy-making and the same is true of the Director of the Research Department.

Was there an *éminence grise* in Conservative tax policy-making comparable to Nicholas Kaldor? Arthur Cockfield comes nearest to meeting this description but falls somewhat short. A former Commissioner of Inland Revenue, who then took up a career in industry, he became almost full-time on Conservative Party councils from 1967 when he retired as managing director of Boots. Whilst the party was in Opposition, and then as Special Adviser to the Chancellor when the Conservatives resumed office, he worked on the CT changes and on the unification of income tax and surtax. As Special Adviser he devised the TC scheme. Subsequently, as Minister of State, he was responsible for the review of capital taxation. But his influence, though great, was not as ubiquitous as that of Kaldor. Thus he played no part at all in planning and introducing VAT.

Just as the Labour Party has its fringe and party-related organisations so have the Conservatives, and with similarly limited effect on tax policy-making. The Bow Group, the Monday Club and PEST* may occasionally interest themselves in taxation and publish a pamphlet on the subject, like the Bow Group's *Case Against a Wealth Tax* (Wallace and Wakeham, 1968). Their main effect is to articulate the points of view of different parts of the party spectrum; they thus constitute part of the on-going process of debate in a mass party.

Comparison of Labour and Conservative tax policy-making

In tax policy-making both major parties rely heavily on policy-making groups containing co-opted specialists and serviced by a Research Department. But, as the earlier part of this chapter indicated, there are major differences between the parties both on the objectives of tax policy and the methods of tax policy-making.

The emphasis of the Labour Party is on taxing the rich, reducing inequality and hitting the speculator and the recipient of high profits. The Conservative emphasis is on reducing tax rates, particularly of direct taxes, providing incentives, simplifying the tax system and

*PEST (Pressure for Economic and Social Toryism) is now incorporated in the Tory Reform Group.

improving the efficiency of tax administration. Both parties show concern for the poor. Nearly all the taxes with which we are concerned (the partial exceptions are SET and the TC scheme) spring from these ideological differences.

The Labour Party structure for tax policy-making, linked to the NEC, is more formal and less flexible than that of the Conservative Party. One result is that policy-making may continue in the Labour Party when the party is in Government; policy-making within the Conservative Party was essentially policy-making in Opposition. Another important difference is that the Research Department of the Labour Party is oriented to the NEC, the party conference and the constituencies. The Conservative Research Department is more oriented towards Parliament and the parliamentary leaders and owes its allegiance directly to the leader of the party. Indeed, during the crucial period of tax policy-making, Mr Heath, as party leader, left the Research Department without a Chairman. The Conservative Research Department has little to do with the constituencies which are the province of the Conservative Political Centre.

This difference is reflected in the service provided by the respective Research Departments both to party leaders and backbench MPs. In the Conservative Party the Research Department 'tax officer', besides acting as secretary to the Tax Policy Committee, becomes effectively a personal assistant to the Shadow Chancellor and services the Conservative Backbench Committee concerned with taxation; also the Research Department will do its best, as far as resources permit, to help individual MPs, for example, those serving on Select Committees like that on Wealth Tax. Labour Shadow Ministers receive less help and other Labour MPs hardly any (Mackintosh 1968; Barker and Rush, 1970).

Whilst both parties co-opt unpaid experts to their tax policy-making committees there are important differences. The Labour Party publishes the membership of its committees and working parties in the annual conference report. The Conservatives do not publish the names of their policy-making groups; there is no requirement that the co-opted members must be party members, and some of their active sympathisers might not wish to be publicly identified with a political party. Whilst academics contribute to both parties in the tax field the Conservatives can call on legal, industrial and accounting skills much more readily than Labour. It is no accident that the dominant tax expert in the Labour Party, Nicholas Kaldor, is an academic macroeconomist; and that description would also fit other leading contributors, such as Professors Robert Neild and Tony Atkinson. The leading experts who advised the Conservatives in Opposition before 1970 and who continued to advise them in office were Arthur Cockfield, a Commissioner of Inland Revenue before he became a leading business man, and Professor G.S.A. Wheatcroft, an academic but also a practising tax lawyer. In opposing the 1965 tax legislation of the Labour Government, Anthony Barber consulted former colleagues at the tax bar; and the Conservative opposition to CTT was notable for expertise provided to them in the Committee stage by a number of leading tax practitioners. The possibilities of this kind of expert support for the Opposition were increased once Finance Bills were partly taken upstairs in Standing Committee (p. 135). Both parties may, on a somewhat haphazard basis, circulate tax proposals to academics or other interested persons for comment. The Conservatives, but not the Labour Party, occasionally contract work to external organisations, but not usually to academics, whose time-scale is not short enough.

Not all tax policies, even when the party is in Opposition, go through the party policy-making machinery. Especially in the heat of the debate on the Finance Bill, parliamentary spokesmen may commit their parties to repeal some part of the Government's legislation. Conservatives fall to this temptation more than Labour because their policy-making procedures are less fettered (witness the promises on SET and CTT), but Labour is not immune (e.g. the promise to restore CGT at death, HC Debates, 20 May 1971, col. 1579). Such pledges are often made without adequate consideration, without discussion of papers and without a full appreciation of the implications. Whilst the promises are not always kept, withdrawal from them can prove embarrassing.

If the Conservatives are more given to making pledges to abolish a tax before they know what to put in its place (witness SET, CTT and also local domestic rates) the Labour Party is more disposed to promise new taxes without adequate preparation (witness CTT and WT). The Conservative Government of 1970–4 had prepared itself much better in Opposition to introduce its tax reforms than either the Labour Government of 1964 or that of 1974. To some extent, this difference may reflect the nature of the specialist inputs (discussed above). Also it may partly reflect the difference in resources between the two Research Departments. The Conservative Research Department is twice the size of the Labour Research Department. Thus, whilst little by way of long-term research is done in either Department, the Conservatives can always manage to find someone for a special assignment for three or six months. Again, they usually manage, along with the usual run of young graduates, to finance a few rather older and more experienced 'desk officers' such as Peter Cropper who worked closely with Arthur Cockfield and Sir Geoffrey Howe on tax policy in Opposition and moved into the Treasury as an adviser to the Chancellor when the Conservatives took office in 1979. He returned to head the Research Department in 1982.

Finally, we might note that, whatever the constitutions may say, in practice similar influences have determined which policy proposals enter the respective manifestos. However, if the views of the Labour left continue to gain ground, the position could well change and the NEC, as the representative of the annual conference, rather than party leader and PLP, could become the decisive voice in deciding the contents of Labour's manifesto.

The Liberal Party

With only a handful of members in Parliament the influence of the Liberal Party has necessarily been peripheral, but at certain stages in the story it has not been unimportant and their approach to the taxes with which we are concerned could be of determining importance in the possible event of the Liberal/Social Democratic Alliance forming a Government.

In fact the Liberals were the first to adopt as party policy proposals for some of the taxes in our study or related taxes. Thus they explicitly committed themselves to VAT whilst the Conservatives were still surveying it with caution. Their interest in negative income tax schemes goes back to Lady Rhys Williams (p. 44), and they continue to support the tax credit approach as the way forward with social security. Also, by 1938 if not before, in *Ownership for All*, the Liberals were advocating an inheritance tax instead of estate duty. They have since regularly reiterated their demand for a legacy duty (donee-based transfer tax) and gifts tax, and latterly have campaigned for a full accessions tax – i.e. a donee-based tax on transfers of wealth during life and at death, the rate of tax being determined by the cumulative total of gifts and legacies received from all sources. A leaflet confirming this policy was issued as recently as February 1981.

The Liberals have also shown a leaning towards a WT as part of a package of tax changes, and John Pardoe, the Liberal on the Select Committee on Wealth Tax, besides casting a vital vote against the proposals of the Chairman of the Select Committee, presented his own Minority Report (p. 178).

Concluding reflections

With new taxes it is clear that the party stage is crucial; most mainstream new taxes originate with the party and become a more or less firm commitment (often long before any details are considered), from which it is difficult, though not impossible, to withdraw. It is therefore important that the party should 'get it right'. The study of the party processes raises, perhaps, four main questions. Are the party resources adequate in total for the task they face? Is there an adequate *range* of inputs into the party tax policy-making process? Do parties realise the importance of considering not only the broad principle of policy but also its main direction and character? How can parties avoid the rash commitment?

In considering the adequacy of party resources we need to have some general criteria in mind. The main parties in West Germany have huge research institutes associated with them, financed by state funds. Do we want this kind of back-up? Putting the point in another way: do we want the parties to prepare taxes in the same degree of administrative detail as the revenue departments? Whilst opinions may differ on the degree of detail appropriate for party tax proposals, there would seem no point in duplicating the civil service in the party organisations. What is desirable in the parties is a clarification of objectives; some consideration of alternative means of achieving the objectives before a choice is made of a particular tax; and enough detailed consideration to ensure the practicality of the tax – i.e. that the objectives can be attained at an acceptable cost, in efficiency, or equity, or resources used in administration and compliance. Without research assistance adequate for this purpose (which implies both a capacity to assess economic effects and to anticipate the practical problems of day-to-day administration) a Shadow Chancellor is likely to be less well-prepared for office and more inclined to the rash commitment. It is also desirable that the party Research Department should be able to give occasional detailed help to backbench MPs, especially to those on Commons committees dealing with taxation.

The Conservative Research Department comes nearer to meeting these criteria than the Labour Party Research Department, but still falls short. Brendon Sewill estimated that about one-quarter of his officers' time was taken up with actual policy research (Ramsden, 1980, p. 6); this compares with under one-fifth in the Labour Party's much smaller Department (p. 57 above). More resources would enable rather more by way of long term research to be undertaken or commissioned and would remove constraints on assistance to backbenchers. Apart from the sheer size of a research department there is a question of quality and continuity. Again, the Conservative Party is better placed than Labour but falls short of the ideal. Research staff in both parties are mainly young graduates, sometimes very bright, on relatively low pay; but the Conservatives do occasionally employ more experienced people on higher salary scales, whereas the Labour Party Research Department is almost wholly staffed by young research assistants and because of the low pay, the turnover is very high. On average, research assistants in the Labour Party Research Department have only stayed about two years: in early 1977 only two members of the Department had been there for eight years or more and one of these was Geoff Bish, the Head. Ramsden (1980) records that about 70 per cent of recruits to the Conservative Research Department have moved on within five years. A high turnover necessarily upsets continuity. There is undoubtedly a case for some state finance for political parties (rather more than the so-called 'Short' money (p. 58)) as recommended in the Houghton Report (1976); but, with the Labour Party's orientation, if more money were made available to the party organisation there is no guarantee that any of it would be used for services to MPs.

The issue of the range of inputs to the party policy-making process, is also one where Labour is more badly placed than the Conservatives. Labour particularly lacks practical inputs (p. 81). It may be that if the party did not publish the names of committee members there might be more professional people willing to offer advice. A possible remedy for insufficient administrative input would be more meetings between Opposition parties and the revenue department. These have often taken place (with ministerial approval) just before elections (p. 91) and occasionally, at other times (p. 78); but, though there are limits beyond which the process could not be taken, the practice could usefully be extended. Other ways by which both parties could increase the input into tax policy-making would be through the secondment of academics for six or twelve months to a party research department. The recognition of the practice by university authorities as respectable and desirable is a necessary prerequisite. The establishment of the Institute for Fiscal Studies in 1969 and the growth of university research in taxation has increased the possibilities of a wider informed input. Also the idea of Opposition Green Papers, toyed with by both parties, could be extended to encompass the views of those with professional tax expertise such as accountants and tax lawyers. However, it is less easy to get individuals and professional bodies to take seriously an Opposition Green Paper, because its implementation is less imminent than a Government Green Paper. Parties in Opposition might also usefully prepare a systematic mailing list of specialists of all kinds willing to comment on Green Papers and other party documents and proposals.

Whilst the measures we have discussed may have some cautionary influence on politicians they will not prevent rash commitments. Perhaps there is no way of doing that; but it is a subject to which we shall return in our final chapter (p. 236).

The evidence from our study reveals that, in some cases, even the objectives of the new taxes had not been clearly worked out before the parties took office. Thus there was scope for the departments to influence not only the details of the new taxes but sometimes the general principles. To the role of the departments in the tax policy-making process we turn in the next chapter.

The Departments

The role of the civil servant

If the main role of politicians and their organisations, the political parties, is to determine the goals of tax policy what is the role of the departments?

The classical Weberian view of the respective role of politician and civil servant is that while the ends or goals are determined by the politicians the means to those ends are determined by the civil servants or 'bureaucrats'.

There is in the Weberian model of bureaucracy the assumption that the bureaucrat in his search for the best means by which political goals are to be achieved will employ economic rationality (*Zweckrational*). But it has been suggested by a number of writers on bureaucratic behaviour (e.g. Simon, 1957; Lindblom, 1959; Downs, 1967) that in practice bureaucrats do not conform to the Weberian model. Rather they behave in a manner alien to it: they do not maximise or optimise, they 'satisfice'; they do not examine policies from the bottom up, they move forward by slow incremental steps. Moreover, some studies (e.g. Niskanen, 1974; Heclo and Wildavsky, 1975) suggest that bureaucrats do not merely respond to externally generated goals – they fulfil their own internally generated goals. This view has been expressed not only by outside academic commentators but also by a number of politicians with experience of office (e.g. Benn and Sedgemoor).

In this chapter we chart the progress of the new taxes through the government departments and attempt to answer some of the questions posed about the goals/means dichotomy, about the actual relationship between the politicians who set the goals of tax policy and the bureaucrats who establish the means to achieve them.

In examining the role of the departments in tax policy-making, it must be recalled that our study relates primarily to new taxes. In so far as party politicians set the goals, we should expect new taxes to originate with them. Moreover, in so far as the administrative approach might be characterised by incrementalism, it would be most likely to apply when changes are being made to existing taxes (some of which may have consequences as important as a new tax). It is therefore not surprising to find that the origins of all the new taxes in our study except SET lay outside the departments, especially within the party organisations. Indeed, as almost all these taxes reflect a particular party ideology, it is wholly in line with civil service tradition that the role of the departments should be their implementation rather than their invention. Nor is it surprising that the exception, SET, which was a product of the pressures of Government, was more concerned with revenue-raising and control of the economy than most of the other taxes, and was freer of party ideology.

There is perhaps one other partial exception: the TC scheme – again a tax with little party ideology about it and one which Anthony Barber hoped would be accepted by all parties. It can be regarded as a partial exception because, whilst there had been a debate in both parties about negative income tax, the Conservatives did not enter office in 1970 with any clearly worked out proposals and what emerged as the TC scheme was rather different from the possibilities previously considered in the Conservative Research Department.

But even to say that SET was an exception and the TC scheme a partial exception to the generalisation that the departments do not originate new taxes is misleading. For both these innovations, although emerging from Whitehall, were the brain children not of the permanent civil service but of the special advisers taken into Whitehall by the Chancellors of the day: Nicholas Kaldor was the architect of SET and Arthur Cockfield of the TC proposals.

Thus, in examining the role of the departments, we are principally concerned to see how the flesh was put on the skeleton taxes by the departments and, sometimes indeed, since the Labour Party in particular committed itself to a new tax on the basis of most inadequate consideration, how the tax wraiths emerging from the party organisations were given both bones and flesh. In so doing we must seek to assess the extent of Whitehall influence on the form of a tax; and how far, if at all, the original intentions were modified by the departmental processing. Furthermore, we must examine whether the departments were responsible for preventing a tax, in this case WT, from reaching the statute book.

Because we are interested in the modifications and amendments to the new taxes in the early years of their existence, we shall also examine the continuing departmental role in amending taxes.

We shall seek to assess the appropriateness of the departmental structure to its role. To do so we need to describe the structure of the executive machinery and the procedures for tax changes, as they are not widely known and understood. This is our starting point.

The executive machinery and procedures

In examining the role played by the central government departments in the tax policy-making process we can usefully distinguish between an 'inner circle' and an 'outer circle'. The inner circle consists of those departments (and persons) concerned directly and specifically with taxes; the outer circle illustrates the functional area, the responsibility of other departments, which may be indirectly affected by tax policy.

The inner circle

At the centre of the web is the Chancellor of the Exchequer assisted by the other Treasury Ministers. The division of responsibilities amongst the Treasury Ministers is the responsibility of the Chancellor, although they can be expected to act as a team on all major issues. For example, Anthony Barber as a tax-reforming Chancellor took the view that whilst each of the new taxes was in the responsibility of a particular minister, all the Treasury Ministers should fully participate in major issues affecting any of the new taxes and that he himself should acquire a detailed grasp of them all, to be able, if necessary, to deal with any question or problem. The Chief Secretary to the Treasury traditionally has responsibility for control of public expenditure and for piloting the Finance Bill through the House of Commons; another Treasury Minister, often the Financial Secretary, may be given responsibility for Inland Revenue affairs, whilst the Minister of State may have special responsibility for Customs and Excise affairs. But these arrangements are not absolute.* A Chief Secretary may lead on a major fiscal change. Thus, Mr Joel Barnett, Chief Secretary in the Labour Government of 1974, because of his special knowledge of taxation acquired as a practising accountant, in addition to the usual functions of a Chief Secretary, carried the burden of the day for the Government on CTT.

For reasons of continuity, too, the pattern may vary. Thus, during Mr Anthony Barber's Chancellorship, when Mr Macmillan moved from Chief Secretary to the Treasury to become Minister for Employment, Mr Patrick Jenkin, who became Chief Secretary (from Financial Secretary) continued to exercise a supervisory role over the new imputation form of CT, whilst Mr Terence Higgins, moving from Minister of State to Financial Secretary, retained the responsibility for indirect taxes (Customs and Excise matters and SET) that he had exercised as Minister of State.

As Figure 4.1 indicates, there are four 'inputs' to the Chancellor in his role as chief policy-making on taxation. The revenue departments, Inland Revenue and Customs and Excise, each have a direct relationship with the Chancellor which is independent of the Treasury as a department. Besides the administration of the taxes under their respective control, the revenue departments have the responsibility to advise on administrative methods and feasibility, on the way a new tax

---

*For an account of the rather different arrangements under Sir Geoffrey Howe, with two Ministers of State, one in the 'other place', see *Hansard* Written Answers, 21 May 1979, cols. 43–44.

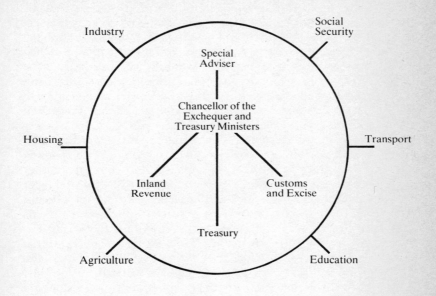

Figure 4.1 Executive machinery

may conflict with existing taxes and on tax legislation – matters which require a detailed knowledge of the tax system. The Treasury has the responsibility for overall economic policy and therefore has the task of assessing the general economic impact of tax proposals.

The Special Adviser to the Chancellor of the Exchequer is someone who will usually have been working on the tax proposals of the Government Party whilst it has been in Opposition and who moves into Government; notably, in our period, Nicholas Kaldor, later Professor Lord Kaldor, Special Adviser to the Chancellor of the Exchequer 1964–8 (Callaghan and Jenkins) and 1974–6 (Healey); and, on the Conservative side, Arthur Cockfield, later Sir Arthur, Special Adviser on Tax Policy 1970–3 (Macleod and Barber) and subsequently, as Lord Cockfield, Minister of State in the Thatcher government of 1979, under the Chancellorship of Sir Geoffrey Howe.

The outer circle
In Figure 4.1 the list of services (with which departments are associated) on which tax policy may impinge is illustrative, not exhaustive. Thus the Department of Health and Social Security may be affected by income tax changes, for example, because of the relationship between the tax threshold and the threshold for various social security benefits (associated with the problem of the 'poverty trap') or by a change in the liability of different benefits to income tax (e.g. the introduction of a tax exemption for war widows' pensions). The Ministry of Transport is most affected by changes in motor vehicle licences, excise duties on fuel, VAT and perhaps by changes in investment allowances. The Department of Education and Science may be affected by VAT but also by rates of income tax, which should bear some relation to the scale for determining the parental contribution to students in further and higher education, because the two together determine the effective marginal tax rate of students' parents. The Department of Agriculture is affected by income tax but especially by capital taxes, CTT, CGT and WT, because of the high capitalisation and low income yield from farming. The Department of Environment, responsible for housing policy, is vitally affected by the mortgage interest relief for owner-occupiers, whilst the Department of Trade and Industry is affected in a wide variety of ways, e.g. by the effect of income tax and CT on profits; by investment incentives provided through the tax system; by the tax treatment of small businesses; by the effect of tax proposals on any industrial strategy and so on.

We could have added other services and departments; for example, Energy is particularly concerned with the petroleum revenue tax (PRT) and excise duties on fuel; Public Buildings and Works, for much of our period a department in its own right, subsequently part of the Department of the Environment, was very much affected by SET, and is affected by VAT and the special income tax rules on subcontractors in the building industry. In addition the Civil Service Department is responsible for arranging the staff establishment for any new tax. Besides government departments the Bank of England is also an ever-present institution in the outer circle.

With any particular tax or tax change some of these departments will be affected, but not others, and the implications for the services of a department may be central or peripheral.

Typical procedures for a new tax
The way in which the machinery works, including the relationship between the inner and outer circles, can be understood by a summary description of the typical procedure for the introduction of a new tax which has been advocated by the Opposition before it gained office. We

shall take the example of a direct tax, which is the responsibility of the Inland Revenue, but a broadly similar procedure is followed by Customs and Excise. For ease of assimilation the description is set out in a series of stages relating to different functions.

(*1*) *The 'research' function*　The Inland Revenue does not have a large research organisation of its own, nor, unlike some other government departments, does it often commission outside research. The Inland Revenue seeks to keep in touch with thinking and developments at home and abroad regarding direct taxes. Under the 1975 reorganisation this duty is particularly imposed on the central division (see below). A watch is kept on what politicians are saying, on the academic literature, on the views emanating from professional associations and bodies such as the Institute for Fiscal Studies. The foreign division in the library keeps an eye on changes in overseas tax structures, and OECD committees and working parties provide information on what other countries are doing.

(*2*) *Monitoring Opposition statements*　Particular note is taken of any commitment made by Opposition spokesmen in parliamentary or other speeches or in a party document, especially a manifesto. Preliminary work is undertaken prior to an election in anticipation of a change of Government.

(*3*) *Possible pre-election meeting*　If and when it is clear that a general election must take place soon, the Chairman of the Board may seek ministerial approval to consult informally with the Opposition to find out more about intended new tax proposals.

(*4*) *General paper*　Shortly after the new Government assumes office, the Treasury Ministers invite the views of the Inland Revenue on their new tax proposals and the Inland Revenue prepares a general paper in which it seeks confirmation that it has correctly understood the Government's intentions; gives an indication of the numbers of tax-payers affected on different assumptions about thresholds etc; estimates possible yields on the basis of the alternative assumptions; outlines the main snags and possibilities of anomalies; suggests the most likely form of administration and the likely extra administrative cost; and analyses the general impact on tax-payers, employers, accountants. The paper raises the question of timing and the related issue of the possibility of public discussion before legislation and the form the discussion might take.

(*5*) *Ministerial guidelines for fuller examination*　One or more meetings is held with Ministers and Treasury officials on the issues raised in the general paper after which Ministers respond by giving guidelines for a fuller examination. The response indicates whether the advice of Departments of the 'outer circle' should be sought and if so when.

(6) *Organisational arrangements in the Inland Revenue and Treasury*   For each tax the Treasury and Inland Revenue will form a view about the appropriate organisation to consider the details, both jointly and in their individual departments. There may be a joint working party. The Inland Revenue may set up a team of officials (Revenue Working Party) probably headed by an under-secretary to work out details of the tax and prepare papers for Ministers (see 8 below); to preserve liaison, an Assistant Secretary from the Treasury might be a member of the team. The nucleus of the team will be those working full-time on the tax. Their job includes drawing up instructions for parliamentary counsel after Ministers have given decisions, parliamentary briefing during the passage of the legislation, and then putting the tax into operation. Another team of officials, with overlapping membership, looks after organisational, management and staffing arrangements. The team will be headed by an under-secretary, depending on the extent of new organisation required (e.g. whether the tax was to be administered through existing local offices or whether a new chain of offices – as proposed for WT – was needed).

(7) *Links with other departments*   The Civil Service Department is likely to be involved at a very early stage to get authority for staffing; with other departments there is no set pattern. Contacts with other departments in advance of any public pronouncement are only made on the specific authority of a Treasury Minister, but nowadays such authority may well be sought if the department in question is likely to be able to offer a significant contribution to the policy-making process. Otherwise the departments with an interest would only be consulted after some publicity had been given to the project.

(8) *Meetings and memoranda*   The Revenue Working Party on tax preparation prepares a series of memoranda for Ministers on different aspects of the tax, drawing attention to decisions required and suggesting alternative solutions. On minor issues the working team indicates solutions it assumes Ministers will want, leaving them to differ if they wish. Much of the agreement of Ministers will be obtained at a series of meetings following the presentation of the memoranda.

(9) *Announcement and response*   Some public announcement is made in a Chancellor's speech, statement or in answer to a Parliamentary

Question (PQ) (probably arranged). If the statement does not indicate that specific arrangements are being made for public consultation (such as a Green Paper) then representations, both written and oral, are likely to follow the announcement. At this stage comment would necessarily be general, e.g. whether the tax was needed at all, whether a particular interest should be exempt.

(*10*) *Consultation pre Finance Bill*   If provision has been made for consultation by means of a Green Paper, this is prepared in the Inland Revenue: more questions are left open for discussion than if the decision has been taken to proceed straight to legislation, and some alternative possibilities outlined. If a select committee is set up, Inland Revenue officials provide it with evidence.

(*11*) *Drafting of Finance Bill*   The Inland Revenue gives instruction to parliamentary counsel for the drafting of the Finance Bill in a series of letters from the Assistant Secretary responsible.* Drafts from counsel are examined and criticised in the Inland Revenue, amendments being effected by further correspondence or meetings.

(*12*) *Finance Bill and Finance Act*   After publication of the Finance Bill representations multiply; documents are received from professional associations etc. and meetings held. These are often on specific aspects of the Bill and are part of the campaign to achieve reliefs through amendments. The Bill proceeds to the statute book as described in Chapter 5 on the role of Parliament.

Procedures for amendment
Once a new tax has been enacted, subsequent amendment of its provisions may result from continued representations by pressure groups; feedback from local tax officers about anomalies and inequities; realisation of the existence of avoidance loopholes which needed to be closed; pressure from MPs (perhaps with particular constituency interests) on Ministers; or the report of a working group set up to consider some particular aspect of the operation of the tax, for example, the Interdepartmental Group on Capital Taxation and Agriculture (p. 104).

If significant political decisions are involved the initiative for amendment comes from Ministers. Otherwise amendments to a new tax already on the statute book are dealt with according to the annual timetable for incorporating the smaller and less controversial items into

---

*For a tax that was the responsibility of Customs and Excise, the responsible person would be someone from the Solicitor's office.

the Finance Bill – items not connected with the 'budget judgement'. The timetable and procedure is as follows:

After July   The two Deputy Chairmen of the Board of Inland Revenue circulate a note to the Assistant Secretaries inviting then to submit 'budget starters'. Perhaps 200 suggestions might be forthcoming, though the number would depend on the circumstances; if it were already clear that the next Finance Bill would contain a major piece of legislation, the note would make it clear that it was only worth considering really strong starters and the response would be less.

September–November   The suggestions are culled by the Chairman and the Deputy Chairmen and may be reduced in number to perhaps about eighty. Unimportant items are omitted and any which (not being of sufficient generality) can be dealt with by means of special concessions. The remainder are grouped into four categories: 'essential', 'highly desirable', 'desirable', 'dispensable'.

November–December   Meetings are held with junior Treasury Ministers who may require the number to be further cut, perhaps to about thirty. The two interrelated constraints are the desired size of the Finance Bill in the light of parliamentary considerations and the shortage both of parliamentary counsel in total, and of those with the special expertise required in particular.

By end January   The general shape of this component of the Finance Bill is clear, although new items may be added (e.g. because of representations from other departments or the discovery of new avoidance devices) up to the last moment and equally a purge of less essential items (sometimes already drafted) can occur late in the day to keep down the size of the Finance Bill. It is thus clear that the departments keep a close watch on subsequent changes to tax legislation, and their continuous influence shapes the process of implementation.

The introduction of the taxes studied
Of the new direct taxes included in our examination, CGT, CT, the modification of CT to the imputation system, CTT and WT (as far as it went) followed very much the pattern for the introduction of a new direct tax as outlined. However, the time allowed for all its stages varied considerably between taxes. With CGT, CT (classical) and CTT legislation was introduced into Parliament within appreciably less than a year of a Government taking office. These taxes all bore the marks of undue haste and required extensive subsequent amendment.

The tax credit scheme

The TC scheme was somewhat different. Work had been done on a negative income tax within the Conservative Research Department (p. 74), but no clear-cut plans existed when the Conservatives took office. Their manifesto of 1970 promised that they would 'make a real effort to find a practical solution' (p. 75). Lord Barber has himself described what happened (Barber, 1975).

The first step was a detailed scheme worked out by Arthur Cockfield, the Chancellor's special adviser on taxation. As Lord Barber writes: 'At that stage the plan, although in considerable detail, had not been submitted to either the Inland Revenue or the Department of Social Security.'

The civil service Heads of the Inland Revenue and of the Department of Social Security confirmed that the scheme would work and the Chancellor and the Secretary of State for Social Services set up a working group of officials known as the Tax Credit Study Group. As well as the author of the proposals, the TCSG included representatives of the DHSS, Treasury, Inland Revenue, CSD and Department of Employment. The Chancellor made an announcement about the scheme in his Budget speech on 21 March 1972; proposed to publish a Green Paper later in the year; and suggested that it be referred to a select committee for study and report.

Value added tax

VAT was the one new tax administered by Customs and Excise. Its introduction followed a similar procedure to that outlined above for direct taxes, but much more detail is available than on the other taxes because the story has been published by one of the principal participants, Mrs Dorothy Johnstone, Under-Secretary in charge of the 'machinery' of VAT (Johnstone, 1975). For this reason, and because of some unique features, notably the unprecedented extent of consultation, an account of its introduction is summarised below.

1. Like the Inland Revenue, Customs and Excise have a Departmental Planning Unit, formerly known as the Intelligence Branch, with the duty of informing itself about developments in indirect taxation; this Unit had collected and studied the foreign literature on VAT.

2. The Customs and Excise Department had provided the secretary for the Richardson Committee (Cmnd 2300, 1964) and had been consulted by the NEDO in preparing its report on VAT (1969).

3. A Departmental Committee, presided over by the Deputy Chairman, had sought to identify and discuss in a preliminary way problems associated with administering VAT. By early 1970 the

Committee had produced a VAT memorandum, of about eighty typed pages, as a basis on which more detailed work could be founded if necessary, and to enable the Department to deal provisionally with VAT enquiries from ministers and others.

4. There was some contact between members of the Opposition's Tax Policy Group and the Customs and Excise shortly before the 1970 general election.

5. When the Conservatives took office they were in a hurry to fulfil their commitment to abolish SET. The Department declared that a workable VAT could be produced in about two years, allowing for consulting the prospective tax-paying population, which was part of the Government's declared intention.

6. The structure for administering VAT included a major division between VAT Liability (VL) and VAT Machinery (VM). VL mainly meant sifting and advising on candidates for special treatment and therefore was of greater political interest at the planning stage. VM meant the rest.

7. Liaison with the Treasury followed the same pattern as for new direct taxes. Treasury representatives were mostly in evidence on VL matters. Most VL matters for political decision were discussed in committees chaired by Mr Terence Higgins, Minister of State and subsequently Financial Secretary; if they were particularly 'hot' the Chancellor was brought in.

8. Professor G.S.A. Wheatcroft was appointed by the Chancellor of the Exchequer as honorary adviser to Customs and Excise on technical VAT problems. He was the medium by which preparatory work on VAT undertaken by the Conservative Tax Policy Group was fed into the civil service machine. Mrs Johnstone (1975) writes: 'He helped us when we greatly needed this help and gradually withdrew as the need diminished (p. 15).

9. Before the Government had committed itself to VAT it was widely known that the Department was working on it (HC Debates, 7 July 1970, col. 470; 24 November 1970, col. 220) and early in 1971 the first tentative meetings were held with trade bodies – the CBI, the Retail Consortium, the NFU.

10. Small delegations visited five foreign countries (France, Germany, Netherlands, Denmark and Sweden) to learn something of the operation of VAT in those countries; the delegations consisted of four or five people led by an under-secretary or assistant secretary and stayed several days.

11. The decision was taken that VAT would go ahead and that this would be announced on Budget Day, 30 March 1971, the tax to begin in April 1973. Thereafter the screen of Budget secrecy was erected around the announcement.

12. Following publication of the Green Paper (which was mainly the work of the VL branch) on Budget Day, 30 March 1971, consult-ation on an unprecedented scale took place. Between March 1971 and March 1972 alone, views were received from over 800 different trade and professional organisations and meetings (often more than one) were held with over 300 of them.

13. A White Paper on VAT, published on Budget Day 1972 (Cmnd 4929, March 1972), contained draft clauses and schedules. It was a device for publishing the VAT portion of the Finance Bill sooner than the Bill itself would normally have been published, so giving the information industry wanted (on rates and coverage) as early as possible compatible with the Budget context.

14. The provision for VAT was included in the Finance Bill 1972. On the VM side the 1973 Finance Bill included four more clauses to fill unintentional gaps in the 1972 Act and rectify one drafting error; the other change was one of policy – the decision to allow a rebate of purchase tax and revenue duties on stocks of goods held on 1 April 1973. The major change was on the VL side: the last-minute decision, as a result of parliamentary and public pressure, to add children's clothes and footwear to the list of zero-rated goods and also those foodstuffs that had been liable to purchase tax.

Selective Employment Tax

The manner in which SET was introduced was completely different from that of any other new tax. SET arose from two (related) needs. The first stemmed from the balance of payments situation: there was a need to promote exports and reduce imports. The Labour Government had ruled out devaluation. It was therefore necessary to find some other means of increasing the international competitiveness of British goods without breaching international agreements by overt subsidisation. The second was the need for additional revenue without raising existing taxes, for in a statement just before the April 1966 election, Mr Callaghan, Chancellor of the Exchequer, had sought to avoid allega-tions that the election was being held just before what would prove to be an unpopular Budget, by announcing that he saw no reason why present taxes should be raised.

The unsatisfactory nature of SET was partly because it was a com-promise between these two objectives – economic management and revenue-raising.

During 1965, to try to deal with the first need, a high-powered Inter-Departmental Committee of officials had recommended a subsidy to employment in manufacturing paid for by a tax on service industries, which, if applied to the Development Areas, could be presented as part of regional policy. The proposal went to Ministers in the autumn of 1965 but no action was taken. Then, following the election, the balance of payments situation worsened and fairly drastic deflationary measures were required. The idea of a payroll tax on services met the Chancellor's need to raise revenue other than by existing taxes. In Michael Stewart's words, SET was 'a device which would seemingly take money out of the economy without making the Chancellor break his word' (Stewart, 1977, p. 65).

SET was a product of the fertile brain of Nicholas Kaldor, the Chancellor's special adviser, who had been influential in the recommendations of the Inter-Departmental Committee examining the balance of payments problem. Kaldor also considered that SET had other advantages. His advocacy was underpinned by economic theory. First, as he was later to explain in his inaugural lecture at Cambridge (Kaldor, 1966), he believed that the slow rate of economic growth of the United Kingdom was the result of 'premature maturity'. The fastest rates of economic growth for a nation are associated with the fast rate of growth of the manufacturing sector – which is an intermediate stage of economic development. The trouble with the British economy was that it had reached a high stage of 'maturity' before it had attained particularly high levels of real income or productivity per head. At the time it was widely believed that industrial expansion was constrained by shortage of manpower. SET was an instrument to get more people into manufacturing.

The second theoretical basis Kaldor traced to a view first put forward by John Stuart Mill about competition in imperfect markets. Kaldor believed that, expressed in real terms, SET would be paid not by reduced consumption or reduced investment but by increased output. In other words the main effect of SET in the retail and other service trades would be an increase in productivity rather than an increase in prices. Whilst the Reddaway Report (1970) went some way to confirm Kaldor's view (p. 32), in the event any increase in productivity served not to increase output but to increase unemployment. The labour released from the service industries did not go into manufacturing either because the assumption was wrong that the constraint in manufacturing output was a labour shortage, or because the labour released was of the wrong sort or in the wrong place.

The Inland Revenue held that they could not introduce a regional payroll tax in under two years because of the congestion in the Department caused by CT and CGT. Kaldor suggested that it could be done by means of a surcharge on insurance stamps. There was a precedent for this approach in an abortive scheme of Mr Selwyn Lloyd as Chancellor in 1961. The Finance Act of that year gave the Treasury temporary power to direct that each employer should pay a surcharge of up to four shillings per week in respect of each insured person employed by him. In fact this power was never used but the section of the Finance Act providing it was the precursor of section 44 of the Finance Act 1966 which introduced SET.

As national insurance stamps had to be provided by all employers, the tax necessitated a procedure by which the tax was collected from all employers and repaid (with a premium) to some.

The question then was which Ministry would act as the general repaying agency; the Ministry of Labour accepted that it could do this through its regional offices, provided that the tax was on an 'establishment' basis.* The Ministry of Pensions maintained that they could produce the increased stamps in three months – hence the tax could come into effect in the summer or early autumn.

Thus SET, which was to be administered by neither of the revenue departments, was agreed on between the election in April and the Budget in early May 1966 to come into effect some three or four months later. It is hardly surprising, in view of the lack of consultation, that the Finance Act differed in major respects from the SET White Paper issued on Budget Day or that, during its short life, SET was the subject of an abnormally large number of changes.

Changes in the Treasury and revenue departments

During the period under review, some important changes in the relationship between the Treasury and the revenue departments took place.

Until 1968 the liaison on matters of tax policy between the revenue departments and the Treasury tended to be haphazard. While the 'budget judgement' was a matter for the Treasury, advice on taxes came directly from the revenue departments to Ministers. Important revenue minutes on tax matters were copied to the Permanent Secretary to the Treasury, but it was unusual for consultation to take place until a matter was put to Ministers. The Heads of the revenue departments and of the Treasury did, however, meet as a Budget Committee.

The view gained ground in the Treasury that the revenue departments lacked a sufficiently comprehensive view on tax policy and that there was a need for the Treasury to involve itself more in tax at the

---

*For a detailed account of the need for this basis and the use of the Standard Industrial Classification in the administration of SET see Pliatzky, 1982, pp. 74–7.

working level. (It might be added that a view held in the revenue departments was that the Treasury considered tax policy from an ivory tower and had little idea how to run a tax system.) Hence, in 1968, a Fiscal and Incomes Policy Unit was set up by Sir William Armstrong, the first Head of which (as an under-secretary) was Mr (now Sir) Douglas Wass, subsequently Permanent Secretary to the Treasury. Following the reorganisation of the Treasury, from 20 October 1975 (see Economic Progress Report no. 67, October 1975) the Fiscal Policy Unit became part of the Counter-Inflation and Public Finance Division of the Domestic Economy Sector, headed initially by Mr Alan Lord as Second Permanent Secretary. The structure of the Domestic Economy Sector as at October 1975 is set out in Figure 4.2

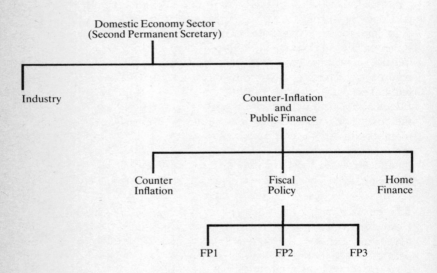

Figure 4.2 Structure of domestic economy section of Treasury after reorganisation, October 1975

Although described as 'Fiscal Policy' units, in fact FP1, 2 and 3 were primarily concerned with changes in existing taxes; FP1 with direct taxes, FP2 with indirect taxes and FP3 provided professional economic advice to the Group as a whole and was particularly concerned with the tax component of 'Budget packages', the distributional effects of taxes and social security payments and the economic implications of tax changes.

The Fiscal Policy Group as a whole was headed by an under-secretary and, in 1978 had about twelve members, with the two administrative divisions headed by an assistant secretary and the economic division by a senior economic adviser. FP1 had close links with Inland Revenue and FP2 with Customs and Excise.

It should be noted that the Fiscal Policy Unit, including FP3, had reported through the administrative hierarchy and in this sense was separate from the sector of the Treasury dealing with other economic policy. During 1980, however, this situation was changed. FP3, which consisted of the economists, was re-named DEU2 (Domestic Economy Economics Unit 2) and brought formally under an under-secretary responsible for economic aspects of a range of policies – on nationalised industries, agriculture, assistance to industry and others. However, the change was one of name rather than function. DEU2 continued to do the same kind of work that FP3 had done and continued in close liaison with FP1 and FP2.

In late 1975 the first stage of a reorganisation within the Inland Revenue was put into effect. This included the establishment of a new Central Division, headed by an under-secretary. As the Board's Report records, the Central Division 'will deal with general fiscal issues, and will have a coordinating role within the Department' (119th *Report of Inland Revenue*, March 1977, p. 19). The new Division incorporated the former Economic Services Section. It has some ten or twelve members including two economists, is concerned with wider fiscal issues in pre-Budget discussions and attempts to look at future developments, for example the desirability and feasibility of an expenditure tax, a broad look at trusts, and so on.

The performance of the departments in tax policy-making
How effective are the departments in the process of policy-making on new taxes and what is the nature of their role? First, are there any deficiencies that stand out as a result of our study?

Coordination within the inner circle
The presence of three separate tax policy-making departments – Treasury, Inland Revenue and Customs and Excise – a feature unusual if not unique to the United Kingdom, requires careful examination. With advice on taxation coming to the Chancellor and his team from three or four different quarters – the Treasury and revenue departments, not to mention the Special Adviser – there would seem to be a potential for conflict and overlap. It is noteworthy that the Chairman of the Board of Inland Revenue and the Chairman of Customs and Excise expressed anxiety when the Fiscal Policy Unit was set up in the Treasury in 1968. The exact division of function between the new

Central Division of the Inland Revenue and FP1 in the Treasury is evolving through practice and day-to-day contact but is not wholly clear. We must therefore ask: 'Is inner circle coordination adequate?'; and 'How does the Special Adviser fit into the picture?' In principle he may assist coordination; or he may be a cause of friction and provide an additional element requiring to be coordinated with the other three.

In fact all our informants were agreed that relations between the revenue departments and the Treasury were 'rarely other than friendly' and the initial anxieties of the revenue departments did not last. Also the two main special advisers were readily acceptable to the departments. But the potential for conflict is there. One Minister stressed the care necessary if this situation is to work – a Minister must consciously make it work. As Dorothy Johnstone (1975) has put it: 'The situation created when an "outside" adviser comes to occupy a room in a government department and look over the shoulders of a group of civil servants . . . is always potentially delicate', the more so when he is personal adviser to the Minister (as distinct from the Department). The Minister must not share with personal advisers confidences he would not share with others. He must bring in people the civil service can work with, considering personalities not just capabilities. Again, on the relationship of the Fiscal Policy Unit and the Treasury with the Inland Revenue and Customs and Excise, the Minister must exercise care and forethought and watch psychological points; for example, the Inland Revenue and Customs and Excise officials are in different buildings and have to come to Great George Street for meetings: the Chancellor must not appear to be sitting at a table with the Treasury on his side and the Inland Revenue or Customs and Excise on the other side.

It has been suggested that it would make for more sensible administration if the revenue departments were incorporated in the Treasury, or alternatively were a completely separate unit, like the National Tax Boards of the Scandinavian countries, concentrating on administration. But the strength of the Treasury lies in its smallness – so that everyone can know each other; this would be destroyed if the revenue departments were subordinated to the Treasury. As for the idea of a complete separation of 'policy' and 'administration', one doubts whether a clear dividing line can in fact be drawn. On the whole, the present arrangements appear to work reasonably well. One feature, however, which appears anomalous, is that the powers of Customs and Excise are considerably wider than those of the Inland Revenue. It is understandable that Customs and Excise need additional powers to combat smuggling, but there seems no logic for differences in the administration of VAT and income tax.* There must also be doubts

*At the time of writing a Committee on Enforcement Powers of the Revenue Departments (the Keith Committee) is sitting, but has not yet reported.

whether, given the desirability of two separate revenue departments, the dividing line has been drawn in the right place. VAT has more in common with income tax than with customs or excise duties. In some other countries, Germany for example, the two taxes are administered by the same office and often by the same officer; elsewhere, for example the Netherlands, whilst the departments are separate, a VAT inspector may join a corporation tax audit team. In the United Kingdom, even the exchange of information between Inland Revenue and Customs and Excise causes hands to be raised in horror and, whilst permitted by law, takes place only with specific sanction at the highest levels. This situation is ludicrous.

One sensible device which has made for smooth cooperation between the Fiscal Policy Unit in the Treasury and the revenue departments has been an interchange of personnel, so that, for example, an Inland Revenue and a Customs official were normally seconded to the Fiscal Policy Unit.

Some particular factors may have reduced the possibilities of friction between personal advisers and the regular civil service over this period. Arthur Cockfield, Special Adviser on Taxation to Chancellor Anthony Barber 1970–3, was himself a former civil servant, a Commissioner of Inland Revenue; he therefore understood the civil service methods and was often dealing with old friends. As for Lord Kaldor, Special Adviser 1964–8 and 1974–6, because of the very high regard in which he was held as an economist, some Treasury economists considered it a privilege to work with him.

The three main contributors to tax policy-making in the departments – the revenue departments, the Treasury and the special advisers – seem to have cooperated without too much friction, yet the evidence of coordination is lacking in some of the recent tax documents. It is unsatisfactory that the Green Paper on Wealth Tax and the White Paper on Capital Transfer Tax, published on the same day, contained only the most scanty reference to each other, although both were capital taxes ostensibly with the same objective. Presumably, each passed independently through its early departmental stages. It is unsatisfactory also that the Green paper included no analysis, even in the most tentative terms, of the possible macroeconomic consequences of a WT. Given the procedures we have described for coordination between Inland Revenue and Treasury, we can only presume that these omissions reflected political decisions.

Coordination with the outer circle
We have seen that in the pre-public stages of planning a new tax, contacts with government departments outside the inner circle are made only on the specific authority of a Treasury Minister (p. 92).

There is thus an element of *ad hocery* about which government departments are consulted and which are not.

The links between the tax system and the services provided by the departments are manifold and important and some appalling examples can be quoted (Sandford, Pond and Walker, 1981) which appear to result from lack of coordination, of which the most notorious is the overlap of social security and tax provisions giving rise to the poverty trap. However, this example relates to existing rather than new taxes and one of the new taxes, the tax credit scheme, was designed to try to tidy up this particular mess.

The biggest danger of inadequate consultation with outer circle departments on new taxes arises if either or both of two situations occur: if a Government seeks to keep the tax secret until Budget Day; and if the Government proceeds to legislate and implement in a hurry.

An example of the former was SET. Conceived between the election of 31 March and the Budget of 3 May 1966, the first public pronouncement on the tax was when Mr Callaghan drew it from his red box on Budget Day. How inadequate was the previous discussion is shown by the three major changes that took place within a week or two of the Budget Day White Paper: agriculture, which at first was to be reimbursed through the annual price review was put into the direct refund category; mining and quarrying were transferred from the 'no refund' to the 'refund' category; and major concessions were introduced for charities. The whole question of the necessity for Budget secrecy is one which we consider later.

CTT was not introduced as rapidly as SET, or with as little prior consultation but, for party political reasons, the tax was very hurriedly implemented. The Labour Government took office after the election on 28 February 1974; Mr Healey announced CTT on 26 March, with immediate implementation for the provisions not yet published relating to lifetime transfers; a White Paper in August 1974 gave details of the proposals; and the tax was enacted in a special Finance Bill introduced in the autumn of 1974. Again, some major differences between the proposals of the White Paper and the tax as enacted, most notably the reduced rates of duty for lifetime transfers, suggest inadequate early consultation. There is also a quite specific example of departmental views altering the tax after its introduction. Although the working party report was never made public, Mr Healey himself in his Budget speech of 6 April 1976 attributed amendments on the treatment of agriculture under CTT to the views of an Interdepartmental Group on Capital Taxation and Agriculture. Such a Group ought surely to have been set up and given time to report before the enactment of the tax. When, as in this case, reliefs are introduced shortly after the introduction of a new tax, an injustice is done to those who would have benefited from them had they been in the original legislation. The tendency to adjust taxes by amendment in subsequent years is considered above (p. 93) and below in Chapter 5.

Strategic planning

It is clear that, in the past, the tendency has been for new taxes to be looked at in isolation rather than in the context of the tax system as a whole and certainly not, as a general rule, in the context of other related policies. Of course, work on a new tax within the Inland Revenue will have some regard to other Inland Revenue taxes if only because members of the Group charged with working out the details of the new tax will have knowledge of other taxes. Similarly with a new indirect tax for which Customs and Excise are responsible. Also each revenue department has a Division with responsibility for taking a broader view of future possible tax changes. But there is no formal mechanism for bringing the two revenue departments together in a strategic planning group, let alone extending it to other departments.

Is a strategic planning group necessary or desirable? The answer must be 'yes'. It is the function of Ministers to determine broad policy issues on new taxes, but a strategic planning group could help to place ministerial proposals for new taxes in a framework which had, as it were, both a horizontal and a vertical dimension; which enabled the tax proposal to be seen against other current tax and related policies; and which also provided a time dimension. Such a group would be the tax equivalent of the Public Expenditure Survey Committee. It would include representatives from other departments likely to be affected by tax changes, and one of its functions might be to estimate the cost of the various reliefs under the tax system (tax expenditures) so that they could be allocated to expenditure programmes.

The Fiscal Policy Group in the Treasury offers a possible basis for such a development, but it would need to be much strengthened and enlarged to include representatives from other departments if it were to fulfil the role indicated.

Characteristics of the civil service role

None of the new taxes we are considering emerged from the established civil service. The civil service role, in the main, was to put clothes on the skeleton taxes emerging from the party organisations. In this process, even with new taxes, one can see some signs of the incrementalist approach which is characteristic of bureaucrats. Thus, for example, CTT emerged as a donor rather than a donee-based tax. Whilst it is debatable (p. 65–6) how far the influence of the civil service determined this decision, it was undoubtedly in line with civil service inclinations to base CTT on estate duty, which was a tax on the donor. Again, civil service incremental thinking doubtless had much to do with the proposed form and organisation of the aborted WT: whereas the universal practice on the European continent is for wealth taxes to be linked to and administered with income tax, in the United Kingdom the view was taken to administer it, along with CTT, from special regional offices and to follow similar procedures, e.g. in methods of valuation. The departmental evidence to the Select Committee on the WT provides numerous examples of the 'difficulties' that would be encountered if other than established procedures were adopted. Even SET, for all its novelty, was partly based on the proposals of Selwyn Lloyd, at an earlier date, to vary national insurance contributions.

Is there any sign of civil service pressures being responsible for a major change in any of the new taxes? Apart from the possibility that this happened with the form of CTT and a measure of civil service antipathy to SET, the main possibility is in relation to WT. Although in his first Budget Mr Healey firmly committed his Government to a WT, the Labour Government of 1974–9 abandoned the idea of introducing one during its term of office. There can be little doubt that the Treasury strongly advised caution. In so doing, however, its views were only in line with almost all those giving evidence to the Select Committee. Above all, the circumstances of high unemployment, low business confidence and high inflation could hardly have offered a less propitious moment for such a tax; and the Labour Party itself in advocating a WT had no clear philosophy on which to base it (Sandford, 1979). If civil service influence helped to lead to the abandonment of the tax this influence did no more than reinforce the arguments of other people and of circumstances. But the fate of the WT is perhaps also an illustration of the need for a party proposing a new tax to have undertaken some serious work on it in Opposition, and clarified the objectives if natural civil service conservatism is to be overcome.

Our evidence indicates that the primary role of the revenue departments is that of administrators and collectors of taxes. They have no research budgets and are not normally expected to perform innovative and imaginative functions.

5 The Role of Parliament – the Floor of the House and the Finance Bill

Constraints on the role of Parliament

Parliament's role in tax policy-making is shaped by a number of constraints. First is a constitutional constraint enshrined in a self-imposed procedural rule. The sole right of financial initiative lies with the Crown (or the Government). This means that only the Government can propose increases in taxation. This constitutional rule is embodied in Standing Order no. 82 of the House of Commons which reads:

> That this House will receive no Petition for any sum relating to Public Service, or proceed upon any Motion for a grant or charge upon Public Revenue, whether payable out of the Consolidated Fund or out of monies to be provided by the Parliament, unless recommended from the Crown.
>
> (Quoted in Reid, 1966, p. 41)

Modern interpretation of this rule means that if any amendment that would involve any member of the public paying more taxes is proposed to the Finance Bill other than by a member of the Government on its behalf, then that amendment is out of order (Reid, 1966, p. 133). 'Amendments must not exceed the scope, increase the amount or extend the incidence of any charge upon the people' (Erskine May, 17th edn., p. 826). The effect of this rule is that no amendments to increase taxation can be moved by backbench members of the House. They can now, however, move amendments which can have 'incidental or consequential changes . . . which may arise from provisions designed in general to afford relief from tax' (*Select Committee on Procedure*, 1970–1, para. 6). It is, therefore, not surprising to find that a feature of the Committee stage of any Finance Bill is that large numbers of amendments are tabled calling for concessions and reliefs from taxation.

A further constraint on the role of the House of Commons is the rule that all legislation, of whatever nature, must have passed all its stages by the end of the Session, otherwise it will fail. That is, no Bills can be carried over from one Session to another. But taxation legislation is especially constrained in time by the provisions of the 1968 Provisional Collection of Taxes Act which updated the 1913 Act. The Act gives the Government the right to collect taxes announced in the Budget (usually March or April) even though they have not, strictly speaking, legal force because the Finance Bill has not yet passed all its stages. Under the Provisional Collection of Taxes Act the stages of the Finance Bill must be completed by early August. The effect of this peculiar time-table means that effectively Parliament has little more than three months in which to consider the Finance Bill. Thus the whole procedure leaves little time for reflection and for second thoughts when anomalies or errors are spotted. Substantial changes often have to be built into the following year's Finance Bill (see for example, the 1976 amendments to the CTT).

Parliament is further constrained in its consideration of new taxes by the convention that new taxes should be presented together with changes to existing taxes in a single Finance Bill.* Although they are of a very different nature and require different legislative treatment, clauses that relate to new taxes are considered by the same people in the same arena at the same time as those modifying existing taxes. This juxtaposition inhibits orderly and reasoned Second Reading debates on the merits and principles of a new tax.

Finally, the traditional adversary style debating procedure used both on the floor of the House and in standing committee reduces the capacity of the House to give a coherent and sensible consideration to complex and technical legislation; and this deficiency is a :ntuated by the inability of the House to call witnesses at the committee stage and by lack of expert advice available to members. As taxes have become more complex in recent years this constraint has become more severe. Select committees in which an investigatory style is employed are not invariably used prior to the introduction of new taxes (see Chapter 6).

Assessment of parliamentary influence

Those writers who have hitherto attempted to assess the influence of Parliament in the process of taxation have concentrated upon the ability of members to put and achieve amendments during the passage of the Finance Bill (for comparison with the USA see Surrey, 1957). While the Government's spending proposals are *never* altered by Parliament, its taxing proposals *are* occasionally altered. The Government does not see every amendment to a Finance Bill as a vote of confidence. It has

---

*The practice of introducing all taxes for the year in a single Finance Bill dates from 1861. Before that date there was a separate Bill for each new tax. In 1860 the House of Lords rejected the Paper Duty Repeal Bill. As a consequence Gladstone put all his financial measures into a single Bill in 1861 (including the lost Paper Duty Repeal) so that the Lords 'must either accept the whole or try the impossible performance of rejecting the whole' (Morley, *Life of Gladstone* vol. 1 p. 674). In 1909 the Lords did reject the Finance Bill thus precipitating a constitutional crisis. As a result they lost their financial powers. Even though there is no longer a constitutional justification for a single Finance Bill the precedent set by Gladstone in 1861 is still adhered to.

been argued, in one of the rare works on the influence of Parliament on tax policy-making (Mackintosh, 1973) that members can exert a significant influence on the shape of tax policy by achieving amendments to Finance Bills. Mackintosh gives examples of amendments that he considers were of more than passing importance. These include amendments made in 1937, 1961, 1962 (including the tax relief for blind persons), 1964, 1965 (amendments to CGT and CT) and 1968 (aggregation of children's income with that of parents). Had he lived to write a second edition of his article he could have added the famous Rooker and Wise amendment to the 1977 Finance Bill which obliged the Chancellor of the Exchequer to update the personal allowances against income tax each year to take account of inflation unless he otherwise announced. But, if we look at these 'successes' very closely we find peculiar circumstances obtain; notably that the issues cut across party lines or, as in the case of the Rooker–Wise amendment, result from a Government majority in the standing committee on the Finance Bill so small (reflecting the composition of the House) that the revolt of two Government supporters was sufficient to secure the passage of the amendment against the wishes of the Chancellor of the Exchequer. Very often 'successes' are reversed by later amendments introduced by the Government (see, for example, the 1975 Finance Bill which reversed defeats in the 1974 Bill on investment income surcharge and the exemption for trade union provident funds).

Mackintosh's theme was taken up by David Millar (1976) who argued that a significant link between pressure groups and Parliament arises from the possibility of changes in a Finance Bill at the Committee stage. Millar quotes from Reid (1966): 'Pressure groups, to their satisfaction, still find members of Parliament capable of influencing taxation law during the Parliamentary process' (Millar, 1976, p. 202). But, Reid, Mackintosh and Millar simply accepted that a few examples of Government defeats on amendments to Finance Bills provided sufficient evidence of parliamentary influence over tax policy. They did not test their hypothesis (for this is what it is) by examining the proportion and overall significance of changes made to Finance Bills by backbenchers in the Committee stage, and above all, they did not examine the *process* of amendment. By considering only amendments that succeeded as a result of a vote they concentrated their discussion on the influence of Parliament in a very narrow focus and took as evidence a very narrow measurement. Reid (1966) was aware of this limitation but contended that any estimate of influence in a more general sense was likely to be 'subjective'.

Although it is undoubtedly difficult to give an estimate of the general influence of Parliament on tax policy in precise quantitative terms, the way in which Members use their opportunities for debate and the subjects of tax policy on which they concentrate can be described. Indeed, such a description is necessary if we are to present a full and balanced picture of the role of Parliament. Many of the amendments brought forward by the Government itself are the result of representations made by MPs in debates, in Committee, in the corridors, or formally to Ministers, and by pressure groups prior to and during the Committee stage. A steady stream of parliamentary comment encourages frequent adjustment to tax legislation.

The flow of comment is diffuse rather than focused and concentrated. It generally begins many years before a new tax is introduced and continues for many years following enactment. The Government receives a continual stream of messages through parliamentary questions, early day motions and, above all, debates. Those debates at which Government and Opposition front bench spokesmen are present, especially Budget debates when the House is considering the Chancellor's Budget statement, provide the most concentrated forum for individual members to present their ideas about new taxes. There is normally only one Budget each year, and therefore only one annual opportunity for Members to focus their attention on taxation policy. However, in some years, especially election years, there have been two Budgets and two Finance Bills (1974 for example) and sometimes also Chancellors have felt obliged to introduce 'mini-budgets' when some particular change is required to meet a crisis situation.

With simultaneous publication on Budget Day in 1980 and 1981 of the White Paper on Public Expenditure, which now also contains some information about tax expenditures, the pattern of the Budget speech is beginning to change; but the traditional pattern of Budget debates, and that which prevailed in the years most relevant to our study, has been that the Chancellor presented a general appraisal of the economic situation, briefly nodded in the direction of public expenditure, and gave a detailed account of the changes he was proposing to existing taxes. On existing taxes he indicated the new rates, thresholds and allowances and often indicated specific exemptions and alterations. On new taxes, however, he was often somewhat vague in the Budget speech itself, choosing to put the details of his proposals to the House in a White Paper issued after the Budget speech but before the debate on second reading of the Finance Bill. Thus in some cases members know by the time of the Budget debate that a new tax is to be introduced but little about its shape and form. This was particularly true in 1966 with SET, and in the March 1974 Budget when CTT and the commitment to a WT were announced. This lack of information can notably impede any sensible consideration of a new tax during the Budget debate.*

*In recent years there has been a growth in the number and detail of press releases immediately following the Budget which can be of help to MPs in preparing their speeches for Budget debates, but they have little time in which to absorb the material.

In a Budget debate, MPs are invited to consider the details of some tax changes and the general principles of others, as well as various aspects of the state of the economy such as the level of demand, the rate of inflation or the balance of payments. In some Budget debates quite extraneous subjects may take up much of the debating time. Thus in 1965 the cancellation of the TSR 2 was announced during a Budget debate and in 1969 Barbara Castle took the opportunity to spark off what one member described as a 'second reading debate' on the proposed industrial relations legislation embodied in 'In Place of Strife'. Members' views on new taxes are thus dotted about, often apparently at random, among speeches on quite different subjects. Like debates on expenditure (Robinson, 1978) debates on taxation are usually incoherent and fragmented. One speaker is not followed by another dissecting his case and argument. Members perform like a concert party which relies for its effect on the contrast between each item.

Budget debates

Before the 1960s Budget debates contained references to some of the principles of the new taxes which were to follow from 1964. Thus the *Final Report of the Royal Commission on the Taxation of Income and Profits* (Cmd 9474), published in 1955, was the subject of parliamentary comment. VAT had a brief airing in the 1961 Budget debate and in 1962 debate centred on the short-term CGT introduced by Selwyn Lloyd. But it was the 1963 Budget debate which really set discussion going on new taxes. From that time until the mid-1970s comments on tax reform increased in scope and intensity. In the following sections the new taxes are considered broadly in the order in which they first appeared with some frequency in parliamentary debates rather than in chronological order of enactment (or, with TC and WT, formal proposal).

Value added tax

In his 1963 Budget statement the Chancellor of the Exchequer, Reginald Maudling, initiated a decade of debate on the subject of VAT. Against the background of Britain's declining share of world trade, and the relative fall in Britain's living standards compared with those of the EEC countries (who, in the person of de Gaulle, had rebuffed one attempt at British entry to the club), a number of economic commentators (including NEDC, 1963) had suggested VAT as a possible device for promoting growth and encouraging exports. It was pointed out that the TVA (VAT) was used by some Common Market countries and that it provided for the rebating of tax on exports. Whilst, by the time VAT was introduced in 1973, the emphasis had shifted to the desirability of a wider base for indirect taxation and a more neutral tax structure (p. 115), in the 1963 debate the thrust of the argument was on the encouragement VAT might give to exports.

VAT was mentioned by a considerable number of speakers in the 1963 debate and many who favoured it (mainly Conservatives) saw a connection between VAT and the recent economic success of our European competitors. Some also noted the EEC connection.

On the other hand leading Labour Party spokesmen were not enthusiastic. Mr Callaghan, who had originally favoured the idea, had changed his mind (4 April 1963, col. 645) on the grounds that the administrative inconvenience of collection could outweigh any fiscal advantages. Anthony Crosland (4 April 1963, col. 703) was uncertain of its effects as an export incentive.

Chancellor Maudling, in his Budget statement was also sceptical:

I have never been convinced that the substitution of an added-value tax, either for profits tax, or for purchase tax, would provide, in practice, an effective incentive to exports in the sense of an opportunity to our manufacturers.

(3 April 1963, col. 467)

Since, however, he was aware that many people were advocating this new tax, he announced the setting up of the Richardson Committee to investigate the proposals. Some Labour members expressed their preference for purchase tax, and many of them feared that VAT would be a widespread tax covering essentials such as food.

In the following year's Budget debate Mr Maudling indicated that the inquiry of the Richardson Committee on VAT showed that 'in the circumstances in this country, the purchase tax is superior . . . there is no advantage either to exports or to the economy generally in introducing VAT' (14 April 1964, col. 249). In considering the use of VAT as a broadly-based tax he indicated that, of goods at present untaxed, not less than four-fifths were food and fuel; and that there were many services that would not be widely considered as suitable subjects for taxation. However, he made a perceptive comment about his capacity to collect what he needed from existing taxes:

Looking at the future trend of public expenditure and the pattern of consumer spending, I think that there is some substance in the argument that at some time the basis of indirect taxation will have to be widened.

(20 April 1964, col. 1007)

VAT was little considered in further Budget debates until 1968. In 1967, following the SET debacle, two Labour MPs, David Marquand and David Owen, had called for a Green Paper on VAT and Marquand, an ardent pro-European, who later left the House of Commons to become an EEC Commission official, linked the need for VAT in the United Kingdom to our possible membership of the EEC. In the 1968 debate a number of Members mentioned VAT as a possible broadly-based tax. Like SET it would permit services to be included in the tax net. It was gradually becoming clear that if SET, which no one liked, were to be scrapped, it would have to be replaced with some other tax which was a good revenue-raiser and offered a broad base. By the time of the 1968 Budget debate Members had brought together the main arguments for VAT (below): that it might encourage exports; that it was the system used in the European Community; and that it was a broadly-based tax better adapted to raising revenue than purchase tax. By 1968 too, Iain Macleod had replaced Reginald Maudling as Conservative Shadow Chancellor and, unlike Maudling, he was not against the possibility of introducing VAT (20 March 1968, col. 439). We thus see a degree of support for VAT emerging in the House of Commons by this time, especially among Conservatives and pro-Europe Labour members. The Liberals, too, suggested that VAT might boost exports (J. Thorpe, 20 March 1968, col. 461). Those who opposed VAT were primarily concerned with its means of collection. Comments on this topic were repeated many times both in this debate and later.

By the 1969 Budget debate VAT was being favourably contrasted to the unpopular SET. Unlike SET it would bear more evenly and not have to be changed at every Budget. In the 1970 Budget debate, it was noted that VAT was proposed by those anxious to see Britain as a member of the EEC, and some Labour Members suggested that it would increase the cost of living. By the next Budget, in 1971, there had been a general election, and the Conservatives were in office. Their manifesto commitment to VAT had been conditional (p. 74), but their intentions about the EEC and SET clear. Mr Barber stated that there was a manifesto commitment to abolish SET:

as part of a wider reform of indirect taxation, possibly involving the replacement of purchase tax by a value-added tax.

(30 March 1971, col. 1392)

By 1971 the Government was clearly committed to the introduction of VAT, but the details were yet to be worked out and a period of consultation (p. 97) would be permitted before VAT appeared in a Finance Bill. Hence comments on VAT in the 1971 Budget debate could be only of a general nature. Harold Wilson, Leader of the Opposition, attacked the Chancellor's proposals. He alleged that the change from SET and purchase tax to VAT would mean very large increases in the cost of living for the average family. It might be, he said, the price that we would have to pay, along with the Common Agricultural Policy, for entry to Europe, but Mr Barber had announced the change *before* we knew what terms we might be offered to enter Europe.

VAT was the most frequently mentioned new tax in this debate, being mentioned by no fewer than some twenty speakers. At last the debate on VAT had reached significant proportions.

The arguments for and against VAT in the 1971 debate can be summarised as follows:

Arguments in favour of VAT   (mostly from the Government side)

1. VAT is more straightforward than SET and PT. It is the 'least imperfect' tax, being broadly based and neutral.
2. The experience in other countries shows that it works.
3. It is a requirement of entry to the EEC.

Of these arguments the first, that VAT is better than the alternative forms of indirect taxation, was most frequently mentioned.

Arguments against VAT   (largely from the Opposition)

1. VAT is administratively cumbersome, expensive to collect and a burden on traders.
2. It will increase the cost of living and particularly harm pensioners and the low paid.

At this stage there were few references to particular interests that might be affected by VAT, except that Mr Jo Grimond (Liberal) urged that there should be no VAT on transport.

Members in the 1971 Budget debate urged the Government to consult widely before new taxes were introduced. Recalling the experience of the introduction of SET (1966) it was suggested that in future both Green Papers and select committees should be used. David Marquand noted the particular need for select committees on corporation tax and VAT because they contained exceedingly complex proposals. But the Chief Secretary to the Treasury, Maurice Macmillan, said that as the Government intended to legislate on VAT 'this autumn' there would be no time for a select committee on VAT, although the Government would consider setting one up for CT.

Introducing his second Budget in 1972 Mr Barber noted that in January 1973 Britain would become part of the EEC. There had been a Green Paper and extensive consultation but no select committee on VAT. A VAT White Paper was to be published immediately following the Budget speech. Thus members had some concrete information on VAT before them for the 1972 Budget debate.

It is not surprising, since they had the details before them, that members paid a good deal of attention to VAT in the 1972 Budget debate. In reply to the Chancellor's speech Mr Harold Wilson announced 'total and unremitting opposition' to VAT. Party lines had been drawn on VAT. The Opposition, as Mr Wilson had indicated, was firmly against it; the Government was firmly for it. The arguments in the 1972 debate can be summarised as follows:

Main Government arguments in favour of VAT

1. It allows for a shift from direct to indirect taxation so that people can keep more of their earnings. It allows more emphasis on tax on spending.
2. It is less discriminatory and is a broadly based consumption tax.
3. It is as unregressive as possible.

Main Opposition arguments against VAT

1. A shift from direct to indirect taxation is undesirable.
2. It will sacrifice fairness to efficiency.
3. VAT is regressive.
4. It will add complexity to the tax system and create new anomalies.
5. VAT is the Tory price for joining the EEC.
6. It will increase the cost of living.
7. It will be an administrative burden on industry and commerce.
8. Much special pleading emerged from constituency interests on subjects as diverse as chocolate biscuits, freight, horticulture and the arts.

Special pleading in Budget debates provides early warning signals to the Government and to pressure groups. As a rule it is not until after the second reading that special pleading becomes sufficiently focused to emerge as a concrete amendment. The story of zero-rating children's clothes is instructive here. Mentioned in general terms in the Budget debate together with other items, and likewise at second reading, by the time the Committee stage took place publicity and pressure group activity had succeeded in persuading MPs from both sides of the House to put down amendments (p. 216). These failed in Committee but eventually the Government introduced an amendment of its own in 1973 to zero-rate children's clothes. Announcing this change the Chancellor confessed:

I can sum up my decision by saying on Shrove Tuesday, the traditional day of repentance: 'I was wrong.'

(6 March 1973, col. 275)

By the 1973 Budget debate VAT was enacted and about to come into operation in the following month. Much comment in the debate centred on VAT. Opposition speakers claimed once again that it would increase the cost of living, an allegation denied by the Chancellor (12 March 1973, col. 1024). A number of special cases were displayed where VAT would have adverse effects: on professional sport, on miner's boots, on charities and, through the administrative burden of collection, on small firms.

Once VAT was in operation, references to it did not disappear from Budget debates. Firstly, when Chancellors alter the rate of VAT (Denis Healey's higher rate for example) an opportunity to discuss VAT in relation to its general economic effects is opened. Secondly, some of the special cases where demands for reliefs have not been met, such as the zero-rating of housing repairs and maintenance (including churches), continue to have claims pressed on their behalf, and attempts are regularly made to reduce the compliance costs to small firms. But the general principle of VAT is now widely accepted and rarely questioned.

Corporation tax I and II

Reform of company taxation had been mentioned from time to time in the House of Commons before the mid-1960s (following the Royal Commission for example). In his 1963 Budget statement Mr Reginald Maudling foreshadowed a reform of company taxation, but made no firm proposals (3 April 1963, col. 466).

Some members, including his predecessor Mr Selwyn Lloyd, who had stated in his 1961 Budget that he intended to examine the idea, and Douglas Houghton on the Labour side, were disappointed at Mr Maudling's lack of interest in this reform. However, Mr Maudling returned to the question in his 1964 Budget. He announced that the Inland Revenue and the experts were now examining the possibility of placing the taxation of company profits for income purposes onto an accounts basis and promised a White Paper outlining the scheme before introducing legislation. The major Opposition spokesmen, James Callaghan (15 April 1964, col. 433) and Roy Jenkins (15 April, col. 487) called for fundamental reform of company taxation. But few other members made even a passing reference to the subject in 1964.

The Opposition, having expressed a desire for reform, found themselves in Government by the next Budget debate. Mr Callaghan, making his first Budget speech as Chancellor, in 1964 foreshadowed his new corporation tax. By now the party lines were clearly drawn on this issue. Mr Callaghan took his cue from the Minority Report of the Royal Commission on Taxation (and followed the arguments of Crosland). He thought that a corporation tax should favour undistributed profits to encourage companies to reinvest. He also linked CT to his objective of an incomes policy; if wages were to be restrained, so in fairness must distributed profits. For the Opposition, Sir Alec Douglas-Home put the contrary view. He drew the attention of the Chancellor to the Majority Report of the Royal Commission which said that profits should be distributed so that the money could be reinvested in the most profitable enterprises.

Replying to the Chancellor next day Mr Maudling opposed both the idea of a separate CT and the particular version of it outlined by Mr Callaghan:

I cannot feel that it can possibly give any encouragement to British industry to invest further.

(12 Nov 1964, col. 1208)

The promised reform made its appearance in the 1965 Budget speech. CT was dubbed 'the most fundamental of the tax reforms in this Budget' and was introduced under the heading of 'Efficiency'. The Chancellor rehearsed the arguments against the idea of a separate CT but maintained that the existence of profits tax had already made nonsense of them. He went on:

There then remains the question of how to frame the tax on company profits. As soon as it is divorced from the taxation of individuals, we are free to draw it up on principles most conducive to economic growth and efficiency . . . The two ways open to us of raising the same amount of revenue from corporation tax are, either to confine the tax to undistributed profits and levy it at a relatively high rate; or alternatively, to impose a tax on the whole profits, irrespective of distributions, at a much lower rate.

(6 April 1965, col. 255)

Mr Callaghan thought that the latter type of tax, the so-called classical system, had a much greater economic and incentive value than the former:

A tax confined to undistributed profits penalises investment and growth; it severely handicaps the young and dynamic companies which must rely on ploughed-back profits for expansion. A tax on the whole profit has the opposite effect. It makes it possible to shift the burden of taxation in such a way as to relieve the faster growing companies, which are generally low distributors, and thus enable them to expand even faster. It will place more of the burden on those which are high distributors. It gives a strong incentive to all companies to plough back more of their profits for expansion. Finally, the incentives to cut costs and to raise efficiency through new investment are much stronger, and must be much stronger when a lower percentage of additional profits is taken in taxation than under the present system, where $56\frac{1}{4}$ per cent of any additional profit would go in tax.

(6 April 1965, col. 255)

The real arguments began on the second day of the 1965 debate when Edward Heath clearly brought out the basis of the Conservative opposition to the classical form of the CT. This speech, the first of many from the Conservative benches, contains most of the arguments that were used over the next six years until 1970 when the Conservatives, regaining office with Edward Heath as Prime Minister, made their own reform of CT. Mr Heath thought that the 'first real purpose' of CT (and of the CGT introduced at the same time) was to 'secure a redistribution of income'. The other 'real purpose' of CT was, he said, to deter overseas investment (7 April 1965, col. 495).

He objected to CT as introduced precisely because it would encourage firms to retain profits. This was not the best way to encourage investment. An expanding firm, he argued, needs to get its funds for growth from the capital market. To get dynamism into industry, money must be paid out, saved and reinvested. This process would permit firms to grow. Otherwise, he argued, in a phrase that was repeated later by others, all that would happen would be 'the survival of the fattest' (7 April 1965, col. 497). Mr Heath preferred the German system (with a lower rate of CT on distributed profits) which resembled more the existing British system than the new proposals.

A number of members referred to CT in the ensuing debate. The arguments used in favour of the classical system can be summarised as follows:

Government side   (Labour members)

1. CT can (with CGT) play a positive part in securing an incomes policy.
2. CT will encourage investment by favouring the ploughing back of profits.
3. CT will discourage overseas investment (left-wing Labour view).
4. The Germans had no capital market so they used the form of CT to create one. We already had a capital market and so did not need to shape our CT to create this effect.
5. The proposed form of CT would encourage efficiency and growth.
6. Distributed profits do not necessarily make their way back onto the capital market – they are treated as income and spent.

The argument most frequently used in favour of CT was the need to encourage firms to plough back their profits.

Opposition (Conservative members)

1. The real purpose of CT (and CGT) is disguised.
2. The retention of profits makes management too comfortable, too idle, it encourages merely caution and 'the survivial of the fattest'.
3. There is a need to distribute profits, to create mobility of capital, to ensure dynamic growth in the economy.

4. Overseas investment and companies trading overseas ought to be encouraged.

5. Directors will spend too much of their time examining the capital structure of the firm and too little on becoming more efficient producers.

6. The West German system of CT is better.

7. The yield of the tax will be small.

On this side of the House, the most frequently used arguments were on the desirability of encouraging capital to circulate to create dynamism in the economy. There was by this time no real opposition to a CT as such (Maudling himself had been the real stumbling block to reform). The Liberals, in this debate, supported the Conservative views about the desirability of maximum mobility of capital.

Important amendments to CT were introduced in 1966 so it remained an issue for debate that year, although SET was the dominant feature of that year's Budget debate; and in the ensuing years to 1970, the Conservatives continued to complain about the form of CT.

In his first Budget Mr Barber proposed the reform of CT. Introducing the new tax, he said:

From the moment when the introduction of corporation tax was announced, we made it clear why we were opposed to the particular form which had been chosen. Nothing that has happened since then has caused us to alter that view, and I therefore intend to reform the structure of the tax.

(30 March 1971, col. 1383)

Mr Wilson, for the Opposition, restricted himself to the comment that if the Chancellor thought that an encouragement to increased dividend payments would contribute to:

a more united and harmonious industrial situation and to better chances of an incomes and prices policy on a voluntary basis, he is wrong.

(30 March 1971, col. 1406)

A number of speakers in the debate made some reference to the proposed changes in CT, mainly continuing the complaints about the adverse effects of Labour's CT. Calls were made for consultation before the new tax was introduced, including a Select Committee, which was established (Chapter 6). In his 1972 Budget speech Mr Barber announced his acceptance of the Select Committee recommendations of the imputation system for CT which would be included in the 1972 Finance Bill (21 March 1972, col. 1358). A White Paper containing the details of CT was to be published before the Finance Bill. Thus members had no firm information before them on the details of the tax for the Budget debate that followed. A number of the Select Committee members, among others, referred to CT in the debate. Some Labour members of the Select Committee complained of its narrow terms of reference and of the Government's commitment to the reform before the Select Committee was established. Following the reform of CT comments, largely of a technical nature and on the increasing complexity and falling revenue of CT, have continued in Budget debates. As a result of continued complaints, demands have been made for the further reform of this tax. A Green Paper, long awaited, was issued in 1982 (Cmnd 8456).

Wealth tax

Wealth taxes, in one form or another, have been recommended to governments for many years. In the period from 1963 we find that WT was always lurking in the minds of some MPs. At times the debate has been conducted in a very low key; at other times it has reached a crescendo. (There was, in 1982, still no wealth tax, although it remained on the political agenda.) There were a number of references to it in the 1963 Budget debate, for the idea had recently been given an airing by Mr Callaghan. A number of Conservatives expressed their fears about the consequences of such a tax. They complained both about the general idea, and about the particular effects on, for example, farmers (4 April 1963, col. 762). Mr Callaghan continued to promote the idea throughout 1963-4 (although it had no blessing from the party leadership at the time) so it attracted a considerable amount of attention in the 1964 Budget debate. Many Conservatives expressed shock at the very idea of a WT; Edward Heath was among them:

So far this is the only proposal that can be tied to the Hon Member, but now it has been banned by his Leader. The one child – strangled at birth – or has it been quietly boarded out for the time being?

(15 April 1964, col. 454)

Whilst Douglas Houghton commented:

What a morbid interest many people have in the Labour Party's intentions about this tax.

(20 April 1964, col. 896)

But, when a few months later Mr Callaghan became Chancellor of the Exchequer he seemed to have forgotten the idea. His taxes for 'social justice' were to be CGT and CT, not WT. WT, perhaps surprisingly in view of the interest it had aroused a few months earlier, received no mention in the 1965 debate. It was not until four years later, in the 1968 Budget that the issue surfaced again to any noticeable extent. The references to WT in 1968 arose largely because the Chancellor, Mr Jenkins, had found it necessary to impose a 'special charge' in the form of a surcharge on investment income. This was intended to apply for one year only. In the highest brackets it meant that some people would have to pay more than 100 per cent of income in tax, a fact appreciated by the Chancellor who recognised that:

In the higher range it will be a small tax upon capital
(19 March 1968, col. 299)

Mr Joel Barnett agreed but thought the charge might be:

a simple administrative method of collecting a Wealth Tax
(21 March 1968, col. 733)

Mr Jenkins considered that, if used for consecutive years, the charge might lead to a shortage of investment funds. However, he did not think that the effect of such a tax should preclude:

the further exploration of the ways in which the taxable capacity of those who possess wealth should be differentiated from that of those who depend primarily on wages and salaries
(19 March 1968, col. 300)

He thought that if some sensible means of taxing wealth could be found, it might then be possible to reduce the highest rates of tax on income. But congestion in the Inland Revenue from his predecessor's measures was such that he could only say of the possibility of a WT:

I will not spend time on a discussion on the merits of such a tax since it would be quite impracticable at present because of the problems of valuation which would be involved.
(19 March 1968, col. 299)

By 1969 Mr Jenkins considered that there would be great administrative costs from a WT with little revenue or demand effect. And he said:

I must continue to give great attention to the overstrain which persists in the Inland Revenue. The two major and worthwhile changes of 1965 were a heavy meal to digest and the process is still not yet complete.
(15 April 1969, col. 1016)

There were only a few muted references by other speakers in this year's debate. Few Conservatives took the possibility seriously.

In 1970, Mr Jenkins's last Budget, several Labour members called for a WT and one complained that after five and a half years of Labour rule there was still no sign of it from the Chancellor. Once the Conservatives took office in 1970, calls for a WT vanished from Budget debates for a while. In 1974, however, Mr Healey became Chancellor in the new Labour Government and proclaimed that he would 'squeeze the rich until the pips squeaked'. The Labour Party, he said, had pledged itself to achieve a major redistribution of both wealth and income:

The Government intends to introduce an annual wealth tax on the rich . . . I
believe that it should be introduced only after a thorough public discussion
about the precise form it should take.

(26 March 1974, col. 312)

This promise of a WT attracted many speakers in the 1974 debate.
Some on the Government side expressed disappointment that the tax
itself did not appear in the 1974 Budget and that all they had been
offered was a Green Paper. As Mrs Renée Short pointed out, there had
been Green, White and Red Papers on the subject produced from
Transport House. But others on the Labour side welcomed the publication of a Green Paper. David Marquand called for the subject to be
sent to a Select Committee for investigation. Some signs of unease were
expressed from the Labour benches. Denzil Davies (28 March 1974,
col. 702) doubted whether a WT, with its attendant problems of
valuation and exemptions, would achieve its object of redistribution -
he preferred a simple capital levy. Significantly, Douglas Jay, who was
shortly to become the Chairman of the Select Committee on a Wealth
Tax, thought that a WT ought to be based on investment income alone
and that the Government should not bother with the valuation of art
and jewellery and other assets because the bureaucratic efforts would
not be justified by the results (1 April 1974, col. 92). On the other hand,
Conservatives Robert Carr and P. Grieve were not against WT in
principle if accompanied by reductions in income tax and death duties
(27 March 1974, col. 495 and 28 March 1974, col. 698). The points
made in this debate were to prove prophetic of the later work in the
Select Committee. Opposition from other parties would be muted so
long as the WT was accompanied by other tax changes, but considerable disquiet was felt about the effectiveness of such a tax, bearing in
mind the practical problems. Thus the debate anticipated the experience of the Select Committee.

There were numerous comments on WT in the November 1974
Budget debate. Some Labour Members were disappointed once again
not to see the WT in this Budget and some referred to the Social
Contract with the unions, pointing out, once more, the relationship
between capital taxation and wage restraint. For the Liberals, John
Pardoe welcomed the Select Committee on the WT and put forward his
view:

We are favourably disposed to the idea of a WT . . . it can replace almost all
other forms of capital taxation.

(14 November 1974, col. 645)

The story of the Select Committee on a Wealth Tax is told in Chapter
6. A WT continues to be suggested from time to time in debates of the
House.

Capital gains tax

This tax was debated in the House of Commons for some years before introduction in its present form in 1965. In 1961 Selwyn Lloyd introduced a short-term CGT in response to the considerable disquiet at the gains made during the period of stock market and property boom. It was suggested then and later that something more than a short-term tax was required. The 1964 Budget debate is interesting in making clear the link in some Labour Members' minds between capital taxation and incomes policy. Douglas Houghton, for example (16 April 1964, cols. 890–1) pointed out that if they were to get an incomes policy the Government would have to show that it was fair in the treatment of *all* income, whether earned or unearned. Profits, dividends and gains should all be subject to taxation. Some Conservatives were not averse to seeing all capital gains taxed so long as the rates were low. Roy Jenkins expressed a view not dissimilar to that of some Conservatives and Liberals when he said:

I should like to see the question of capital gains looked at again and an effective tax brought in here, but as part of this general scheme . . . Had we a really imaginative re-casting of our taxation system in which loopholes were closed, capital gains dealt with effectively, and a small annual capital tax considered, it might, alongside this, have been possible to come to a real remission of taxation on people who wanted to save a substantial part of their income.

(15 April 1964, col. 487)

Capital gains tax came in the following year, when Mr Callaghan became Chancellor after the election. Announcing in his autumn Budget his intention to introduce a CGT in his spring Budget of 1965 he said:

The dividing line between capital and income has become blurred. The income tax system has been misused by some to avoid paying income tax by entering into arrangements which dress up income, which is taxable, to look like capital, which is mainly untaxed. The Right Hon and learned Gentleman, the Member for Wirral, caught a fleeting glimpse of this when he made short-term capital gains chargeable to tax . . . Therefore in my spring Budget, I shall introduce proposals for the taxation of capital gains . . . This measure will bring to an end the state of affairs in which hard work and great energy are fully taxed while the fruits of speculation and passive ownership escape untaxed. I hope, therefore, that it will have a substantial effect in helping wage and salary earners in this country to accept the need for an incomes and prices policy.

(11 November 1964, cols. 1039 and 1040)

Several Government supporters echoed Mr Callaghan's view that 'the necessity and purpose of a CGT is to get an incomes policy' (Tom Iremonger, 11 November 1964, col. 1115).

But this being a relatively short debate, few others considered the matter. CGT was, in any case, overshadowed by CT in the year in which it was enacted. During the 1965 Budget debate when both CGT and CT were introduced, the arguments in favour of CGT from the Government side (which were frequently bracketed with arguments for CT) were that it would play a positive part in securing an incomes policy; that it was an act of justice and fairness to other heavily taxed people; and that the effect of inflation on CGT is no different from the 'fiscal drag' which adversely affects income tax payers. For their part, the Conservatives argued that its purpose was a disguised one of redistribution (this point has been made subsequently with increased emphasis in relation to the 'inflation tax' effect of CGT); that it would deter small savers; that it would only tax inflation; and that its yield would be small.

There was, however, no real opposition to the idea of CGT as such. Conservative members seemed to accept much of the argument that there should be equity of taxation as between those who earned their incomes and those who obtained them through capital gains. In the late 1970s and early 1980s, however, members began to complain more vigorously that without indexation CGT had come to be an inflation tax, not a tax on real capital gains. In 1982 provision was made for indexing CGT thereafter.

Capital transfer tax

The problems associated with death duties have long occupied speakers in the House of Commons. The defects of estate duty had been noted in Budget debates over many years before there appeared to be any practical prospects of reform. As early as 1964 we find Conservatives urging an inheritance tax in order to bring greater equity into the system because estate duty had become largely avoidable and arbitrary (16 April 1964, cols. 671 and 673). Labour members from time to time pressed for a gifts tax but during the 1960s demands for this particular reform remained muted. In 1969 Mr Jenkins was of the opinion that, together with the WT proposal, a gifts tax would be too much for the Inland Revenue to digest especially since it would produce little revenue and cost a great deal to collect because of the requirements of valuation. By the early 1970s slightly more references are made in Budget debates to the alternatives to estate duty with some Conservatives preferring an inheritance tax and Labour supporters emphasising a gifts tax. Although the demands for this reform based on arguments of equity were not so pressing that they were irresistible, by the time of the 1974 election reform of estate duty was perceived by many Labour members as an essential element in a package of new taxation on the rich.

On attaining office in 1974, therefore, the Chancellor lost no time in announcing the reform of estate duty. His March 1974 statement emphasised the technical improvements that CTT would bring:

> I intend to take measures to close the loopholes which prevent estate duty from performing the role assigned to it . . . the estate duty has always been a largely avoidable, indeed a voluntary tax . . . I therefore propose to introduce this year, in my second Finance Bill, a tax on lifetime gifts . . .
>
> (26 March 1974, cols. 312 and 313)

CTT was to apply immediately to lifetime gifts although the actual legislation was not to be brought in until later in the year. This immediate operation of the tax was designed to prevent avoidance. In spite of the unusual step of immediate imposition of a tax which would not be enacted until a second Finance Act of the year, this tax attracted much less comment in the 1974 Budget debate than did the less definite promise of WT (p. 122). There was no clear clash of party views on CTT at this stage. The real clashes began during the passage of the Finance Bill when CTT was attacked by the Opposition piecemeal. By then it was perceived by the Conservatives as an ideologically motivated tax and not a reform primarily to satisfy the demands of equity, and they set out to destroy it by undermining it.

By the November 1974 Budget debate, following a White Paper on CTT published in August 1974, members had a better idea what the reform would entail. However, the new tax was only a minor item in the Budget debate, for this was the period of the oil price rise, rapidly rising prices at home and the start of the feeling of economic crisis. All these factors drew members' attention away from consideration of CTT although some were interested in its details. One Conservative warned that it might not be an effective revenue raiser (13 November 1974, col. 474) and one that the combination of CTT and the foreshadowed WT would discourage investment (13 November 1974, col. 503). Most of the comments from both sides of the House concerned exemptions. One Labour and one Welsh Nationalist MP welcomed exemptions for working farmers as did several Conservatives who also urged exemptions for woodlands. In later years following the enactment of CTT special pleas and calls for exemptions have continually been made by speakers in Budget debates, and with much success. The concern for detail displayed during the enactment of CTT has persisted throughout its history and has had a profound impact on the effectiveness of this piece of capital taxation (pp. 41–2).

Tax credits

The idea of tax credits in some form (or a negative income tax) had been around in general terms for a long time before the period of tax reform with which we are mainly concerned and there have been, therefore, references to it from time to time for many years. Many of the references are made by people who have long been particularly attached to the idea, Sir Brandon Rhys Williams for example. Most, however, refer to TC as an attractive idea to which they themselves have not given particular attention. Mr Joel Barnett spoke of TC in 1968, saying:

In the long run, the only way to get a simpler and better tax system is to have a negative income tax . . . computers are not yet available in the Inland Revenue to make that possible.

(21 March 1968, col. 733)

Mr Barnett later sat on the Select Committee on Tax Credits but did not, in the event, put his full weight behind the idea (p. 169).

Tax credits attracted a considerably increased attention in the 1969 Budget debate. Some members considered that it merited serious study. In 1972 Mr Barber announced that he hoped to introduce a system of tax credits to effect an integration of the social security and income tax systems:

It is obvious that immense difficulties are involved in trying to bring these two separate systems together in a simpler and more general system. But, there can be few in this House who have not at some time or other been attracted to the idea of some form of negative income tax . . . It would provide a smoother graduation from the area of benefit to that of taxation, and so it would avoid some of the worst features of what has become known as 'poverty surtax' . . . I therefore propose to publish later in the year a Green Paper setting out the scheme in detail. I hope that the House will in due course agree that it should be referred to a Select Committee for study and report.

(21 March 1972, cols. 1383–4)

Replying, Mr Harold Wilson thought that the question of negative income tax had 'eluded the ingenuity of successive Chancellors' (21 March 1972, col. 1394) but welcomed the possibility of a Select Committee. A number of speakers in the subsequent debate expressed interest and/or delight that the scheme was forthcoming and welcomed the proposal to set up a Select Committee. By 1973, however, it was clear that the scheme was hanging fire. It was still being examined by the Select Committee (p. 165). Almost all who spoke in the debate on the subject, however, were in favour of TC. Some spoke of the advantages it would bring to pensioners and to others on low incomes. One Opposition Member raised the matter, then under consideration by the Select Committee, of whether benefits for children should be paid through the employer to the father or through the Post Office to the mother.

By 1974 the Select Committee had reported, the matter was shelved and a general election had put the Labour Party into office. Mr Healey explained his Government's position on the TC scheme:

We believe, as we explained at length in Opposition, that there are serious drawbacks to the tax credit scheme proposed by the previous administration.

They were fully described in the Minority Reports of the Select Committee. We have not taken any decision against the principle of a negative income tax, which was the subject of considerable study under the previous Labour Government, but our immediate priority has been to carry out the major increase in National Insurance benefits which I have referred to. We are also pledged to improve the present provision for children, but this must wait for a later Budget.

(26 March 1974, col. 312)

Members speaking in the debate expressed sorrow that the idea of TC appeared to have fallen by the wayside. For the Liberals, Jeremy Thorpe, John Pardoe and Cyril Smith all spoke in favour of a TC scheme. According to John Pardoe it was 'the only way to redistribute incomes' (28 March 1974, col. 688) and Cyril Smith saw it as the way to tackle poverty. John Roper from the Labour benches and Keith Joseph from the Conservatives also spoke in favour of a TC scheme.

Selective employment tax

Unlike the other taxes in our case studies SET was not the subject of parliamentary comment before its introduction because it was a novel idea of Nicholas Kaldor (p. 98). But, from 1966 until its repeal in 1972, it took up a high proportion of all Budget debates and dominated that of 1966, the year of its introduction. The analysis of comment in the House reveals how discussion can encourage the demise of a tax as much as encourage its birth.

Of all the taxes we have studied SET was the most generally unpopular. That unpopularity was apparent from the day of its announcement. Members on both sides of the House complained both about the general basis and specific aspects of the tax and continued to do so throughout its life. These complaints had their effect in the alterations made to its form each year.

In his Budget speech the Chancellor introduced his new tax, selective employment tax, to provide a new *source* of taxation. The House had no prior warning of SET and for details it had to wait for the White Paper. So those who heard the Chancellor's speech learnt only of the basic principles of the new tax, which in the Chancellor's words:

Must be able to do three things. First, avoid the adverse effects of increases in purchase tax and income tax. Second, broaden the tax base. Third, make a positive contribution to the long-run structural changes we need in order to achieve a healthy balance of payments . . . These requirements have led me to consider the position of services in our tax system . . . virtually all services lie outside the scope of indirect taxation . . . The existing arrangements have tended to shift the pattern of consumer spending in favour of services and hence to produce a similar shift in the pattern of output and employment. Manufacturing output has been seriously impeded by labour shortages, and this has hampered the growth of productivity.

(3 May 1966, cols. 1453–4)

A payroll tax would not, he thought, make the most effective use of manpower. What he wanted was a differential tax which would increase the cost of labour in services and reduce the cost of labour in manufacturing.

Mr Edward Heath, by now the leader of the Opposition, replied to the Chancellor's speech. Until he had studied the White Paper, when it appeared, Mr Heath could only give preliminary reactions. But he pointed out that the effect of SET might not be to encourage economies in manpower in the distributive trades, but rather to increase the cost of food, clothing and other essentials. The effect then would be like an extension of the purchase tax. He was also concerned about the effect on the tourist trade, and on the most outlying areas of the United Kingdom:

Eighty per cent of activities in the Highlands of Scotland are concerned with services . . . It will affect those areas which rely on tourists, and on services in particular. Once again there is a contradiction in the Government's policies.

(3 May 1966, cols. 1475–6)

Much of the time in this year's Budget debate was taken up with the SET although members still had no details of the new tax. In fact, in contrast to the previous years, the Chancellor's speech had been very short, with SET the only item of note in it. However, even had the Budget contained other new items, much of the debate would still have concentrated on SET which raised strong feeling on both sides of the House. An analysis of the criticisms and praises shows how far views cut across party lines.

Government   (Labour Members)

Arguments in favour of SET

1. A bold, imaginative and highly novel means of raising revenue.
2. A desirable broadening of the tax base.
3. A means of rectifying an imbalance in the economy which was becoming too biased towards service industries.

Arguments against SET

1. It would raise prices.
2. It adversely affects the distributive trades, especially the co-ops.
3. It adversely affects the regions – especially where there are large concentrations of service industries.
4. It has adverse effects on hotels and tourism.
5. It may encourage manufacturers to hoard labour.

Opposition (Conservative Members)

No arguments in favour

Arguments against SET

1. It raises prices as the tax will be passed on to the housewife.
2. It places a burden on the distributive trades.
3. It has adverse effects on the regions.
4. It has adverse effects on hotels and tourism.
5. It will not reduce overmanning in manufacturing industry.
6. It extends taxation to goods not previously taxed.
7. It has adverse effects on agriculture.
8. It fails to include the civil service and nationalised industries.
9. It adversely affects invisible exporters such as banking services and insurance.
10. It has adverse effects on rural transport.

With this form of tax the Government had clearly stirred up a veritable hornets' nest, giving tremendous scope to Members to express their special interests and the needs of their particular constituencies. It was a classic example of the tax doomed before it starts because of the extent to which special interests can press their claims. Many of the remarks critical of SET were accompanied by comments on its adverse effects in that Member's own constituency. The continual barrage of special pleading went through all the stages of the 1966 Finance Bill and throughout all subsequent Budget debates and Finance Bills until the tax was finally abolished in 1973. Hardly any economic activity was without at least one defender. Mr Laurence Pavitt, perhaps the most consistent opponent of the tax from the Government side, commented in 1967:

I was surprised to find that coffin makers are in an anomalous position because of SET. If one's coffin happens to be made by someone in association with a funeral undertaking, the workers are taxed but if a carpenter makes one's coffin separately, this comes within order XIII Minimum List Heading 479, relating to other wood manufacturers, and not only is the tax not paid, but a premium is received for it.

(11 April 1967, col. 1063)

(For an account of the technique and method of collecting SET see Pliatzky, 1982.)

Whilst SET certainly did have the effect of raising substantial revenue, particularly in its later years, there is no doubt that this particular tax, with its discriminatory characteristics and built-in anomalies, offered a unique opportunity for MPs to press the Government to make changes. The Government, trying to cope with all these pressures on details of the tax, was rather in the position of the Dutch boy, trying to stem the flood by a finger in the dyke.

In 1967 the Chancellor referred in his Budget speech to the proposal for regional differentiation in SET which later became embodied in the 'regional employment premium' designed to take account of the numerous and strong criticism of the effect of SET on employment in the regions. In some regions – the least developed as a rule – service industries formed a large section of the economy. The intention of REP was to encourage extra investment in manufacturing industry in such areas in an attempt to correct the balance between classes of employment. The Chancellor also announced other important changes to SET including relief for part-time workers.

Complaints about specific aspects of SET continued to rumble on. Although the 1968 Budget contained no proposals for new taxes, the debate was notable for the re-awakened interest in new taxes. Some members by now had begun to link the introduction of VAT with the possible abolition of SET. VAT, like SET, had the merit of being more broadly based by the inclusion of services, than purchase tax. SET continued to take up much time in the 1969 Budget debate. It found one friend on the Government side because it was cheap and easy to collect (R. Roebuck, 15 April 1969, col. 1118) but most comments were, as in the past, critical.

On the broad aspects of SET Mr Edward Milne, a Labour Member, put the argument concisely when he said:

The shake-out and transfer of labour from one industry to another has not occurred. Moreover, SET has been passed on to the consumer in many of our service and distributive trades.

(15 April 1969, col. 1052)

He was supported from the Opposition by Sir Tatton Brinton:

It was a bad tax when it was introduced, and it is getting worse with every increase, because it is selective, because it differentiates arbitrarily between different forms of enterprise with an unforeseen end result. I agree with the Hon Member for Blyth in deploring this bad tax.

(15 April 1969, col. 1057)

Laurence Pavitt continued his campaign:

Tonight I speak with bitterness and anger. SET has come up for the third occasion. It is a totally ill-conceived tax which has not yielded the results it was thought it would yield in the first place . . . SET marks the first time that any Government has ever put an indirect tax on food . . . I speak as a Co-operative member, one of the eighteen-strong Co-operative Group . . . the Government have persistently produced an ill-balanced economy by trying to separate services from production.

(15 April 1969, col. 1087)

SET was also frequently mentioned in the 1970 Budget debate. Whilst a few loyal Government supporters held that the Reddaway Report (1970) had 'vindicated' SET the complaints still abounded. Members continued to complain that the tax penalised tourism, the Scottish economy and the theatrical industry, among many other examples.

Relief came with the change of Government in 1970 and the introduction of VAT. Announcing the forthcoming change, Anthony Barber said:

We have frequently explained why we consider SET to be a thoroughly bad tax. It is unfair and it is arbitrary . . . The distinction between manufacturing and services is in fact quite untenable . . . Purchase Tax has some obvious advantages, but it also has one major disadvantage, and that is that it bears particularly heavily on a limited number of goods and not at all on services. The desire to broaden the base of indirect taxation was, I believe, one of the reasons why the previous Government decided to raise additional revenue from SET . . . we have made it clear that food will be relieved of the tax (VAT).

(30 March 1971, cols. 1393–4)

A feature of the 1971 debate was the relatively large number of references to the need for consultation before new taxes were introduced. Both Green Papers and select committees were advocated because CT and VAT were exceedingly complex proposals. Sir Henry D'Avidgor Goldsmid commented that, because CT and CGT were introduced by the previous Labour Government without Green Papers, there had to be 600 Government amendments in the first year and 300–400 in the following year (5 April 1971, col. 87). The experience of SET's introduction had made its mark and future references to that tax were to its hasty and ill-considered mode of enactment.

Postscript

The November 1974 Budget proved to be the last in the 1970s to see the introduction of new 'mainstream' taxes. The Select Committee on WT failed to produce a majority report (p. 178) and the tax was subsequently abandoned for the duration of the Parliament (p. 207).

The continuing gravity of the economic situation deflected the attention of the Chancellor from tax reform, which would in any case have been increasingly difficult for a minority Government. CT remained as amended by the Conservatives, the negative income tax idea languished, and VAT established itself as a vital element in the taxation system besides income tax. Members of Parliament in Budget debates subsequent to that of 1974 continued to make speeches about possible tax reforms, but at no further time during the 1970s did they have any actual proposals on mainstream taxes before them to focus their attention. The main thrust of debate on taxation after 1974 concentrated upon the perceived need for adjustments to existing taxes.

The Finance Bill

The House of Commons finally gets down to the detailed business of considering the new tax proposals in the Finance Bill. The six new taxes were passed in four Finance Acts. CGT and CT (classical) were passed in the 1965 Finance Act, SET in the 1966 Act, CT (imputation) and VAT in the 1972 Act, and CTT in the 1975 Act.

Second reading

The first substantive part of the Finance Bill procedure is the second reading. This usually occupies one day and about six hours of parliamentary time. In relation to the Budget debates, therefore, it is not very significant as an opportunity for continuous influence. And indeed, second readings of Finance Bills often appear simply to continue the Budget debate and are used in the same way. Second reading debates cannot focus and concentrate upon the principles and desirability of new taxes. They are about an entire Finance Bill and hence do not afford members a suitable arena in which to fight out the principles of a new tax. There are however a few significant differences between the second reading of the Finance Bill and the Budget debate. The second reading concentrates on taxation (omitting the expenditure side and general debate on the state of the economy) and by the time the second reading is held (generally about two weeks after the Budget debate) the Bill has been published and members have an idea of the real nature of any new taxes and of their detailed provisions, and can better assess how various groups and interests will be affected by the legislation.

The second reading of the 1965 Finance Bill (CGT and CT) consisted of another rehearsal of the arguments already displayed in the Budget speeches. There were also protests about the length and complexity of this Finance Bill.

The second reading debate was very general in nature and was followed by a committee stage also on the floor of the House. The 1965 Finance Bill was, in many ways, a watershed in the parliamentary consideration of taxation. The introduction of two significant and complicated new taxes, CGT and CT, in a single Bill, which at the same time contained many adjustments to existing taxes, was almost too much for many members to contemplate. It took up more parliamentary time than any previous Finance Bill: $21\frac{1}{2}$ days (211 hours), all of it on the floor of the House. Between 1945 and 1950 the Finance Bill averaged 4–5 days for all its stages. By 1961 the average had risen to 9 days. The 1965 Bill strained the procedures of the House to their utmost. The two new taxes were not simple instruments that could easily be passed through the House, but introduced a host of technical complexities, which had required skilful drafting and needed very careful parliamentary consideration. That the House realised its inadequacy for the task is evident from the *Report of the Select Committee on Procedure on 'The Finance Bill'* (HC 382, 1966/7) which reflected the experiences of the 1965 and 1966 Finance Acts.

The second reading of the 1966 Finance Bill which contained the SET legislation is also worthy of examination. SET was, as John Diamond for the Government put it, 'the main talking point of the Finance Bill'. Mrs Thatcher, for the Opposition, agreed that SET was 'Entirely the core of this Budget' (26 May 1966, col. 490). Mr Diamond argued that SET was a contemporary tax that took account of contemporary conditions, particularly full employment (26 May 1966, col. 482). But the tax had been so hastily put together that there had been no time for the customary pre-legislative 'consultations' with all of the special and affected interests (p. 189). Much of the consultation process thus had to take place while the legislation was winding its way through Parliament between the announcement of the tax in the Budget and the Bill's report stage. As Mr Diamond indicated (26 May 1966, col. 488) the Chancellor would be meeting with the charities (an affected group) after Whitsun. Diamond in his introductory speech also forestalled some of the coming tide of criticism from special interests likely to claim exemptions. He said that the tax on mining enterprises would be refunded as it would on agriculture, horticulture and forestry. These interest groups had already been consulted. He listed so many exemptions already promised that a Conservative Member asked whether all these decisions ruled out further amendments in Committee.

Further candidates for exemptions were mentioned by Margaret Thatcher, including tourism, hotels and catering, charities, religious bodies, insurance and finance, education, nursing homes, the disabled, the theatre and part-time workers. 'I have had representations from the Church of England, the Free Church and the Synagogues' she said (26 May 1966, col. 496). In the course of the Bill she warned that her party would table many amendments to mitigate the effect of the tax on people who were deserving cases (26 May 1966, col. 494). Many of these amendments, she correctly remarked, were not party political matters at all.

In the subsequent speeches all the pleas for special cases and exemptions came tumbling out – music and the arts, part-time workers, the disabled, the Cooperative movement, the building industry, charities, hotels, the over-65s, insurance and Development Areas. And, indeed, the pleas came from both sides of the House. Winding up, Mr Callaghan did his best to bat back. He was clearly somewhat rattled on the question of charities since their case had been widely supported by both sides of the House. 'We must find a way in which they can be recompensed,' he said (26 May 1966. col. 655). On hotels and tourism, however, he considered that much of the criticism was misplaced. And the cooperatives (whose case was made forcefully by Coop and Labour Members) would have to be treated like other retail outlets. As for the other deserving cases such as pensioners and part-time workers, 'All these matters can be reviewed, not this year, but as the tax proceeds. I cannot recommend any concessions on these matters this year.'

We see the special pleaders out again in force in the second reading of the 1972 Finance Bill which introduced CT and VAT. Most of the special pleading was directed towards VAT and can be seen as a continuation of some of the points made in 1966 with respect to SET. VAT, after all, was to replace SET, and would tap many of the same sources of taxation. Although a large part of the Finance Bill was taken up with CT the debate on the subject was by now old hat. Anthony Barber held that nothing had happened since 1965 to change the Conservative mind about the form of this tax. Denis Healey, replying for the Opposition, said little about CT but attacked VAT as 'a bad tax for a country which had an effective sales tax'.

During the second reading of the 1974 (No. 2) Finance Bill enacted as the 1975 Finance Act, the Chief Secretary of the Treasury remarked that the preparation of the CTT legislation had been 'a mammoth task' and that there had been insufficient time to deal with some matters in the Bill as published (17 December 1974, cols. 1379–80) including avoidance through the medium of close companies, and various categories of trust that ought to qualify for a measure of relief. The main Opposition speech was once again by Margaret Thatcher, who criticised the principle of such a tax in the light of current economic circumstances.

Defects of the second reading stage
The experience of the passage of new taxes reveals that the inclusion of new taxes in a Bill with other measures does not permit a proper consideration of the principles of a new measure as would a separate second reading. This defect is particularly serious if the tax is desired for ideological reasons. Not having to defend its principles clearly and unambiguously·in a proper second reading, the Government can less easily resist demands for concessions and reliefs. By this time the special interests have had time to consider the Bill, to assess its effects upon them, prepare arguments for amendments and find MPs willing to table them.

The committee and report stages
The committee stage of any Finance Bill is its most important stage and its longest. It is convenient to consider the committee and report stages together for they are both concerned with detailed amendments. The third reading stage is a mere formality as a rule. Although the legislation

has to be rushed through in a mere three months or so, the Committee stage of a Finance Bill can occupy up to fifteen or twenty days of the session and thus come to dominate the timetable during the summer months. Table 5.1 summarises the progress of Finance Bills from 1961 to 1975. The four Finance Bills that included our new taxes afford an interesting comparison. The first two, 1965 and 1966, had their entire Committee stages in the Committee of the Whole House. The other two, 1972 and 1974 (No. 2), were taken by the new procedure under which the committee stage was divided and the main classes taken in the Whole House (that is the clauses dealing with broad matters of principle), the detailed clauses being taken in the standing committee. The new procedure was introduced as a result of Members' complaints.

This change had first been recommended in 1959 (HC 92, 1958/9) but resisted by the Treasury. In 1965 (HC 276, 1964/5) the Select Committee on Procedure once again recommended that the Finance Bill be divided and part of it sent to a standing committee. This proposal was not adopted by the Government. So the 1965 and 1966 Finance Bills were taken under the old procedure. In the 1966/7 session the Procedure Committee yet again examined what could be done to improve the passage of the Finance Bill. It proposed the division of the Bill as one of three possible new procedural devices. The main argument from politicians against division of the Bill was that it would prevent all Members from having their say on the fundamentally important questions of taxation. Mr Whitelaw stated in his evidence (Q.59) that division of the Bill, with part considered by a small standing committee, would amount to 'taxation without representation'. It was argued that taxation 'affects the interests of all the constituents of every Member, unlike many other Bills, which are sectional in scope' (HC 382, 1966/7, p.v). This, of course was the Treasury argument. The Treasury maintained that 'the major tax proposals . . . may be of universal application to every citizen of the country' (HC 382, 1966/7, p. 3). The Select Committee in its 'conclusion' came down firmly on the fence. The alternative to sending a Finance Bill to standing committee would be a 'voluntary timetable'. In the event the Government decided to take the route of dividing the Bill and sending part of it to standing committee. Under the 'split' procedure the general clauses of any new tax embodying its principles are taken in committee of the Whole House and the technical clauses in standing committee. Taking the main clauses in the committee of the Whole House injects something of the nature of a second reading debate into that section of the proceedings.

The Committee and report stages of the 1965 Finance Bill took a total of twenty-one days, reflecting the complexity and scope of the two new items of legislation that it contained. The 1965 Bill was the longest for 55 years with 90 clauses and 19 schedules in 226 pages.

Table 5.1 *Progress of Finance Bills to Finance Act*

Year	1st Reading	2nd Reading	Days in Committee WH = Whole House SC = Standing Committee	Reported	Report stage	3rd Reading	Royal assent
1961 (session 1960/1)	25.4.61	4.5.61	WH 15.5.61 16.5 1.6 7.6 8.6 (9)	21.6.61	3.7.61 4.7 (2)	6.7.61	19.7.61
1962 (1961/2)	16.4.62	3.5.62	WH 15.5.62 16.5 21.5 22.5 (8)	5.6.62	2.7.62 3.7 (2)	6.7.62	1.8.62
1963 (1962/3)	10.4.63	6.5.63	WH 14.5.63 15.5 16.5 21.5 23.5 (8)	30.5.63	25.6.63 26.6 (2)	28.6.63	31.7.63
1964 (1963/4)	21.4.64	7.5.64	WH 2.6.64 4.6 9.6 10.6 15.6 (5)	18.6.64	30.6.64	3.7.64	16.7.64

Table 5.1 (contd.)

Year	1st Reading	2nd Reading	Days in Committee WH = Whole House SC = Standing Committee	Reported	Report stage	3rd Reading	Royal assent
1964 (No. 2) 1964/5	17.11.64	24.11.64	WH 30.11.64 1.12 2.12 (3)	2.12.64	7.12.64	7.12.64	17.12.64
1965[a] (1964/5)	13.4.65	10.5.65	WH 17.5.65 18.5 20.5 24.5 25.5 26.5 27.5 31.5 (16)	24.6.65	12.7.65 5.7 6.7 7.7 8.7 (5)	15.7.65	5.8.65
1966[a] (1965/6)	10.5.66	25.5.66	WH 15.6.66 16.6 20.6 21.6 22.6 27.6 29.6 30.6 4.7 (9)	4.7.66	12.7.66 13.7 (2)	28.7.66	3.8.66

Table 5.1 (contd.)

Year	1st Reading	2nd Reading	Days in Committee WH = Whole House SC = Standing Committee		Reported	Report stage	3rd Reading	Royal assent
1967 (1966/7)	18.4.67	2.5.67	WH 1.6.67 6.6 7.6 8.6	12.6 14.6 15.6 21.6 (8)	21.6.67	27.6.67 28.6 (2)	30.6.67	21.7.67
1968 (1967/8)	25.3.68	24.4.68	SC 1.5.68 2.5 3.5 8.5 13.5 15.5 20.5	22.5 24.5 27.5 28.5 29.5 11.6 12.6 (14)	13.6.68	4.7.68 3.7 2.7 1.7 (4)	4.7.68	26.7.68
			WH recommitted 18.6 19.6	20.6 (3)				

Table 5.1 (contd.)

1969 (1968/9)	21.4.69	6.5.69	WH 13.5.69 14.5	20.5 21.5 (4)	26.6.69	15.7.69 16.7 17.7 (3)	18.7.69 24.7.69	25.7.69
			SC 11.6.69 16.6 18.6 24.6	23.6 25.6 26.6 (7)				
1970 (1969/70)	20.4.70	5.5.70	SC 12.5.70 13.5	26.5 27.5 (4)	27.5.70	27.5.70	27.5.70	29.5.70
1971 (1970/1)	5.4.71	28.4.71 21.7.71	WH 28.4.71 11.5 12.5	18.5 20.5 (5)	22.6.71	5.7.71 6.7 7.7 (3)	7.7.71 28.7.71	5.8.71
			SC 24.5 26.5 9.6 14.6	15.6 16.6 21.6 (7)				

Table 5.1 (contd.)

Year	1st Reading	2nd Reading	Days in Committee WH = Whole House SC = Standing Committee	Reported	Report stage	3rd Reading	Royal assent
1972 (1971/2)	27.3.72	20.4.72	WH 9.5.72 16.5 10.5 17.5 11.5 (6) 15.5 SC 23.5.72 19.6 24.5 21.6 25.5 22.6 5.6 24.6 8.6 27.6 12.6 28.6 14.6 (14) 15.6	28.6.72	10.7.72 11.7 12.7 (3)	12.7.72	27.7.72
1973[a] (1972/3)	12.3.73	2.4.73	WH 10.4.73 10.7.73 11.4 11.7 (2) (2) SC 2.5 16.5 7.5 21.5 9.5 28.5 14.5 (7) (2)	28.5.73	11.7.73 (2)	24.7.73	25.7.73

Table 5.1 (contd.)

Year	1st Reading	2nd Reading	Days in Committee WH = Whole House SC = Standing Committee	Reported	Report stage	3rd Reading	Royal assent
1974 (1974)	1.4.74 22.7.74[b]	9.5.74 30.7.74	WH 16.5.74 24.6 17.5 25.6 21.5 27.6 10.6 1.7 13.6 2.7 17.6 3.7 19.6 20.6 (14)	16.7.74 17.7	22.7.74 30.7 (2)	30.7.74	31.7.74
1974 (No. 2)[a] (1974/5)	14.11.74 11.3.75	17.12.74 13.3.75	WH 15.1.75 20.1 12.1 23.1 (4)				

Table 5.1 (contd.)

Year	1st Reading	2nd Reading	Days in Committee WH = Whole House SC = Standing Committee	Reported	Report stage	3rd Reading	Royal assent
1974 (No. 2)[a] (1974/5) (continued)			SC 25.1 28.1 30.1 31.1 4.2 5.2 (11)	18.2.75	3.3.75 4.3 5.3 6.3 10.3 (5)	10.3.75 13.3.75	13.3.75
1975 (1974/5)	21.4.75	8.5.75	WH 9.5.75 20.5 10.6 (3) SC 12.6.75 13.6 19.6 24.6 26.6 (8)	3.7.75	16.7.75 17.7.75 (2)	17.7.75	1.8.75

Source: Public Bills Book, HC
Notes: [a] New tax introduced in session
1965 Corporation Tax; Capital Gains Tax
1966 Selective Employment Tax
1973 Corporation Tax; Value Added Tax
1974 (No. 2) Capital Transfer Tax

Up to 1965 eight or nine days had generally sufficed for the committee stage of a Finance Bill and a further one or two days for its report stage. Third reading generally took one day. The progress of the CGT and CT in committee indicates the scope of the problem that the Government had set before the House. On CGT alone there were over 1200 amendments tabled; 440 by the Government and 680 by the Opposition. 145 Government amendments were considered. Of these 138 were agreed, 6 on divisions. Two new clauses were proposed by the Government. 131 Opposition amendments were considered in committee, of which 10 (mostly drafting and clarifying changes) were agreed to, 36 were withdrawn, 30 negatived and 55 defeated on divisions. The Opposition proposed three new clauses; one was withdrawn and two negatived. The debate on CGT in committee centred on the distinction between short and long-term gains, limits of exemption, valuation and rates of tax for unit trusts. Among the Opposition amendments were proposed exemptions from CGT for vintage cars, postponement of payments for livestock, and allowances to be made for CGT in the determination of estate duty. The Bill was considerably altered by the Government during its passage through the House.

Edmund Dell (15 July 1965, col. 834) expressed his concern that 'amendments which were accepted often followed discussions between Government and outside interests which have taken place not inside the House'. Indeed the discussions and representations on this legislation took place not only *before* the Bill was drafted, as is common, but also continuously during its passage through Parliament. Mr Heath (22 June 1965, col. 715) claimed that the Chancellor was constantly capitulating to pressure and another member described the Bill as 'a leaking sieve' (15 July 1965, col. 873). Joel Barnett, for the Government, admitted that the Bill had been considerably improved during its committee and report stages. 'I do not dispute that when the Bill was introduced it had bad parts' (15 July 1965, col. 869).

The CT provisions were also subject to much change by the Government during their committee stage. Many Opposition amendments were of a technical nature designed to point out desirable changes in the hope that these would be incorporated by the Government in the final stages of enactment. Anthony Barber said (15 July 1965, col. 900) 'The Bill will be remembered as one of the most complicated and slipshod.' It was generally agreed that the Bill had not been fully worked out before its presentation to the House.

But if the experience of the committee stages of the 1965 Finance Bill had upset members, they had more to come with the 1966 Bill. Both CGT and CT had at least been expected and foreshadowed; they had been discussed, at least in principle, for some time. They also, to some extent, replaced and built on existing taxes. SET was quite different. It was a completely new tax which was sprung on Parliament without any pre-legislative discussion. The committee stage of the 1966 Bill did not take so long as the committee stage of the 1965 Bill (which had included two new taxes) but the nature of the legislation aroused strong feelings of opposition. SET was not welcomed by the Opposition and many Government supporters were lukewarm or even hostile.

Mr Callaghan, continuing Diamond's theme (in the second reading debate) of the 'contemporary' tax admitted that it might need adapting. He said:

There is scope for changes in the tax in the future . . . for improvements in the light of experience . . . to adapt to changing needs of the economy.

(28 July 1966, cols. 1980–2)

But he was not willing to permit major amendments in the first year. Three days of the committee stage of the 1966 Finance Bill were reserved for discussion of SET. The arguments continued in committee exactly as they had been expressed in the Budget speech and in the second reading of the Bill. There were calls for concessions and members pointed out each particular group that would be harmed by the tax. Yet few amendments of any substance were achieved. At the third reading the Opposition expressed regret that the Bill 'was amended so slightly' (28 July 1966, col. 1968).

The real amendments to SET came, as Mr Callaghan had fore-shadowed, in subsequent Finance Bills. One significant change to come in a later year was the regional employment premium (REP). In 1967 the Government published a Green Paper on *The Development Areas: A Proposal for a Regional Employment Premium*. REP would be paid using the machinery established for the administration of SET. Although the Chancellor called 1967 an 'off year for tax reform' (12 April 1967, col. 1002) he had begun the task of watering down SET. Part-time workers had been 'the subject of most of the representations I have had'. Employers were allowed to reclaim part of their payments (p. 33). By 1968 the new Chancellor Roy Jenkins was not too sure about SET and set up the Reddaway Inquiry to investigate it. Meanwhile he proposed refunds to hotels in Development Areas. The experience with SET reveals that the influence of Parliament is measured not so much in amendments achieved when a new tax is first created, but in amendments achieved during the lifetime of that tax. Governments with safe majorities are reluctant to accept defeat on their legislation. But if a good case is made they can, in subsequent years, present changes as their own and claim the applause for them.

By 1968 the committee stage of the Finance Bill had been reformed. Part was now taken upstairs in standing committee. The first standing committee to consider a Finance Bill had fifty-two members (the number was subsequently reduced to thirty-five or thirty). The experience of the first two standing committees deserves some consideration although they did not have new taxes to study. The 1968 standing committee met on thirteen occasions and twenty-three amendments were made, most of them on drafting and minor changes. At the beginning of the first day of the new procedure the Members debated points of order including the 'shirtsleeves' issue. They talked for a full five hours without ever looking at the Finance Bill. By the third meeting they were still complaining about poor ventilation and lack of space. But in spite of the drawbacks of their new surroundings members soon saw that they had some advantages. In particular it is much easier for members to communicate with interest groups and advisers in the committee rooms than it is on the floor of the House. Members can see their advisers, they can walk over to talk to them or to representatives of pressure groups. In the House there is no such ease of communication for the Opposition, although civil servants may be 'on hand' to advise Ministers. The importance of expert advice on taxation law was apparent in the passage of the 1965 Act. Mr A. Duffy (Labour) congratulated the Conservative Opposition on its successes 'backed up by obviously good and thorough staff work' (15 July 1965, col. 846). 'On many occasions', he said, 'I envied them. They were well briefed.'

During the 1968 standing committee proceedings members continued to complain about the effects of SET on the retail trades, and on the hotel trade. Endless pressure groups paraded their needs; for example there was reference to the pleas of the 'Association of Circus Proprietors of Great Britain' (11 June 1968, col. 1832) and 'Every Member of the Committee will have received a letter from Securicor' (11 June 1968, col. 1832). Roy Jenkins defended SET because it raised revenue and was cheap to collect. Also, he said there was a very real need to tax services that would otherwise escape purchase tax (11 June 1968, col. 1873). In reply Iain Macleod (11 June 1968, col. 1903) maintained that 'The logic of events driving us to a widely-based sales tax or a VAT seems absolutely inescapable.'

For the 1969 Finance Bill the standing committee membership was reduced to thirty. Many amendments tabled in this standing committee, as indeed in others on Finance Bills, do not seem primarily directed at success, but rather are intended to serve as pegs for general debate. Even when the rate of CT was under discussion and an Opposition Member (Peter Horden) decided to give a discourse on the money supply, the Chairman exclaimed (11 June 1969, col. 180) 'I hope the relation of speeches to corporation tax will be clear to me.' Sir

Henry D'Avigdor Goldsmid hoped that 'I should not be considered a spoil-sport if I reverted to the subject of the amendment. We have had a variety of interesting speeches dealing with almost everything except corporation tax' (11 June 1969, col. 180). The long-standing theological debate about the best form of CT was also continued in this arena. Altogether the general debate, more like a Budget debate than anything else, continued for three hours and thirty-three minutes. This was not in any sense a technical discussion of the CT, let alone the amendment. So the idea that a standing committee might permit more detailed and careful examination of clauses is not borne out by the behaviour of members on this occasion. The same dreary, uninformed debates that go on on the floor of the House may be simply transplanted upstairs to a committee room where there is even greater scope for points of order and irrelevance.

Changes on CGT in the 1969 Finance Bill prompted more technical discussion. On some of the more highly technical points, especially of capital taxation, the Opposition can occasionally score a success and achieve an amendment. But it is often achieved indirectly. Occasionally the Opposition persuades the Government to accept the point; more often there is a promise to bring in an amendment of their own at a later stage. Government promises are not always fulfilled, but they are from time to time; it depends on the way in which the promise is couched. Dick Taverne, for the Government in the 1969 committee said 'I am happy to undertake to move on Report an amendment to enable clearances to be applied for.' That firm sort of promise spells success for the Opposition although it will be recorded as a Government amendment. Thus some Government amendments, often of an obscure or technical nature, are really Opposition amendments in disguise. The degree of technicality that had crept into taxation legislation by 1969 is well illustrated by an amendment by Richard Wainwright (Liberal) for 'Exemption on Insurance Companies from Corporation Tax on Capital Gains in respect of Unit Trust Holdings'! No wonder some members preferred to use the committee stage for broad debates on the money supply.

In 1972 it was the Conservative Government's turn to introduce new taxes in their Finance Bill. They introduced VAT and the new CT. The CT change was simply the culmination of all their efforts since the original CT of 1965. But they had preceded the legislation with a select committee inquiry (p. 160). VAT had not been the subject of a select committee inquiry, but it had been the subject of many years' discussion and of considerably detailed pre-legislative planning. The main clauses of principle of CT and VAT were taken in Committee of the Whole House, and the details (the bulk of the legislation) considered in standing committee. The standing committee (which had thirty-five members) met on twenty occasions, on twelve of which it considered VAT. CT occupied most of five sittings.

The committee stage of the 1972 Bill was characterised by the efforts of the special pleaders to gain concessions for the groups and interests they represented. Among other requests amendments were tabled to achieve zero-rating on catering, works canteens, pubs and clubs, fish and chip shops, confectionery, beer, newspaper deliveries, sports admission charges and many others. None of these were successful at the time. Of all the Opposition amendments only twenty-one were brought to a decision. All were lost. Even the one great victory of the special pleaders for relief from VAT – the zero-rating of children's clothes – failed as an amendment in committee. It was not until just before the tax was due to operate a year later that the Government finally announced that children's clothes would be zero-rated for VAT. This case is interesting because in the standing committee the conditions for success for the amendment were all present. Even if the Government could use its majority to defeat any amendment it was the sort of case where one might have expected the Government to give during the committee stages one of its 'we will look at this at a later stage' promises. The Opposition had some support from Government members. In particular Mrs Kellett-Bowman moved an amendment of her own on children's shoes (10 May 1972, cols. 232–8). But the Government's promise to look into an alternative did not come until towards the end of the stages of the 1972 Bill. Between the enactment of the 1972 Finance Act and the operation of VAT in 1973 pressure was maintained on this issue. It was brought up during a supply day debate on 5 December 1972. It was also the subject of a debate on 14 February 1973 on the motion by Joel Barnett 'That this House considers that Value Added Tax should not apply to children's clothing'. There was also an early day motion on the subject signed by 142 members. This notable amendment apart, the whole of the committee stage on VAT resembled the Budget debate and the second reading debate. It could not really be said to have provided a really detailed analysis of the new tax.

The part of the committee stage taken on the floor of the House resembled a second reading debate. Clause one of the Bill laid out the principles of VAT. Chancellor Anthony Barber stated that the debate on 'clause one of the Finance Bill is a debate on the general merits of VAT and Government policy governing indirect taxation'. Mr Healey did not really take up the challenge and confined much of his remarks to the powers of enforcement (10 May 1972, cols. 1162, 1169). The powers of enforcement, like the provisions and incidence of the tax itself, had roused the interest of pressure groups.

Thus Mr Percival commented:

My Hon friends and I who table Amendment No. 79 together with the CBI, the Law Society, the Bar Council, the Finance Committee of Conservative Back-benchers, the Society of Conservative Lawyers and others are seriously concerned about the enforcement provisions.

(10 May 1972, col. 1175)

Pressure did ultimately have some effect. Several amendments were made by the Government during the passage of the VAT legislation. Among other things concessions were made on talking books for the blind, the Royal National Lifeboats, land adjacent to ports. hearing aids and some second-hand goods. Mr Healey commented:

Almost every concession made by the Government was one which was refused in Committee, but when finally put into an Opposition Amendment, the concession was made when we came to the Floor of the House.

(19 July 1972, col. 646)

In fact the relief for hearing aids (following pressure from the Hearing Aid Council) had originally been proposed by Jock Bruce-Gardyne (Conservative). He tried to withdraw his amendment but the Opposition forced a division which was lost. But some of the special groups that had long pressured the Government for tax concessions had no success. The churches still have to pay VAT on repairs and are still (1981) trying to obtain relief. CT had a much shorter and smoother passage through its committee stage in 1972. The arguments when they came were almost exclusively technical or reverted to the broad issues that had dominated debate on the subject for ten years – which method of CT was most desirable. The Opposition to CT had, by 1972, lost its spirit. Joel Barnett for the Opposition, did not really think that the reform of 1972 was a party political issue. Debate in the standing committee was so good natured on CT that Patrick Jenkin (28 June 1972, cols. 1729–30) commented 'This has been one of the most civilised of standing committees since the introduction of the new procedure.' Perhaps one of the reasons for the good nature of its proceedings was that it always ended before midnight!

The same could certainly not be said of the committee stage of the 1974 (No. 2) Bill when CTT was introduced. Three major clauses were debated in Committee of the Whole House: clause 17 announcing the new tax, clause 33 establishing the rate of tax (subsequently amended in third reading), and clause 40 establishing domicile for tax liability. The rest went to standing committee which considered CTT in ten of its twelve sittings. Its twelve sittings occupied 132 hours, an average of eleven hours for each. What was worse, many of the sittings went on all night, ending at 8.18 am, 8.24 am and 9.11 am the following morning on three occasions. The CTT legislation was extremely complex, not particularly well drafted, and raised many technical issues. The Government itself had to table many amendments. Altogether some 830 amendments were put down. Many of the Opposition amendments were highly technical and proposed by noted Conservative tax specialists backed up by expert advice. Some of the Opposition amendments and at least one from the Government's own backbenches (Denzil Davies and Cledwyn Hughes – relief for small farms in Wales) sought relief from tax for special groups and cases, among them trusts, charities, political parties, small businesses, agricultural property and woodlands. The Opposition, with its expert backing, made the running in this committee. The Government in the 1974–9 Parliament was working with a slender majority and so the Opposition pushed as far as they could go. Perhaps, with a stronger majority, this particular piece of legislation would have had an easier time in the standing committee. Whilst it might have been possible for members to grapple with this complex piece of legislation during daylight hours, it was almost impossible for them to follow the proceedings in the middle of the night. After one particularly obscure discussion on the sale of assets by trustees 'at arm's length' and below value, Mr Nicholas Ridley called for the presence of the law officers to help the Ministers explain the meaning of the Bill to the committee. Sir John Hall commented:

This episode emphasises that the Bill is becoming more and more complicated . . . [it] should have gone to a select committee . . . Many of the topics that have been raised are not understood by either side of the committee or even by the Minister.

(17 February 1975, col. 1772)

Nevertheless, the Conservatives did by dint of continued effort and expertise make a good show at exposing the shortcomings of the Bill. At the close of the committee stage on CTT David Howell called it 'an Alice-in-Wonderland Committee'.

I have never seen a Bill so torn to bits, so shot to bits by the devastatingly superior knowledge of my Hon and Right Hon friends . . . The Chief Secretary and the Financial Secretary have been fighting on the most changing ground . . . in a situation where they simply have not had information or the knowledge to meet the criticism of my Right Hon and Hon friends.

(18 February 1975, col. 2302)

Report and third reading
The report stage of Finance Bills offers the Government the opportunity to put their finishing touches to the legislation and permits them to return to those aspects of the Bill which they had promised in committee to consider 'at a later stage'. It is at this stage that many of the concessions which are to be allowed during the initial year of the legislation are written in. By getting the Opposition to withdraw its amendment and introducing their own the Government can correct deficiencies in drafting and can gain two advantages for itself. It can

avoid the loss of face accompanying defeat in a standing committee (like defeat on the floor of the House this is taken seriously), and it can share some of the praise from interested parties for the generous manner in which it has made the concessions. The operation of party voting in the House of Commons ensures this double victory for the Government.

The third reading of Finance Bills is little more than a formality allowing Ministers to wind up with praise for themselves and their supporters' efforts and permitting the Opposition to claim success in 'improving' the legislation.

Defects of the Committee and report stages

The experience of the standing committees considering new taxes reveals some of the defects of this procedure. Firstly, there is generally inadequate information on the details of the new tax. 'Notes on clauses' are provided to Ministers, one for each clause, explaining its purpose in detail and how the wording achieves that purpose. These may be published in the White Paper accompanying legislation, as they were for CT (Cmnd 2646, 1965), Reform of Personal Direct Taxation (Cmnd 4653, 1971) and Reform of Corporation Tax (Cmnd 4955, 1972) (Johnstone, 1975). This was not done, however, for VAT. There were, however, some papers available for VAT that provided an explanation of some sections of the Bill. But even with the 'notes on clauses' members are often not much helped. Notes on clauses are short background notes, not detailed explanations of complex legal points. Notes prepared for Ministers by civil servants do not always help them out when unexpected difficulties of a highly technical nature arise. At such a point they may need to obtain further elucidation from their civil servants. For Ministers the problems in standing committee are similar to those experienced during a particularly difficult question time. For civil servants the problem is that, with only a few hours' notice, they must consider each amendment, judge its validity, estimate its cost and write a brief for the Treasury Minister. Secondly, most members find it difficult to understand tax law. Only a few experts are able to grapple with arcane topics such as trusts. These expert MPs are almost exclusively found on the Conservative side of the House. Conservative Members are much more active in tax committees than Labour Members and it is not surprising that so much of the criticism of current financial procedures emanates from their side of the House. Thirdly, expertise, even where available, cannot be brought to bear in a balanced manner in a standing committee because there is no cross-examination of witnesses and special interests do not have to defend their case. Expertise may thus be used in an unbalanced way, as it was on CTT to support the claims of some groups in society while the needs of others are weakly presented. Finally, the standing committee is a microcosm of the House. Members are obliged to attend, and voting is controlled by the Whips. As on the floor of the House, an adversarial style of debating is used – although it may be toned down somewhat in committee. But adversary politics does not encourage collective efforts to improve the form of tax legislation. Sir Geoffrey Howe (1977) said of the standing committee stage:

Because of the debating nature of the proceedings, the Minister often feels no compunction about glossing over questions that are beyond him.

(Howe, 1977)

A debating style as used in the British Parliament does not mean reasoned argument. Certainly the need to understand new tax legislation is not served well by taking the detailed consideration in a standing committee.

But where else could the details of a tax Bill be more satisfactorily considered? Some sort of committee stage is essential. The floor of the House, the traditional venue, is certainly not suitable when taxes such as SET, VAT and CTT affect certain specific and particular classes of tax-payer. Standing committees permit particular cases to get a better hearing but obscure the consideration of general principles, and fail to encourage a satisfactory use of expertise. The effect of current procedure, as Sir Geoffrey Howe said in 1977 is that:

We are in danger of being drowned in a sea of exemptions and concessions. One man's allowance quickly becomes another man's anomaly.

(Howe, 1977)

Christopher Sandy writing in *The Times* (17 November 1978) said of the sort of topics that get most coverage, 'Few of these are concerned with significant amounts of tax revenue and often only a handful of tax-payers are affected, albeit that the effect upon those particular individuals may be dramatic . . . the specific is crowding out the general.' The effect of concession piled upon concession and of changes to details is particularly serious when a tax has been desired by a Government for ideological reasons. If the Government bends to the blandishments of specific groups and interests it runs the risk of watering down its own proposals so much that they are unsuitable for achieving its political goal. Analysis of the types of amendment that are made to tax bills, and the way in which they are made reveals how much the principles of a legislative instrument can be thwarted by changes to its details.

The significance of amendments
An outstanding feature of the four Finance Bills that contained new taxes is the vast number of amendments (many of them from the Government) that are tabled at committee and report stages. Analysis of the content of amendments suggests a useful typology.

Types of amendment

1. Drafting amendments. These alter words, clear up ambiguities. They form a high proportion of the total especially from the Government side.

2. Paving amendments. Many of the amendments (for example to the CTT legislation) serve to pave the way for subsequent amendments. The Opposition may, by one of its amendments, clear the way for a Government amendment at a later stage.

3. Probing amendments. These are intended to discover what the Bill means. MPs are frequently at a loss to understand financial legislation. For example, on CTT the following questions were put through amendments: 'What is a gift?' 'What is a spouse?' If the proposer of such an amendment receives an answer, he will generally then withdraw his amendment.

4. Proving amendments. These are designed to make the Minister prove why he needs such and such a regulation. This sort of amendment occurred frequently during the Committee stage of the VAT legislation because there was much opposition to the tax on the grounds of the difficulty of collection and the harshness of the means of enforcement.

5. Debating pegs. Some amendments are put down which the mover knows perfectly well will not succeed but which allow him to make debating points. Examples include amendments about the exemption rather than the zero-rating of food for VAT. The Opposition wanted to see food outside the scope of VAT completely.

6. Substantive amendments. These are intended to alter the legislation in a substantive way. Amendments that completely alter the character of the legislation are, of course, out of order at the committee stage (such amendments may be put at second reading only). But amendments to tax legislation that grant reliefs and concessions are substantive amendments. A cumulation of such changes may alter the general character of a tax.

The process of amendment

Of all the hundreds of amendments very few will ever be brought to a division in standing committee (twenty or thirty divisions being a high number). Extremely rarely does an Opposition amendment of substance succeed. However, the measure of parliamentary influence used by Mackintosh (1973) and accepted by Millar (1976) (p. 109) greatly underestimates the role of Parliament in the tax policy-making process because it fails to distinguish between different functions of amendments. Although the influence of Parliament is broader than a mere count of successful substantive Opposition amendments would suggest, one cannot go to the other extreme and claim a much greater role for Parliament in the process of developing tax policy simply because over the years ideas mooted in Parliament eventually find their way into legislation. But, together with the activities of pressure groups and publicity from the media, Parliament does play a broad part in the adjustment of tax policy. The process is perhaps best described as a multi-staged one. Ideas are aired in general debates. Sometimes they are concerned with general principles; often they reflect special interests (generally once the details are known). Amendments are proposed (and almost always lost) at committee stage. A very few amendments of a substantive nature are taken up by the Government and put forward at report and third reading. Many appear in subsequent Finance Bills. (See especially the 1966 Finance Bill which had two whole schedules to amend the CT and CGT of the previous year, and the 1976 Finance Bill which had forty-one new clauses to add to the previous year's legislation on CTT.)

The real effect of Parliament on tax policy can thus only be seen by tracing back the alterations to a tax during its lifetime. In the case of CTT, for example, it was obvious to many MPs from the start that it would provide an infinitely malleable tax which within six years has been transformed by amendment after amendment to resemble nothing so much as the tax it replaced (p. 42). During the standing committee stage of CTT Nicholas Ridley said of it, 'This is a nice tax . . . one would benefit from so many loopholes . . . there is to be relief for farmers and historic houses, wealth distributed and bequests to widows.' (18 February 1975, col. 2144).

CTT is a particularly interesting tax, for a detailed case study of the process of amendment shows quite clearly the various routes by which parliamentary activity has its impact on tax policy.

1. Government defeats on Opposition amendments. This route to amendment is rarely successful.

2. Introduction of amendments in order to prompt the Government into action. Very often as a result of an amendment introduced at committee stage, the Government will agree to introduce a similar measure of its own 'at a later stage'. That 'later stage' may mean the report or third reading stage. We can find a number of examples of this sort of amendment process from CTT. A number of amendments first suggested from the backbenches and subsequently introduced by the Government, made a real reduction of liability:

a. the introduction of a new scale of tax for gifts made by an individual not less than three years before his death, involving significantly lower rates of tax in the lower brackets;

b. the relief from tax on successive transfers of the same property within four years.

c. the relief for woodlands;

d. the exclusion from tax of certain dispositions for maintenance of a donor's family;

e. the tax credit for the periodic charge on certain trusts, and the special low rate of tax on early capital distribution;

f. exemption for special classes of trusts, and the relief for sales and mortgages of reversionary interests;

g. the exemption of outright gifts up to £100 to any one donee in any one year;

h. the increase of the exemption for marriage gifts by parents of the parties from £2500 to £5000;

i. the increased exemption for gifts to charities and the introduction of an exemption for gifts to political parties.

Some of these major changes that appeared during the original passage of the Bill can be traced to Opposition amendments, woodland relief for example. The exemption for certain classes of trust was pushed for by the TUC and trades unions, political parties by the Labour and Liberal Parties, and the relief for charities had all-party support.

3. Government introduces amendments in a subsequent year. Some of these may be traceable to amendments tabled when the Bill was first considered.

In the case of CTT many amendments were made in the 1976 Finance Bill. This Bill contained forty-two CTT clauses to be added to the original thirty-one clauses. Conditions for relief on historic houses (temporary reliefs had been granted pending the result of the Select Committee on the Wealth Tax) were set out in detail. There were also exemptions for maintenance funds. Greater relief was given for agricultural property and the methods of calculating its value were simplified Exemption limits were raised. Some concessions which in 1975 were said to be impossible appeared in 1976 as Government amendments (e.g. relief for business property).

Conclusion

The experience of CTT in 1974 confirmed the view of Iain Macleod writing in *The Times* on 18 June 1968 of earlier tax legislation: '. . . The Treasury seem reluctant to accept even incontestable propositions in the year of their birth. They are noted, filed away and appear years later as Government amendments.' Some commentators (*The Guardian*, 4

March 1975 for example) thought CTT was introduced in too much of a hurry. But haste is only part of the explanation for the great number of changes made to the original CTT legislation. The fact that such changes are a regular feature of the tax legislation process points to deeper underlying factors. The bulk of amendments to CTT, as to others of the new taxes, are of a technical and drafting nature. Amendments generally are of such a character. Proportionately few out of the large numbers tabled are of much substance. But this small proportion of substantive amendments can over a period of years utterly transform a tax so that it no longer fulfils its original objectives, as they did with CTT. Our case studies indicate that both the nature of much recent tax legislation and the procedure by which it is considered in Parliament are together responsible for the ultimate legislative product.

It has been suggested that select committees would afford the prospect of a more rational and better drafted tax legislation for they, using an investigatory procedure, could conduct a pre-legislative examination of draft proposals. It is argued that this process would eliminate much of the poor drafting of tax law which currently makes it so complex and ill-suited to its purposes and could relieve the struggle to comprehend that is evident on the floor of the House and especially in standing committee. The select committee procedure is superficially an attractive alternative to a procedure that has been described by Sir Geoffrey Howe as 'weary' (Howe, 1977). But while on the surface the select committee might look like a device for more considered and rational appraisal of tax policy proposals, it may also provide an enhanced opportunity for special interests to put their case. We shall consider this dilemma in Chapter 6.

6 The Role of Parliament – Select Committees

The role of select committees in the making of taxation policy

In the nineteenth century Parliament made wide use of select committees as investigatory bodies. They were established to inquire into great matters of social and economic concern arising from the industrial revolution and the demands of a rising democracy. As a consequence their reports form one of the major sources of nineteenth-century history and tell us much about conditions in unreformed Britain.

Taxation appears as one of the great concerns studied by *ad hoc* select committees from time to time during the nineteenth and twentieth centuries. Among the taxation topics considered during the period from 1800 to 1970 were income and property tax, passenger duty, window tax, taxation of Ireland and of Scotland as well as local matters such as rates.

Towards the end of the nineteenth century the practice of referring important matters of state to select committees fell somewhat out of favour and an extra-Parliamentary device, the royal commission, became much more popular. The investigatory function gradually passed from the parliamentary arena. But a number of taxation matters continued to be referred to select committees during the early decades of the twentieth century. The most notable were those on Luxury Duty (1918) and on Increase of Wealth (War) (1920). (A list of Select Committees that have considered aspects of taxation in the twentieth century follows the bibliographical references at the end of the book.) But for major studies on income tax (Cmd 615, 1920) and on the National Debt and Taxation (Cmd 2800, 1927) the Government went outside the House of Commons. The Select Committee on the Medical Stamp Acts (1936) was the last select committee specifically established to consider a question of taxation until the 1970s. From 1936 to 1971 the only occasions when select committees looked at taxation matters were when established select committees such as the Estimates Committee happened to choose a topic connected with the taxation system. The Estimates Committee, whose terms of reference were wide enough to include scrutiny of the activities of the revenue departments, considered for example, PAYE in 1945, Customs and Excise in 1956, Schedule A in 1960 and the Cost of Collection in 1963. More recently, the Public Accounts Committee has expressed concern about the cost of collecting VAT and abuses of the PAYE system; the Inland Revenue regularly features in the reports of the Parliamentary Commissioner for Administration; and the Expenditure Committee (1970–79) discussed taxation from time to time. But these inquiries were primarily concerned with the *administration* of taxation rather than with broad questions of taxation policy, or with details of specific taxes. These subjects of inquiry, chosen by the Members of the select committees themselves, reflect the view that committees, in an executive-dominated Government, should generally keep their activities to scrutinising and criticising the administration of policy rather than the policy itself (Coombes, 1966; Johnson, 1966). In the nineteenth century, select committee inquiries sometimes preceded legislation. But the House of Commons has never been established true pre-legislative committees on the American model that could examine the details surrounding specific legislative proposals from the Government. The idea of a pre-legislative committee stage that could hear evidence from witnesses from outside Parliament and that could tease out the factual basis and consequences of Government legislation has never appealed to the British House of Commons. It has always been thought that such committees might detract from the floor of the House and weaken the grip of party control. So, although suggestions on these lines have been made to the House of Commons from time to time, it preferred throughout the nineteenth and twentieth centuries to use *ad hoc* investigatory committees when there was general commitment to particular legislative proposals. The relationship between the inquiries of select committees and legislation was thus always somewhat distant. Moreover, no system of select investigatory committees existed until 1979 when the departmental select committees were set up to monitor the work of the central government departments. Now that there is something like a system of select committees, *ad hoc* committees for special inquiries can still be established. The current system does not cover every aspect of governmental activity and in particular the requirements of taxation policy are only indirectly covered by the Treasury and Civil Service Committee. This may reflect a lack of interest in structural changes in taxation: e.g. it has not looked at the Green Paper, *The Taxation of Husband and Wife* (Cmnd 8093), issued in December 1980.

The House of Commons still has no permanent machinery to study tax proposals and to review the structure of the tax system. Parliament has however paid some attention to the legislative processes by which it considers taxation proposals. Several select committees on procedure have inquired into financial procedure and in particular the Finance Bill. In doing so they have commented on the way in which Parliament currently considers taxation measures and have made recommendations for improvements in procedure.

A number of Members who are interested in management of the economy have proposed from time to time the establishment of a select committee on economic affairs which could, *inter alia*, consider taxation structure. This proposal was first made in the evidence of the Study of Parliament Group to the Select Committee on Procedure in the session 1964/5 (HC 303). In 1967 the idea was again aired by Michael Ryle in his article 'Parliamentary Control of Expenditure and Taxation' in *Political Quarterly* (Ryle, 1967). It appeared again in the evidence to the Select Committee on Procedure in 1968/9, 1969/70, and 1970/71 (HC 410, HC 302, HC 276). The idea has also been widely promoted in the press and in journals by politicians and commentators (Mackintosh, 1973; Raison, *Daily Telegraph*, 26 February 1977).

A few reformers, however, have concentrated on the special requirements of tax policy-making that are separate from general economic policy. In their memorandum to the 1968/9 Select Committee on Procedure, the Clerks Assistant put forward the view that a separate select committee on taxation was more appropriate than a combined expenditure and taxation committee (i.e. an economic affairs committee). They had grasped the fact that some questions of taxation changes are properly in the hands of the executive – the changes of rate necessary for short-term demand management – but that these aspects of specific policy are separate from and different to the questions of long-term changes in structure.

The Treasury, for its part, has consistently objected to the House of Commons considering taxation policy in Committees. First of all, as indicated in Chapter 5, it opposed, for many years, the idea that some parts of the Finance Bill should be taken in standing committee. It also disliked the idea of a select committee considering taxation. It thought that a select committee on economic affairs which could consider changes in taxation might trespass on the area of political initiative properly reserved to the Government (see HC 276 of 1970/71, pp. 1–47 and Millar, 1976). This view of the Treasury was coloured by the concept of taxation as primarily an instrument of short-term demand management. The replies of Sir Douglas Allen to questions from the Select Committee on Procedure in 1968/9 make it clear that while the Committee members themselves were groping towards the idea that a select committee might consider new taxes and the tax structure (mention was made of VAT and of negative income tax) the Treasury was only concerned with the significance of changes in tax rates. The obsession of the Treasury and some Ministers with the tools of demand management, and with maintenance of the special conditions of Budget secrecy that obtain in Britain, discourages an open attitude to the long-term planning of taxation policy.

As a result of the evidence received, and in the light of their own views (expressed during the questioning of the Treasury witnesses) the Procedure Committee (1968/9) recommended the establishment of an expenditure committee without taxation functions instead of a committee on economic affairs. They decided to examine the procedure for scrutinising taxation policy as a separate matter (HC 410, 1968/9).

The Procedure Committee returned to the question of taxation again in the 1970/71 session when it reported on *The Scrutiny of Taxation* (HC 276). It heard suggestions from some witnesses that technical changes to existing taxes should be considered separately from new taxes. The official witnesses pointed out that in 1945, 1964 and 1968 separate Bills from the main Finance Bill were introduced to effect various revenue reforms and changes. In 1945 the system of capital allowances was passed in a separate Act, in 1964 a separate Act was passed for the Inland Revenue machinery for collection (Income Tax Management Act); and in 1968 the Revenue Act changed the basis for Selective Employment (SET) payments and abolished the export rebate. All of these were classified as 'Revenue Acts' (see the evidence by Sir Norman Price, p.38). In 1970 the Income and Corporation Taxes Bill which was passed in November, changed the rates of taxes with effect from the succeeding April. But none of these examples compare with the new taxes in our survey such as SET, VAT and CT. All the examples of separate Acts referred to the creation of administrative machinery, not of a new tax.

The Select Committee on Procedure considered the need for a select committee to 'inquire into proposals for new taxes or for major alterations to the structure of existing taxes' (para. 32, p. xvii). In recent years, such proposals had on occaision been published by the Government in White or Green Papers, but since 1945 the only debate in the House had been that in June 1967 on the proposals for a regional employment premium, which was contained in a Green Paper on the Development Areas (HC Debates 1966–7, col. 651). But the Treasury was not in favour of creating a permanent select committee to consider tax proposals. It thought that many of the issues would be politically highly charged (para. 36, p. xx), and that such a committee would place too great a burden of work on Members, Ministers and officials. The Treasury, however, advocated a return to the practice of the years between 1900 and 1939 when the Chancellor referred specific proposals for new taxes or restructuring to *ad hoc* select committees, and also supported the use of Green Papers for new taxes. The Procedure Committee, faced with Treasury opposition to the idea of a permanent taxation committee, but not thinking that the *ad hoc* proposals went far enough to permit continuous scrutiny of taxation structure, opted for a compromise by advocating that an extra sub-committee be added to the Expenditure Committee to consider taxation. The Expenditure Committee should then be re-named the Expenditure and Finance Committee, and its order of reference amended by inserting the words: 'to consider the existing system of taxation, proposals for major changes in the structure of existing taxes and proposals for new forms of taxation, to consider the economic implications of different forms of taxation' (para. 43, p. xxiii).

This proposal was not accepted by the Government. Both the Government and the Treasury felt that a permanent select committee either on economic affairs, or specifically concerned with taxation, might encourage the development of expertise among MPs and thus eventually produce a counterweight to the Government's view on management of the economy. However, the Government was as dissatisfied as many backbenchers with the way in which some of the new taxation of the 1960s had reached the statute book. The long drawn out parliamentary stages of CGT and CT in 1965, the haste and lack of calculation that had heralded SET in particular, left a nasty feeling that some taxes required more careful preparation and a longer, more 'open' pre-legislative stage. Some of the ideas currently being canvassed for new taxes by academics, commentators and politicians had not been fully considered or worked out in detail (tax credits, for example). Thus the Government saw much merit in the use of the select committee as an *ad hoc* investigatory tool in those cases where it had a mind to legislate but had some reason to expect either political opposition or serious administrative difficulties, or where it wished to have a public airing of the effects of a new tax on particular individuals and groups.*
Thus the Government decided to revive the use of the *ad hoc* select committee for consideration of new tax proposals, linking the select committee inquiry to the publication of a Green Paper. This permitted interested parties to study the proposals and prepare evidence for the select committee. The first *ad hoc* tax select committee was appointed in 1971 to consider the Green Paper on the reform of corporation tax. Thereby the House of Commons had reverted to the earlier practice of itself, rather than an outside committee (such as the Richardson Committee on VAT) or a royal commission, examining Government proposals for reform of the taxation system.

The Select Committee on the Corporation Tax

When CT was first introduced in 1965 there was no public machinery such as a select committee set up to look at alternative proposals or at the possible effects that the Government's provisions might have. As the debates on CT reveal, there was a very deep ideological division of

*For the classic account of why a government might establish a committee to inquire, see Wheare (1955).

opinion on the best method of company taxation (p. 118 and p. 119). Even had the option of a select committee occurred to the Government in 1965, there would therefore have been little point in taking the CT proposal to a select committee where consensus would have been impossible to achieve. Moreover, when a Government is sure it knows what it wants to do, as the Government was with CT in 1965, to open up the subject for detailed discussion might only reveal difficulties and cause delay. Thus, all the debates on the classical form of CT, including its detailed effects, had to take place in Parliament *after* the Chancellor had announced his commitment to a particular scheme.

Throughout the years of CT's operation, Conservatives were un-convinced that the scheme introduced by the Labour Party had been the right one. They continued to believe that industrial development was encouraged more by distribution than by retention of profits. Thus, before they won the election in 1970, they set about devising proposals for the reform of CT (p. 74). When they returned to power in 1970 they were ready to undertake their own reform, Having strongly objected to the manner in which the previous Government had introduced CT without adequate prior consultation, they wanted to find some means of achieving more 'open' Government. Like the Labour Party, however, they were firmly committed to the basic shape that the tax should take. Nevertheless they were willing to leave open the technical means by which the tax should be calculated and collected. Thus the Green Paper on the Reform of the Corporation Tax, published in March 1971 (Cmnd 4630), contained a firm commitment to 'remove the discrimination against distributed profits' but left open issues of implementation. Then a select committee was established to examine the best means by which this objective could be achieved. By such means the Government was able to control the atmosphere in which the Select Committee worked. It minimised the possibility of conflict among the Members of the Select Committee by assigning them a narrow and technical task.

The Green Paper indicated three systems which would achieve the Government's objective: the two-rate system, the imputation system, and the pre-1965 system. The Government indicated that it did not wish to return to the pre-1965 system, or any variants of it, and that its preference was for the two-rate system. Both the two-rate system and the imputation system could be designed to afford relief from double taxation of profits earned by UK companies trading overseas – an important point of dispute when the Labour Government had origin-ally brought in CT in 1965 (p. 118–19).

The Committee was chaired by a Conservative Member, Sir Henry D'Avigdor Goldsmid, a bullion broker and company chairman. Table 6.1 shows the Members of the Committee and their backgrounds. All

Table 6.1   Members of the Select Committee on Corporation Tax and their relevant expertise

Conservative	
Sir Henry d'Avidgor-Goldsmid (Chairman)	Bullion broker. Chairman of Anglo-Israeli Bank and Pergamon Press
Kenneth Baker	Industrial consultant
Sir John Foster	Barrister
Peter Rees	Barrister, tax expert
Sir Tatton Brinton	Chairman of carpet manufacturing company
Eric Cockeram	Company director
Labour	
John Roper	Economist
David Marquand	Opposition front bench spokesman on economic affairs, 1971–2
Denzil Davies	Barrister
Dr John Gilbert	Economist, accountant

the other Conservative Members on the Committee had business connections. Three were company directors, one an industrial consultant and one, Peter Rees, QC, a noted tax lawyer. On the Labour side two members, David Marquand and John Roper, had long displayed an interest in the way in which Parliament scrutinises taxation and expenditure. David Marquand had been a member of the 1968/9 Select Committee on Procedure and of the 1970/71 Select Committee on Procedure which examined the proposals for a select committee on taxation. Of the other two Labour members, one was a barrister and the other an accountant and both later became Treasury Ministers. All of the Select Committee members were therefore well equipped to tackle the complexities of CT.

However, it is clear from the activities of the Members of the Committee that the Conservative Members as a whole took a greater interest in its work, were more active in the evidence sessions, asking considerably more questions of witnesses than their Labour counterparts (see Table 6.2). The lack of vigorous Labour Party behaviour is perhaps curious when it is recalled that the Select Committee was sitting during the life of a Conservative Government which meant that the Labour Party could choose from among its entire contingent of MPs whereas the Conservatives, by the very nature of things, were obliged to field a 'second eleven'. The Labour Members of the Committee were however 'moderates', two of the four are now in the Social Democratic Party. In

Table 6.2 Select Committee on Corporation Tax: attendance and participation of Members according to political party

Conservative	Attendance (%) (max = 9)	Participation score[a]	Labour	Attendance (%) (max = 9)	Participation score[a]
Sir Henry d'Avigdor Goldsmid (Chairman)	100	27.8	John Roper	100	7.4
Kenneth Baker	100	14.0	David Marquand	89	6.8
Sir John Foster	100	10.0	Denzil Davies	100	6.4
Peter Rees	100	9.0	Dr John Gilbert	67	3.4
Sir Tatton Brinton	89	4.8			
Eric Cockeram	100	3.1			

Notes: [a] Average number of questions asked per session attended
In total 812 questions were asked, of which the Chairman asked 250, the five Conservative Members (excluding the Chairman) asked 363 and the four Labour Members asked 199.

any case the majority of the Labour Opposition no longer saw this question as one of 'party politics' (Joel Barnett, p. 148).

Two factors affected the levels of activity in this Committee. Firstly, the principle of the tax was not under debate. Thus any really strong Opposition behaviour was inhibited. Secondly, the question before the Committee was a highly technical one and, on balance, the Conservatives had the greater weight of specialised expertise among their Members. Their representatives on the Committee had more intimate knowledge of the intricacies of company taxation. The Labour Members, on the other hand, although interested in general economic questions, had less specific expertise on taxation. Thus the Select Committee could be effectively dominated by the Government supporters whose task was merely to adjudicate between different technical devices.

In order to discover why the Committee reached its particular conclusion we must examine the evidence presented to it and the sources of that evidence. Important witnesses were the Inland Revenue (which gave oral evidence on three occasions), the Building Societies Association, the Life Officers Association, Shell, the Association of Unit Trust Managers, the British Insurance Association, the International Chambers of Commerce, the Confederation of British Industry and the Institute of Directors. The Revenue, in its evidence, put the case for the two-rate system favoured by the Government. But most of the other witnesses to the Committee preferred the imputation system although some favoured a different version from that put forward in the Green Paper. The Committee found that in a closed economy there would be no real difference between the two systems but:

The arguments in favour of the imputation system spring basically from this country's position as an international trader and investor . . . the imputation system was preferable to the two-rate system as a basis for the renegotiation of double taxation agreements . . . the imputation system would be the more favourable to the UK balance of payments. British investment abroad is much more substantial than foreign investment in the UK . . . Finally, your Committee think that it is likely that harmonisation within the EEC would be in the first place facilitated by the adoption of imputation here.
(HC 622, 1970/71, pp. xiii and xiv, paras 23, 24 and 25)

Thus the Select Committee found in favour of the system recommended by most of the witnesses that it heard. Most witnesses, like the Government, were clear in their own minds that they supported some system that favoured the distribution of profits. However, the Committee did have a contrary view presented to it by Lord Kaldor who favoured a tax regime that encouraged retention of profits. Because of their narrow terms of reference the Committee was able to ignore this evidence.

In assessing the effect of the Select Committee's report on the subsequent legislation it is perhaps worth quoting at length from the Chancellor's Budget statement of 21 March 1972 in which he foreshadowed the introduction of the new CT in the 1972 Finance Bill. Mr Anthony Barber recalled that he had, at first, favoured the two-rate system:

Having said that, the fact is that the majority of those with whom we consulted clearly favoured an imputation system. So did the Select Committee, by a unanimous recommendation . . . I have, therefore, reconsidered the matter in the light of this advice, and have come to the conclusion that the advantages of the two-rate system are not sufficient to outweigh the arguments that have been put forward in favour of the alternative. I therefore accept and endorse the Select Committee's main conclusion that the form of corporation tax to be introduced in this country ought to follow the imputation system set out in the Green Paper . . . I have been keeping closely in touch with developments in the Community, which is engaged in a programme to harmonise the structure of its company taxation. It has not yet reached a conclusion, but the choice which we have made puts us in line with both France and Germany.

(HC Debs, 21 March 1972, col. 1358)

In fact, of course, the same people, companies, associations, etc. made representations to the Chancellor as gave evidence to the Select Committee. It is not surprising, therefore, that the Select Committee's recommendations were in agreement with the Chancellor's own conclusions.

The Select Committee on Corporation Tax proved a successful experiment from the Government's point of view. It fulfilled the demands for more careful consideration of details and for more 'open' tax policy-making without permitting an open discussion of the broad principles of company taxation structure. Opportunity for party conflict was removed by excising the root basis of party difference from the terms of reference. The consultation process was brought out into the public gaze. If, in the end, difficulties arose with the legislation, the Government could always claim that these questions should have been examined by the Select Committee and that all interested parties had had full and public opportunities to state their case. It seemed an attractive way to proceed.

The Select Committee on Tax Credit
Once the reform of CT was under way the Government turned its attention to another scheme that had long been on the books – tax credit. The idea had been worked out into a practicable scheme in 1971 by Arthur Cockfield, Anthony Barber's special adviser on taxation (p. 95). A working group (the Tax Credit Study Group) of senior officials was established to develop it further. However, it soon became clear to

the Chancellor that the TC proposal had far-reaching and broad economic implications. Moreover the Chancellor wanted to establish a consensus in favour of the tax credit system before introducing legislation and hence it was a particularly suitable case for an 'open' pre-legislative consultation phase. A Green Paper, *Proposals for a Tax Credit Scheme* (Cmnd 5116), was published in October 1972 and a Select Committee appointed on 1 December 1972 'to consider the Green Paper on proposals for a tax credit system and to report thereupon'.

The Labour Party this time fielded a top ranking team (see Table 6.3) which included Mrs Barbara Castle who had been Secretary of State for Employment from 1968 to 1970. According to Richard Crossman (1977, p. 705) Mrs Castle was not ill-disposed to the idea of tax credits; 'She hates the contributory system and she thinks this (tax credit) is a solution I shouldn't rule out.' Joel Barnett had also spoken favourably about the idea in the House of Commons (p. 126). The Labour contingent played a very active part in this Select Committee. After the Chairman, Mrs Castle was the next most active participant in its proceedings and other Labour Members were more active than the Conservatives (see Table 6.4). The Opposition was not shackled by restrictive terms of reference. The question before them was more 'open' than had been the case in the Corporation Tax Select Committee, and it raised questions on which the Labour group had a wide expertise (social security and the problems of the poor) and access to well qualified outside advisers.

The details of the scheme as outlined in the Green Paper are set out in Chapter 2 (p. 45–7). The tax credit scheme would replace the income tax personal allowances, the existing family allowances and family income supplement. Many existing social security benefits would, however, remain.

In the event the Committee received a huge volume of evidence. In order to attract as wide a range of evidence as possible the Select Committee, after its first meeting on 7 December, issued a press statement inviting individuals and representative bodies to submit their views without restriction. This invitation produced a remarkable response. As well as formal evidence the Committee received nineteen petitions with nearly 50,000 signatures in all. The petitions were all in favour of the payments of child credits to mothers (rather than to fathers who might be the sole wage-earner). The Committee also received nearly 500 letters, many of them multi-signed, again all concerned with the payment of benefits for children to mothers. The Tax Credit Study Group likewise received large numbers of submissions on this point, 35 petitions with about 45,000 signatures and some 1500 letters. In addition a petition with some 300,000 signatures was

Table 6.3   Members of the Select Committee on Tax Credit and their relevant expertise

Conservative	
William Clark (Chairman)	Opposition front bench spokesman on economic affairs 1964–6, accountant, director
David Price	Economist
Alfred Hall-Davies	Company director
Marcus Worsley	Farmer, landowner, company director
Peter Trew	Author, director
Mrs E. Kellett-Bowman	Barrister, farmer, social worker
Labour	
Mrs B. Castle	Secretary of State for Employment 1968–70
Joel Barnett	Accountant
Douglas Houghton	Former Secretary, Inland Revenue Staff Federation, Ex-Minister
Robert Sheldon	Company director
Liberal	
John Pardoe	Company director, member of London Metal Exchange

formally presented to the House of Commons. The public expression of a desire to pay some of the tax credits for children to mothers was further backed up by research done on behalf of the Child Poverty Action Group. A survey of mothers with children had demonstrated how reliant many of the poorest were on their weekly family allowances. For many families this was used for essentials such as food. It was often the only personal income that a wife with children could entirely rely on receiving regularly. Thus a powerful case, backed up with strong empirical evidence, was made out for a system that ensured an income for mothers. Several people interviewed for our study, Members of the then Government and of the Select Committee among them, felt that it had been an error on the Government's part to omit from the original scheme in the Green Paper a clear commitment to the payment of benefits for children to mothers. The opposition thus stirred up to the scheme might well have been responsible for the dissension on the Select Committee. But, in fact, there were also other powerful arguments against the scheme that emerged as the Committee's inquiry proceeded.

Table 6.4 *Select Committee on Tax Credit: attendance and participation of Members according to political party*

Conservative	Attend- ance (%) (max = 17)	Partici- pation score[a]	Labour	Attend- ance (%) (max = 17)	Partici- pation score[a]	Liberal	Attend- ance[a] (max = 17)	Partici- pation score[a]
W. Clark (Chairman)	100	63.4	Mrs B. Castle	88	11.27	John Pardoe	76	4.1
David Price	94	10.0	Joel Barnett	82	9.4			
Alfred Hall-Davies	94	4.7	Douglas Houghton	94	5.9			
Marcus Worsley	100	2.8	Robert Sheldon	94	5.0			
Peter Trew	100	2.5						
Mrs E. Kellett- Bowman	100	2.3						

Notes: [a] Average number of questions asked per session attended
In total 1982 questions were asked, of which the Chairman asked 1077, the five Conservative Members (excluding the Chairman) asked 374, the four Labour Members asked 476 and the one Liberal Member asked 54.

While much of the evidence heard by the Select Committee broadly accepted that tax credits were desirable, there were many powerful arguments against the scheme as proposed. Some witnesses, notably Lord Kaldor, thought the scheme misconceived. Most of the evidence, however, pointed to the effects that the new scheme would have on particular classes and groups of citizens. As a result of the great torrent of evidence on behalf of mothers the Committee recommended that, if the scheme were implemented, all child credits should be payable to mothers. Other groups identified as requiring special treatment were married women who were earning, the blind, overseas dependents, single parent families, the self-employed, and those at the lower end of the income scale and in receipt of other means-tested benefits not replaced under the tax credit proposal. By the time that the problems of each of these special groups had been considered the Committee report said:

It may be asked how much is left of the original scheme, in view of the modifications that have been proposed . . . it would have been attractive to introduce a system which sought as far as possible to produce a single payment through the employer or government agency . . . the total effect of all direct taxes and all benefits in each individual case would have been apparent to the individual on the face of the pay slip . . . This aspect of a negative income tax will no longer be obvious, to the extent that child credits are paid on a universal basis outside the system and perhaps to the extent that artificial qualifications for entry to the scheme are devised . . . we see dangers if the process of extension is carried beyond reasonable limits; the result might be to export particular difficulties inherent in the benefit field into the taxation field as a whole.

(pp. 39–40, para. 119)

Not only did the Select Committee propose modifications to the scheme as outlined in the Green Paper, on the basis of evidence received, it also pointed out a number of consequential effects on those in receipt of war and disablement pensions, retirement pensioners, married women with small earnings (part-time workers), those paying higher rates of tax, those (mainly employers) who would have to administer the scheme, and effects on insurance companies, building societies and banks (part III, paras, 122–77).

By the time that the draft report had been produced it was clear that, if the modifications were accepted the proposal for tax credits would not be the administrative simplification originally intended. Three of the Labour members (Joel Barnett, Barbara Castle and Robert Sheldon) were sufficiently unhappy with the proposal by the end of the Committee's deliberations to propose draft alternative reports of their own. Joel Barnett and Robert Sheldon worked together to produce a draft report. Their main objections to the scheme were its lack of progressivity, the belief that the additional revenue required could be better spent, the failure to present a revenue-neutral scheme, the loss of the flexibility of PAYE, and the fact that only one of the forty-four means-tested benefits would be totally displaced; they therefore recommended rejection. Their draft report was lost, voting being 6–3 (the Liberal, John Pardoe voting with the Government majority). Mrs Barbara Castle in her draft report concluded 'An examination of the social implications of the tax credit scheme shows that it would do far less to relieve poverty where it is most acute than the expenditure of £1300m on further reforms of social security.' The scheme, she thought, as outlined in the Green Paper, simply failed to meet its objectives: it would be better to improve the system of income support for poor people; it would eliminate few means-tested benefits if introduced on a revenue-neutral basis and would have regressive elements. Her draft report, like that of Joel Barnett and Robert Sheldon, was rejected by 6–3. The Chairman's draft report was then adopted by a 7–3 vote, the Liberal voting with the Government.

Once the Chairman's draft was accepted by the Committee Mrs Castle and Mr Houghton proposed many amendments. None was accepted. Their amendments, however, reveal their considerable reliance on the evidence from Professors Kaldor and Atkinson and the Child Poverty Action Group; this evidence had swayed their minds against the tax credit scheme.

Strictly, a select committee cannot have any but an agreed report. The so called 'minority reports' are in fact only draft reports but they appear as part of the published proceedings. When members of a select committee have particularly strong views against a proposal there is much advantage to be gained from bringing forward a draft report, getting it 'on the record' and having it available for use at a later date if required.

The effect of the agreed Chairman's report has to be evaluated in the light of a number of considerations. Firstly, the majority of the Committee accepted the general idea of tax credits, but proposed a number of significant modifications to the Government proposals. They pointed out that the scheme as designed by the Government was rigid, that it would only be a start towards the simplification of the relationship between tax and social security, and that some groups would require special treatment. Secondly, the agreed report was not unanimously accepted by the Committee. There were also on the record two minority reports which, in effect, rejected the proposals. These were, moreover, supported by substantial evidence and argument. Thirdly, and most important for the Government, the report and its mass of often complicated evidence, far from clearing up the inherent difficulties that might appear in the scheme once legislation was announced (and which might therefore require concessions and create anomalies), simply raised more questions. The report was unusually long and complex, the evidence even more so. The Government had always been thinking of this particular reform on a long time scale (1977 was the earliest date that it could have been put into effect), but the extra complexities revealed by the Select Committee report must have pushed the timetable back even further.

In the event an election early in 1974 robbed the Conservative Government of its majority. By the time that they framed the 1979 election manifesto they were no longer fully committed to a tax credit scheme (p. 78). There were, moreover, administrative costs to the tax credit scheme. The computerisation of the Inland Revenue was put off by Chancellor Barber in 1971 while the tax credit scheme was under consideration and was still barely under way ten years later. The scope for any fundamental change on the lines of tax credits is now effectively ruled out for another ten years or so until the computers are operating.

The experience of the Tax Credit Select Committee was very different from that of the Corporation Tax Committee. There was plenty of scope for party differences and they were fully exploited by the Opposition Members. Labour Members, backed by well researched advice, were able to dominate many of the evidence sessions (the Chairman apart). This particular tax issue was not about the usual tax complexities of trusts and companies but was in essence about social security benefits, income maintenance and the best way of caring for the poor, sick, elderly and children. It was, therefore, traditional Labour Party ground.

Thus, in many respects the Tax Credit Select Committee presents an interesting contrast to the Corporation Tax Select Committee. It confirms the view held by many academic observers (and also many Members of the House of Commons) that select committees are most likely to be successful when they have a narrow remit and can work in an atmosphere conducive to consensus.

The experience of such 'pre-legislative' select committees has not been one of uniform success, and we consider that their value is probably greatest in areas outside acute party controversy and where there will not be a strong Government attitude towards the final Bill.

(Select Committee on Procedure, HC, 1977/8, p. xiii).

Such comments raise the question 'What is success for a select committee?' Is a select committee only to be judged successful if it says there is one clear and undisputed answer to a complicated question? Perhaps, before the Labour Party appointed a select committee to consider a complicated and controversial tax it ought to have been more aware that, given a difficult question, select committees cannot always produce a clear-cut answer. On the other hand, perhaps the Government well knew what it was about when it appointed a select committee to consider its proposal for a WT. For one thing a select committee can do, if its members work hard and have the benefit of excellent outside help and advice, is to stop ill-considered and ill-worked out schemes of tax reform before they are rushed onto the legislative conveyor belt.

The Select Committee on the Wealth Tax

The Select Committee on Corporation Tax was presented with a Green Paper which committed the Government to a particular type of tax and left the Committee to choose between two alternative ways of implementation. The Select Committee on Tax Credit was presented with a Green Paper which outlined in some detail a particular scheme for the proposed changes but did not prevent the Committee from recommending alternatives. But, when the Select Committee on the Wealth Tax was established in 1975 to consider the Government's Green Paper on Wealth tax, they were presented with two objectives (p. 50), carrying different implications about the structure of the tax, with no indication of the relative importance to be assigned to each. Consequently, although the Green Paper contained much detail on the tax unit, rates, thresholds, ceiling provisions, scope of the tax, relief for particular assets, form of administration and so on, it was all framed in terms of 'might' or 'possibly' or 'illustrative provisions'. Almost the only hard commitment was that there should be a wealth tax.

The Committee faced a daunting task. A wealth tax – or rather the large number of different wealth taxes compatible with the Green Paper – raised fundamental issues, some of which were not immediately apparent but emerged during the course of the inquiry. There was the problem of what should constitute wealth for tax purposes, e.g. should it include the value of pension rights. There were the possible economic consequences – to saving and to the existence and growth of private firms – which could alter the very nature of the economy. There was the possible threat to the national heritage. The tax also posed a host of technical problems and needed to be examined in the context of other possible changes in the tax system. The Committee had therefore both political and technical questions to resolve.

These issues could not quickly be settled; and the political issues were likely to divide members of the Committee on party lines. The experience of previous select committees established to consider taxation of wealth (Select Committee on Luxury Duty, 1918, and Select Committee on Increase of Wealth (War), 1920) should have been a warning that no commonly agreed answer to such questions was likely to emerge.

In the event the whole select committee process took up the best part of a parliamentary year. The amount of evidence presented was large. Like the Tax Credit Select Committee, the Wealth Tax Committee issued a press statement inviting individuals and representative bodies to submit their views. On such an emotive topic as the taxation of wealth much publicity also ensued during the proceedings, and by April 1975 the Committee asked for power to appoint sub-committees so that all the evidence that they required to hear could be taken in the course of the current parliamentary year. This request prompted a rare debate on taxation select committees (HC Debates, 6 May 1975, cols. 1358–9). From 14 May 1975 evidence was taken through sub-committee 'A' which studied the effect of a wealth tax on productive assets, and through sub-committee 'B' which studied its effect on the national heritage. Altogether the Committee took oral evidence from forty-eight representative bodies and from eleven individuals. The Committee had also appointed a specialist adviser, Professor J.R.M. Willis (a former deputy chairman of Inland Revenue) and were able to rely on the work (recently commissioned and published by the Institute for Fiscal Studies) by Professor Willis and others – *An Annual Wealth Tax* (Sandford, Willis and Ironside, 1975).

The number of interest groups giving evidence and their variety was much greater than for the two earlier taxation select committees. The wealth tax proposal drew the attention of many business and private interests and landowning, farming and artistic groups as well. Although many of the bodies that gave evidence were previously in existence and had previously given evidence to other select committees this particular Select Committee actually generated a new pressure group and certainly gave a great boost to what has become known as 'The Heritage Lobby'.

The term 'heritage lobby' is used to cover those representing the interests of owners of historic houses and their associated gardens, pictures and other objects of fine art, and rare books and manuscripts. It may be thought remarkable that a sub-committee had to be set up for the purpose of considering evidence on this topic alone. But the heritage lobby, although not previously so well organised, has always been in the background. In *The Future of Socialism* Anthony Crosland quotes from Sir William Harcourt's Budget speech of 1894 to illustrate how, when capital taxation is proposed, the 'National Heritage' argument is immediately raised:

Large historic mansions provide a pertinent example. The community has a strong interest in their proper upkeep, and the present rate of decay and destruction is appalling.

(Crosland, 1964)

Feeling itself under attack in 1975 by the prospect of a WT the heritage lobby rose to the challenge. In fact just over one-third of the oral submissions to the Committee were primarily concerned with the national heritage and similarly one-third of the sixty-two memoranda received from representative bodies were about the protection of the national heritage. In addition two individuals gave oral evidence and a further half dozen sent letters on the subject.

In bringing together people interested in the maintenance of the 'heritage' and forcing them to articulate their interests and demands in the media, the wealth tax debate ensured that the heritage groups were far better placed to defend their interests in subsequent Finance Bills. One new and influential group was 'Heritage in Danger'. In his letter to the Clerk of the Select Committee, the Secretary (Hugh Leggatt, the art dealer) said:

'Heritage in Danger' is an organisation spontaneously brought into existence by the widespread fears that a wealth tax as that proposed in the Green Paper must inevitably lead to an extensive dispersal overseas of works of art . . . and the destruction of our national heritage generally.

The membership of the Committee, too, represented special interests, especially the Conservative members who were handpicked to represent every sort of interest (from small businesses to the owners of stately homes) that might be affected by the introduction of a WT. Table 6.5 shows the membership and changes in membership of the Committee, and Table 6.6 the sub-committee membership. Table 6.7 shows Members' expertise and interests. The Labour Members (among whom the turnover was high) on the whole had little background expertise in matters of taxation or wealth. Two of them were, it is true, very wealthy men themselves, but neither of these were particularly active in the Committee. The Conservative Members, on the other hand, appear to have been selected with much care. Members of two of Britain's best-known family businesses (the publishers Macmillan and the grocers Sainsbury) were included in the Conservative team, as were representatives of farming and land holding, historic houses and tax law. Because the Labour Party was the Government it was in the same position as the Conservatives had been for CT: it had to field its second eleven. But, in contrast to the Conservative team on CT, which did a competent job on a limited topic, the Labour team for the WT did not play at all well. They really seem to have lacked the will to win. It is notable that on such an 'ideological' topic the Government did not consider it necessary to put on the Select Committee Members who were known to have a strong commitment to a WT. Few of those who served on the Select Committee were other than Labour Party 'moderates'; indeed five are now in the Social Democratic Party. It is surprising that there were not more trade union members or

Table 6.5 Membership of Select Committee on Wealth Tax

Membership of Committee as appointed on 12 December 1974

Labour	*Conservative*	*Liberal*
Guy Barnett	William Clark	John Pardoe
Jeremy Bray	Robert Cooke	
Ray Carter	Ian Gow	
Tam Dalyell	Sir John Hall	
Denzil Davies	Paul Hawkins	
John Horam	Maurice Macmillan	
Douglas Jay	Robert McCrindle	
Mrs Millie Miller	John Nott	
Colin Phipps	Timothy Sainsbury	
John Roper		
Brian Walden		

18 December
Sir John Hall replaced by
Peter Rees

15 January 1975
Guy Barnett replaced by
Robert Kilroy-Silk

17 January
Brian Walden replaced by
Mrs Ann Taylor

24 January
Tam Dalyell replaced by
John Garrett

5 March
Mrs Ann Taylor replaced by
John Cartwright

7 March
John Nott replaced by
Nigel Lawson

21 March
Mrs Millie Miller replaced by
R.B. Cant

27 March
William Clark replaced by
T. Skeet

16 April
Robert McCrindle replaced by
G. Dodsworth

24 June
Denzil Davies replaced by
Neville Sandelson
Robert Kilroy-Silk replaced by
Roderick MacFarquhar

Table 6.6   Sub-committees of the Select Committee on Wealth Tax (appointed on 7 May 1975)

Sub-Committee 'A'	Sub-Committee 'B'
Productive Assets	*National Heritage*
J. Bray	R. Carter
R. Cant[a]	R. Cooke [a]
J. Cartwright	J. Garrett
D. Davies	I. Gow
G. Dodsworth	J. Hawkins
J. Hawkins[b]	D. Jay
J. Horam	R. Kilroy-Silk
D. Jay[b]	M. Macmillan
N. Lawson	J. Pardoe
M. Macmillan[b]	J. Roper
J. Pardoe[b]	T. Skeet
C. Phipps	
P. Rees	
T. Sainsbury	

Notes: [a] Chairman
[b] Members of *both* sub-committees

members of the Tribune Group put onto the Committee. 'The Whips', we were told in interview, 'thought that it was best to put onto the Committee people who were themselves rich.' Thus one explanation of the behaviour of the Government side in this Committee is that, on balance, it was not strongly in favour of the proposal for a WT.

Not only were the Conservative Members on the Committee against the idea of an additive WT and very knowledgeable in the relevant areas, they were also very hard-working. They approached their task in a professional manner. They prepared themselves well for the evidence sessions. They had access to their own specialist assistance. At one time three of the Conservative team had their own research assistants (paid by them) working on the WT more or less full-time. None of the Labour Members had such help, nor did they, as in the case of tax credits, draw upon substantial outside evidence to support their case. As a result of their interest, hard work and good preparation the Conservatives were able to make most of the running in this Committee and were by far its most active members (see Table 6.8). They were able to draw out the witnesses to present just the sort of material that they (the Conservatives) wanted to support their position. Thus they were able to build up an impressive body of information and material to support the view that a WT, unless accompanied by special reliefs and changes in other elements of capital taxation, would have very detrimental effects upon many important areas of British life from woodlands to sculpting.

Table 6.7 Members of the Select Committee on Wealth Tax and their relevant experience

Labour

Douglas Jay (Chairman)	Considerable ministerial experience including Treasury and Board of Trade
Jeremy Bray	Formerly Parliamentary Secretary Ministry of Power and Minister of Technology. Company director
Ray Carter	—
Denzil Davies	Barrister. Member of Select Committee on Corporation Tax
John Horam	Member of Expenditure Committee
Millie Miller	—
Colin Phipps	Director of oil companies
John Roper	Economist. Member of Expenditure Committee
Robert Kilroy-Silk	Graduate in economics. Lecturer in Government. PPS Minister for the Arts 1974–5
John Garrett	Management consultant. Vice-Chairman PLP Trade Group
John Cartwright	—
Robert Cant	Economist
Neville Sandleson	Barrister. Formerly director of publishing companies
Roderick MacFarquhar	—

Conservative

William Clark	Opposition front bench spokesman on economic affairs 1964–6. Chairman of Select Committee on Tax Credit. Accountant and financial director
Robert Cooke	Active in campaigns for preservation of historic buildings
Ian Gow	Solicitor
Paul Hawkins	Chartered surveyor and auctioneer
Maurice Macmillan	Former Chief Secretary to the Treasury. Publisher
Robert McCrindle	Banker. Financial consultant
John Nott	Former Minister of State at the Treasury. Barrister. Director of Warburg 1965–7
Timothy Sainsbury	Director of J. Sainsbury Ltd
Peter Rees	Barrister (tax law). Member of Select Committee on Corporation Tax

Nigel Lawson	Financial journalist
Trevor Skeet	Wide interest in trade and industry
Geoffrey Dodsworth	Company director

Liberal

| John Pardoe | Liberal spokesman on economic affairs. Member of Select Committee on Tax Credit. Company director. Member of London Metal Exchange |

Notes: Members who served for less than two months on the Committee have been omitted from this table
— indicates that the qualifications and experience of the Member do not appear to be of particular relevance to the subject of the Committee's investigations

The Select Committee were unable to agree on a report. In the absence of two Labour members in the final stages of the Committee, the members declined to accept the chairman's draft report, as amended. For this they gave three reasons:

1. the failure to ensure that the suggested wealth tax was 'substitutive' rather than 'additive';
2. the failure to ensure that productive assets, in particular, were protected by a 'ceiling' equivalent to not more than the top marginal rate of income tax; and
3. the lack of recognition of the special dangers of introducing such a tax at a time of high inflation and economic crisis.

In these circumstances, the Committee decided to publish with their proceedings all the draft reports which had been before them, including both the unamended and amended chairman's draft. Thus, there is not one report, but five.

The history of the reports, which indicates the degree of support they obtained, was as follows. At the end of the summer recess the members received a draft report from the Chairman, Mr Douglas Jay. This did not appeal to many members of the Committee, and three other reports were prepared as alternatives to the Chairman's. In the order of events, the Liberal report (submitted by the sole Liberal member on the Committee, Mr John Pardoe) was first proposed in place of the Chairman's draft. It was supported by the Conservatives, and lost only by the casting vote of the Chairman. Then came a report submitted by Dr Jeremy Bray; his support was limited to two Labour colleagues, and it was rejected by a very large majority. Then Mr Maurice Macmillan presented a report for the Conservatives. It was supported by Mr Pardoe and defeated only by the casting vote of the Chairman. Finally,

Table 6.8 Select Committee on Wealth Tax: attendance and participation of Members according to political party

Labour	Attendance (%) (max=20)	Participation score[a]	Conservative	Attendance (%) (max=20)	Participation score[a]	Liberal	Attendance (%) (max=20)	Participation score[a]
D. Jay (Chairman)	100	23.0	P. Rees	100	27.6	J. Pardoe	75	6.3
C. Phipps	60	8.1	M. Macmillan	95	20.5			
R. MacFarquhar	100	5.33	N. Lawson	86	17.2			
J. Bray	45	5.1	T. Sainsbury	95	16.4			
D. Davies	35	5.0	T. H. Skeet	77	9.8			
J. Roper	95	4.7	P. Hawkins	90	9.3			
N. Sandelson	100	4.67	R. Cooke	80	5.3			
R. Carter	15	2.33	W. Clark	62	5.1			
Mrs M. Miller	57	1.75	I. Gow	74	4.9			
J. Garrett	35	1.0	G. Dodsworth	75	4.0			
R. Cant	77	0.9	J. Nott	60	2.57			
J. Horam	60	0.7	R. McCrindle	38	0.2			
J. Cartwright	47	0						
R. Kilroy-Silk	0	0						
Mrs A. Taylor	60	0						

Notes: [a] Average number of questions asked per session attended

In total 2870 questions were asked, of which the Chairman asked 459, the twelve Conservative Members asked 1987, the fourteen Labour Members (excluding the Chairman) asked 330 and the one Liberal Member asked 94.

the Chairman's draft was put to the vote and carried – but only by the Chairman's vote. This report was then considered paragraph by paragraph; at the end of this procedure the amended Chairman's report was voted upon – only to be rejected.

There are three features of particular significance in relation to the contents of these reports: the main areas of disagreement between them, the areas of agreement, and, in particular, those areas where the main reports agree, but differ significantly from the Green Paper.

Tables 6.9 and 6.10 summarise, in comparative form, the views of the five reports and of the Green Paper on the important issues. The summary of Dr Jeremy Bray's report (which received little support, and also expressed no views on a number of matters) has been placed at the bottom of the table so that comparison can more readily be made between the others, hereafter referred to as the 'main' reports.

The disagreement on principles between the reports stems primarily from differences of objectives. The purposes of the wealth tax, as set out in the Green Paper, were twofold: to promote horizontal equity by taking account of the additional taxable capacity conferred by wealth as such over and above any income derived from it and to reduce inequality.

The Green Paper gave little indication of the relative importance to be attached to each objective and, at times, appeared to confuse them. The Chairman's draft report made equity its main objective, but also sought to contribute to a reduction of inequality. The Conservatives' report was concerned almost wholly with equity. The Liberal report accepted equity as the major purpose, and wished the WT to make a limited contribution to reducing inequality, but its distinctive feature was the proposal to use a heavy WT as a means of making big reductions in income tax to stimulate effort and enterprise – an efficiency objective. Finally, Dr Bray's report was concerned only with reducing inequality. The differences in the proposals of the various reports on major issues such as rates of wealth tax, allied changes in income tax and ceiling provisions, all stem from these differences of objective.

But, even from these differences of approach, there emerges one very important element common to the main reports. All see equity (horizontal equity) as the major objective, and all accept the conclusion which logically follows. The investment income surcharge (which attempts to tax the additional taxable capacity conferred by wealth, but does so only imperfectly because it fails to tax wealth that yields no income and taxes only lightly wealth yielding a low income) must be completely replaced by a WT. There is no place for both. No continental country with a WT also has a surcharge. This, in turn, implied that the threshold needed to be brought down from the £100,000 proposed by the Green Paper to something like £30,000. On the need for such a change, the difference between the main reports is only one of timing and forthrightness of language. The Inland Revenue opposed this reduction of the threshold wholly on administrative grounds.

A comparison of details shows much in common between the main reports and some significant differences between them and the Green Paper. The elements of agreement and disagreement can be traced out in the tables.

Several conclusions of interest emerge from this detailed analysis.

1. The main reports all differed in substantial ways from the Green Paper. Sending tax proposals to select committees is no rubber stamp.

2. Although there was no agreed report from the select committee, as might have been expected given the nature of the subject matter, there was a considerable measure of agreement in principle on many of the complex technical issues and also a wide measure of agreement on what should be the main objective of the tax.

3. From the recommendations of the main reports (and their divergence from the Green Paper) it is clear that many interest groups were very effective in putting their cases, most notably the heritage lobby.

Finally, there is the question of whether or not the Wealth Tax Select Committee was a 'success'. The answer to this question depends entirely upon what is judged to be a 'successful' select committee. As we have pointed out above (p. 171), it is often suggested that to be successful select committees must reach consensus and produce an agreed report. If they do not then the House is unlikely to take them very seriously. But the experience of select committees suggests that many have, in the past, produced agreed reports which have been ignored and left on shelves to collect dust. When, however, a select committee is given a pre-legislative rather than purely investigatory task the conditions for success are somewhat different. Success means agreeing to some small adjustments to Government plans that will improve the subsequent legislation – as in the case of the Corporation Tax Select Committee. For this sort of success to be achieved, however, a government has first to have a completely firm commitment to the general form of the legislation that it is going to introduce, and secondly it must ask a select committee to perform a specific and well-defined task. Under such a model of select committee function, therefore, the Select Committee on the Wealth Tax, like the Select Committee on Tax Credit could not be judged a success. It was given a task which precluded the possibility of 'success' in these terms.

Table 6.9 Wealth tax: comparison of Green Paper and Select Committee Reports – main principle

	Personal tax unit	Threshold of liability	Rates of wealth tax	Reductions of income tax (and other taxes)
Green Paper	Left open whether married couples should be taxed separately or together. Minor children to be aggregated with parents.	£100,000. Higher for husband and wife if aggregated.	Illustrative scales A — Taxable wealth £000s % 1st 400 1 Next 1500 1½ Next 3000 2 Excess 2½ B — Taxable wealth £000s % 1st 200 1 Next 200 2 Next 1500 3 Next 3000 4 Excess 5	Possible investment income surcharge allowed as offset to wealth tax. Possible reduction of 'high rates of tax on earned income'.
Chairman's draft unamended (9+C:9)	'Quotient system' for husband and wife (twice the tax on half the aggregate on wealth). Minor children to be aggregated with parents, but a modest allowance for each child.	£100,000 – but reduction of threshold over time to eliminate investment income surcharge. Threshold should be kept under regular review.	As scale A of Green Paper, but with wealth under £500,000 taxed AT ½%.	Investment income surcharge should be offset against wealth tax. Objective to reduce threshold and discard surcharge. The 'hope' expressed that income tax reductions will prove possible.
Chairman's draft amended (8:10)	As Chairman's draft.	As Chairman's draft.	As Chairman's draft.	As Chairman's draft except that reduction in income tax 'should be made'.
Liberal Draft (Mr John Pardoe) (9:9+C)	As Chairman's draft.	£30,000 – so as to eliminate the investment income surcharge. Threshold and rate bands should be indexed.	Taxable wealth £000s % 1st 20 1 Next 50 1½ Next 400 2 Excess 2½	Abolition of investment income surcharge. Income tax reduced maximum rate of (Incomes policy to prevent bonanza to high income receivers).
Conservative draft (9:9+C)	Quotient system. If CTT remains unchanged the wealth of minor children should not be aggregated with parents.	About £30,000 – so as to eliminate the investment income surcharge.	Proportion at a rate of between ½ and 1%.	Abolition of investment income surcharge. Income tax reduced maximum rate of Abolition of capital gains tax.
Dr Jeremy Bray's draft (3:15)	Aggregation of husband and wife. Minor children aggregated with parents.	£100,000	Scale B of Green Paper.	Investment income surcharge should be offset against wealth tax.

Note: Figures in brackets below heading of draft reports indicate voting. C stands for chairman.

Ceiling provisions	Special treatment for private business	Special treatment for agriculture	National heritage (heritage objects and historic houses)
Possible ceiling related to income. Alternatively, form of ceiling might take account of yield.	Possibly allowed to defer payment until sale, retirement or death (with interest at commercial rates. which could also be deferred).	Possibly allowed to defer payment until sale, retirement or death (with interest at commercial rates, which could also be deferred).	Possibly allowed to defer payment (with or without interest) subject to public access.
A progressive income-related ceiling (possibly over 100% of income of very wealthy). Should also be a 'floor' to liability.	Rejection of deferment. If no general ceiling, one for productive assets desirable. Reduction of liability where tax-payer's wealth consists mainly of his business (e.g. 1% reduction of tax for every 1% by which business assets exceed 50% of wealth.	Besides provisions as for private businesses, owner-occupied land should be valued at a multiple of rental value (as for CTT). Some further relief or exemption for forestry.	Wealth tax on works of art deferred until sold to a private person and not payable at all if retained until owner's death. Deferred liability restricted to (say) six years. Deferment similarly with historic houses except that on death or gift, wealth tax payable for six years back. Concessions subject to (flexible) conditions for public access.
As Chairman's draft, but without mention of possibility of ceiling over 100%	As Chairman's draft.	As Chairman's draft.	As Chairman' draft, except that one year is substituted for six years. Also where tax-payer is the initial purchaser of a work of art of a living artist, valuation for wealth tax should remain fixed at level of initial purchase in hands of initial purchaser.
No general ceiling provisions (but special ceiling for owners of productive assets.)	As Chairman's draft. Also special ceiling restricted as to frequency (or tax holiday) to allow for new business or older businesses going through a bad patch.	As Chairman's draft plus provisions for private businesses.	Exemption of heritage objects and historic houses subject to (flexible) conditions for public access.
Ceiling in range 0% to 75%.	Rejection of deferment. General proposals adequate to protect productive assets. If these not accepted in full, then concessionary valuation and deductibility of wealth tax from income tax liability.	Rejection of deferment. Favourable valuation of agricultural land. Concession to apply to landlords as well as owner-occupiers. Exemption for forestry and woodlands.	Exemption of heritage objects and historic houses subject to (flexible) conditions for public access. Exemption of funds set aside for maintaining heritage.
None.	None, except for deferred payment (as in Green Paper) at compound commercial rates of interest (establishment of a public agency receiving payment in kind and providing venture capital.)	None.	No exemption; works of art accepted in payment of tax. Revenue from works of art devoted to spending on the national heritage.

	Scope of charge	Trusts	Household effects	Owner-occupied houses
Green Paper	(a) *Resident or domiciled* Charge on world wide assets. (b) *Resident and ordinarily resident but not domiciled* Charge on UK assets. (c) *Other cases* Charge on UK land and permanent establishments.	*Straightforward trusts* Attribution of whole of trust funds to life tenant. *Discretionary trusts* Charge calculated by reference to settler's circumstances, if alive; possible relief by reference to payments. In both cases payment to be made by trustees from trust assets.	Exemption up to certain value of aggregate personal and domestic property.	Taxable.
Chairman's draft unamended	As Green Paper except that where a person is resident and domiciled. but not ordinarily resident, he should be included in category (b) instead of category (a).	Green Paper, as modified by Inland Revenue, by which charge on discretionary trusts should be calculated to greatest extent possible by reference to circumstances of beneficiaries.	Exemption of individual items below £1000 (between £1000 and £2000 value chargeable limited to twice excess over £1000).	Taxable.
Chairman's draft amended	As chairman's draft.	Liability of trust should be that which would arise if a proportion of trust capital corresponding to proportion of trust income received by each beneficiary belonged to the beneficiary absolutely. Payments to be made by trustees from trust assets.	As Chairman's draft.	Taxable.
Liberal draft (Mr John Pardoe)	As Chairman's draft.	As Chairman's draft.	As Chairman's draft.	Taxable.
Conservative draft	As Chairman's draft.	Position simplified by the proposal for proportionate wealth tax. The threshold attributed to individual should be conceded to aggregate assets settled by one settler and attributed proportionately among trusts. Payments to be made by trustees from trust assets.	Exempt irrespective of value.	Exempt.
Dr Jeremy Bray's draft	Special provisions, as necessary, to restrain the movement of capital abroad.	—	As Green Paper.	Taxable.

Note: — indicates no comment made on the topic

Occupational pension rights	Patents, copyrights	Deductions	Administration	Compliance requirements
Exempt.	Taxable.	Debts relating to exempt assets not allowed as a deduction. (Inland Revenue also accepted that tax due or assessed but not yet paid should be deductible.)	New regional organisation. Separate return from income tax.	Full self-valuation and self assessment. Selective examination by Revenue (audit). Re-opening of accounts subject to six year limit, with interest at a commercial rate on tax underpaid (where no fraud).
Only chargeable where they can be valued with reasonable confidence and should attract a lower rate of tax.	Exempt in hands of author or inventor. Artist's stock of own works also exempt. Otherwise taxable.	Contingent liability to development land tax should be allowed as a deduction.	Accept Green Paper proposals 'with some reluctance'. Arrangements to be kept under review. If threshold lowered balance of advantage might shift to administration with income tax.	Work of valuation eased if capital valuation adopted for dwellings. No (or low) interest where tax underpaid because of erroneous (but honest) valuation. Special relief for valuation expenses.
Chargeable, but subject to relief by partial exemption. Concessionary valuation or a lower rate of tax.	As Chairman's draft.	Taxes in respect of past events which should become payable in the future should be deductible. Contingent liabilities to capital gains tax and development land tax should be deductible.	As Chairman's draft.	As Chairman's draft.
Charged at a lower rate; or wealth tax relief for those over retirement age related to size of pension, such that the higher the pension the less the relief.	As Chairman's draft.	As Chairman's draft.	Wealth tax administred from income tax offices. Single return for wealth tax and income tax.	As Chairman's draft.
Taxable on a proportion of their values on the assumption that the employee will retire on wealth tax valuation day (subject to appeal on grounds of ill-health).	As Chairman's draft.	Capital gains tax, development gains tax, development land tax and stamp duty, which would be paid on the realisation of each asset on the valuation date, should be deductible.	Introduction of wealth tax should be deferred until Inland Revenue has been able to devise a satisfactory method of administration.	Inland Revenue must challenge or accept a self-assessment within twelve months. Assessment should be re-opened only in cases of fraud or wilful default. Emphasis should be on conventional valuations. Valuations should be quinquennial.
—	—	—	—	As Green Paper.

But there may be other criteria by which a select committee that is asked to look at a government's pre-legislative proposals may be judged a success. If a government is not quite sure that it does want to do something, or if it thinks that it wants to do something but is not clear as to how to do it, or what its effects might be, then a successful select committee could be one that helps it to postpone or terminate ill-conceived plans. In these terms, the Select Committee on the Wealth Tax could be judged a success. The history of the origins of the WT reveals that the Labour Party (or at least the governmental arm of the party) had only a weak commitment to the idea. Certainly the idea of a WT had long been 'in the air' in Labour Party circles. The Labour 'moderate' Crosland (1964) suggested that a WT be introduced, but his idea was only a very general one. It was intended to have rather different results from the proposals that eventually emerged from the NEC and the TUC who extracted from the Government a promise to enact a wealth tax in exchange for agreement to the 'Social Contract' (incomes policy). The idea of a wealth tax was a convenient rhetorical point which could be used with dramatic effect by Ministers (Callaghan, Healey, etc.) in speeches to show solidarity with the TUC.

But to put the rhetoric into practice was obviously going to be much more complicated than the advocates of a wealth tax (who had made no detailed proposals as to its form) thought. The Select Committee revealed the many complications and effects of wealth taxation. A select committee provides a public forum for the display of the effects of a tax on particular groups in society. It brings out for public use what otherwise would only be circulated privately between interest groups and government. The effect of the Committee's deliberations was to make it difficult for the Government immediately to introduce legislation without considering its effects on particular groups. They did not, in any case, have a sufficient majority to push through legislation that did not appeal to the 'moderates' in the party. By the end of the 1974–9 Parliament the Social Contract was in ruins and so was incomes policy and therefore the Government no longer had to worry too much about keeping its side of the bargain. The Wealth Tax Select Committee can therefore, from some points of view, be regarded as a success because it showed that there was no clear answer to the questions that were before it, that the Government itself had not worked out the basic nature of the wealth that it was hoping to tax, and that any such tax would have to accommodate all sorts of interests and might produce so many concessions and reliefs as to be virtually negated in effect. Since the Government itself did not see the wealth tax as one of its major priorities of policy, the lack of any clear direction from the Select Committee helped it stall on the issue. Following the 'failure' of the Select Committee the Government joined with the TUC (at its urging) in a joint committee to examine the question of a WT further. But this committee did little and no further substantial moves were made to implement this particular reform.

However, should a future Government decide to proceed with a WT it can call to its aid the very substantial work contained in the evidence and reports of the Select Committee.

General conclusions

Following the experiments of the 1970s with the use of select committees to consider new tax legislation, there have been continued proposals for a more 'open' tax policy-making process to be the rule rather than the exception. Sir Geoffrey Howe in a speech to the Addington Society, 16 February 1977, made a plea for more 'open' tax policy-making. 'The first motto of any Chancellor should be "to consult now and draft later".' He suggested that there should be an exposure draft published in advance of a Bill's first reading which would afford an opportunity for interested and informed parties to make representations before it reached Parliament. Significant changes in the structure and shape of the tax system should always be foreshadowed by Green or White Papers or by draft bills. A select committee stage could perhaps be interposed, before, or after, principles had been considered in conventional standing committee, or proposals might be remitted to a regularly appointed select committee with special and continuous responsibility for the tax system.

On the other hand the experience of select committees on taxation reveals some of the dangers that lurk in 'open' committee stages and pre-legislative investigation, especially for a Government that wants to introduce new taxes to which it is committed for ideological rather than for administrative or revenue-raising reasons. The three *ad hoc* select committees veered towards the American experience of pre-legislative committees that open up new avenues for the influence of pressure groups. 'Open' tax policy-making through the use of select committees brings the demands of groups more clearly into the process of shaping taxes. Parliamentary committees provide a splendid public forum – which may also attract the attention of the press – in which groups can articulate their views. Even if select committees are not themselves all powerful in the tax policy process they are *public* which is what interest groups like about them. Any Government that practises 'open' tax policy-making and yet still wants to stick to its principles will have continually to resist the demands of interest groups for concessions and reliefs if it is to attain its primary objectives. In Chapter 7 we shall explore further the processes of consultation between government and interest groups in the shaping of tax legislation.

7 The Consultative Process, Public Debate and Pressure Groups

Introduction

The 'standard' or 'classic' view of the role of pressure or interest groups in the British political system is that they tend to converge on the departments during the formulation and drafting stages of legislation and that they are less active at the parliamentary stages than are their American counterparts. Stuart Walkland has suggested that:

The most effective time for groups to operate is after a decision to legislate has been taken, but before a Bill has actually been drafted and published.

(Walkland, 1968, p. 38)

He further suggests that:

The extent of the Government's consultation with groups is a function not of its political weakness, but of its political strength. Secure in its monopoly of political authority, the Government can afford to consult group and parliamentary opinion widely, knowing that, ultimately, its view of the matter can be made to prevail. Consultation is ordinarily undertaken not because a government or department is weak or insecure, but in order to gain for a policy the widest possible consent before initiating the formal legislative procedures.

(Walkland, 1968, p. 42)

Where government has a firm commitment to legislate, the purpose of consultation from the government's point of view is to obtain consent; also, through the provision of information from groups, the consultation process can assist in the design of the form of legislation – but it cannot alter its principles or purpose. If this model of the role of groups and consultation is correct then the level of consultation is likely to be low and limited, for there is little apparently to be gained by the groups themselves if they cannot obtain substantial concessions or reliefs.

But this is only one view of the role of groups in the policy-making process. Other views assign a very different role to interest and pressure groups and evaluate the consultative process in a very different light. Theories of the political process that see policies as the outcome of group interaction conclude that groups wield real power. They, not the government, which merely acts as broker, determine the shape of policies. Groups, in this model, join in the consultative process because they expect to gain concessions and reliefs if they press their case effectively. If this model is more accurate than the 'classic' model of the role of groups in the British policy-making process, we should expect to see relatively high levels of group activity and extensive consultation.

Some group theorists go further than the simple statement that policy is shaped by groups and suggest that some groups are more powerful and effective than others. Olson (1965) argues that pressure groups have a differential effect on policy outcomes which is dependent upon their size and the extent to which they concentrate their efforts on clearly focused targets. Groups that keep their size, their aims, and their general ambitions in check, he argues, are *relatively* more successful in influencing outcomes than are the large amorphous groups (such as the TUC) which get their fingers into just about every policy that the government initiates. Wootton (1970) argues that in the mixed economy business groups appear indispensible to governments of whatever ideological disposition, because they, unlike trade unions, are ultimately responsible for production. This, he argues, is the root of business influence over policy (p. 95). Producer groups have sanctions: in the case of tax policy if taxation is too harsh production will fall.

Which of these two contrasting views of the role of consultation and the influence of groups on policy fits the case of tax policy-making in Britain? Are pressure groups brought into the process simply to gain consent for the government's measures or do they enter the process in order to obtain benefits, reliefs and concessions for themselves? Can groups, through the process of consultation, exert power or influence to make governments change their minds or introduce legislation of a different nature from that originally intended? How far is the activity and role of interest groups determined by the channels that are available to them? Have changes in the government's structures for consultation altered the behaviour of groups and encouraged their participation?

As we have already seen, at every stage in the process of tax policy-making – as policy is developed in the political parties, shaped in the departments and scrutinised in Parliament – external influences of various sorts are brought into play and may have some effect.

The consultation process

Growth of informal consultation
Informal consultation is a continuous process in tax policy because, unlike other policy areas, there must, by law, be a Finance Bill every year. By 1977 some eighty representative bodies were submitting Budget representations addressed to the Chancellor of the Exchequer or the Board of Inland Revenue, and Customs and Excise also received some annual pre-Budget submissions. Besides trade and professional bodies, submissions are regularly made from pressure groups such as Age Concern, Child Poverty Action Group, the English Tourist Board

and the Historic Houses Association. A number of those submitting written comment regularly discuss their Budget representations with the Inland Revenue: the Association of British Chambers of Commerce, the CBI, the Consultative Committee of Accountancy Bodies (CCAB), the Law Society and the Law Society of Scotland. In 1976 and 1977 the Bank of England coordinated the representations of a group of banks and other financial institutions and bodies concerned with trade and finance (e.g. the Committee for Invisible Exports and the National Association of Pension Funds) and arranged one meeting with the Inland Revenue in 1976 and two in 1977.

These written representations and meetings before the annual Budget are only incidentally concerned with new taxes; and the same is true of the submissions from the CBI, CCAB and others on the actual contents of the Finance Bill and the sometimes extensive series of meetings that follows. However, the growing practice of regular consultations has embedded the habit into pressure group behaviour, and they will respond to most government initiatives. On new taxes, submissions are generally made after the announcement of the intention to introduce a new tax or after a statement of the tax itself. The extent of consultations on new taxes increased greatly with the change in approach signified by Green Papers, and was on an unprecedented scale with VAT. For example, Dorothy Johnstone records that discussions had taken place with trade organisations about the introduction of purchase tax in 1940, though they were curtailed by war exigencies. This enforced curtailment apart, there were other important differences between purchase tax and VAT:

> In 1940 there was no Green Paper on sale from the Stationery Office to any purchaser and containing an open invitation to express views; Customs and Excise decided which trade organisations needed to be consulted about purchase tax and approached them direct and separately, tailoring the approaches to their special interests. In 1971, in contrast, it was part of the official philosophy that the consultations about VAT should be as little restricted or influenced by official preconceptions as they possibly could be.
>
> (Johnstone, 1975)

As we have already noted (p. 97), although sheer numbers are no indication of the weight of opinion expressed, between March 1971 and March 1972 views on the 'machinery' of VAT were received from over 800 different trade and professional organisations and meetings (sometimes more than one) were arranged with over 300 of them. Also, from quite an early stage in the preparation of VAT, Customs and Excise officials accepted invitations from trade and professional bodies to talk and be questioned about it.

Another form of consultation has also grown up in recent years – between the Revenue authorities and experts. In either an old tax or a new an important part of a proposal may concern an area of the economy where the law and/or practice is particularly specialised and recondite. In such circumstances consultations are held with the representative body of the particular field either before legislation is drafted or at the draft clause stage, so that the Finance Bill presented to Parliament may be accurate. An example is on aspects of life assurance, where the Life Officers' Association might be consulted. The consent of a Treasury Minister is always obtained for such meetings.

Green and White Papers

Green Papers are a recent innovation to provide a convenient focus for consultation and discussion. They were invented by the Labour Government in 1967 (Pliatzky, 1982). White Papers are of much earlier vintage. It is generally held that 'White Papers announce firm government policy for implementation. Green Papers announce tentative proposals for discussion' (Pemberton, 1969). Sir Harold Wilson wrote:

> A White Paper is essentially a statement of government policy in such terms that withdrawal or major amendment following consultation or public debate, tends to be regarded as a humiliating withdrawal. A Green Paper represents the best that the government can propose on the given issue, but, remaining uncommitted, it is able without loss of face to leave its final decision open until it has been able to consider the public reaction to it.

(Wilson, 1971)

As applied to taxation these distinctions are at best over-simplifications. All the taxes with which we are particularly concerned (except the TC scheme and WT which have not been implemented) were the subject of White Papers. Some were the subject of Green Papers, and Green Papers were also issued on regional employment premium (REP) which was the first such 'Green' paper (Pliatzky, 1982), and on other tax possibilities (inheritance tax and reform of local taxation) which were not pursued by the government of the day. Where Green Papers were not issued the proposals of the White Papers were often subject to change on major issues. Thus, with SET the treatment of charities, agriculture and mining was all changed within a fortnight of the publication of the White Paper, whilst with CTT a lower rate for life-time gifts was adopted during the passage of the Finance Bill in direct contradiction to the White Paper. On the other hand important elements in some of the Green Papers were presented as 'hard' (see Table 7.1). As Grant Jordan (1977) puts it: 'One believes that one knows the difference between White Papers, Green Papers and their kin, but under close examination they often tend to merge to a uniform grey.' (p. 30).

Analysis of Green Papers

Despite this confusion of colour it can be accepted that a Green Paper is intended as a discussion document with some matters deliberately left open by the government. As such it particularly invites submission from interested parties in an open fashion before the legislation is actually drafted. Table 7.1 attempts to classify all the tax Green Papers before 1976 (whether or not they relate to the taxes with which we are particularly concerned), primarily according to the degree of government commitment. It can be seen that the pattern is immensely variegated. At one extreme is the Green Paper on Local Government Finance which contained neither government commitment nor practical proposals of a kind which might be the subject of meaningful debate. At the same end of the spectrum is the Inheritance Tax Green Paper which, whilst avoiding commitment, did present certain practical alternatives. At the other extreme the Corporation Tax Green Paper excluded discussion of the principle of the change, as did the VAT Green Paper, but left open certain issues of implementation. The most recent of these Green Papers, on WT, apart from the commitment to the tax, was compatible with either a very heavy additional tax burden on the wealthy or indeed simply a rearrangement and possible reduction of tax burdens if income tax reductions and ceiling provisions accompanied a WT. There can be very different WTs for different purposes, and the Green Paper never spelt out the objectives with sufficient clarity. This deficiency doubtless reflected the lack of work and thought, and the ambivalence towards the tax, at the party level (p. 208).

Why no Green Paper for CTT?

Although since the first Green Paper on taxation (REP, 1967) new tax proposals have generally been accompanied by Green Papers, this has not been an invariable practice. Development Gains Tax and Development Land Tax were not so accompanied nor was Petroleum Revenue Tax. These taxes may be regarded as outside the main stream of taxation and have not been our particular concern. More significantly, CTT was not accorded Green Paper treatment.

Mr Joel Barnett, Chief Secretary to the Treasury, explained in an article in the *Financial Times* (12 March 1975) why there was neither Green Paper nor select committee on CTT. The Labour Government had to make the tax operative from the date of the Chancellor's first budget to avoid forestalling – i.e. gifts that would avoid the new tax. 'Then' Mr Barnett writes

Once the tax was announced and operative we had to get the provision for it on the statute book as quickly as possible. We should have liked to have dealt with it in the same way as the wealth tax and had a Green Paper and a parliamentary select committee before legislation was prepared. But circumstances simply did not allow this.

The argument is not wholly convincing. It is arguable whether the danger of forestalling required the Government to make the tax operative so soon after its arrival in power. The detriment from forestalling has to be set against the inconvenience, inequity and possible economic harm arising from hasty legislation. (For example, the Finance Act following the enactment of CTT contained improved reliefs for agriculture and new reliefs for private businesses. Presumably, with more time for consultation and reflection, these reliefs would have been contained in the original Act; those whose farms or businesses became subject to CTT before the change have good reason for feeling aggrieved, and there may also have been economic damage.) Once the decision was taken to apply the new tax from the date of the Chancellor's first Budget, it is still arguable that a Green Paper would have been possible; but it would have meant the Inland Revenue preparing both Green Paper and legislation at the same time. The White Paper of 8 August 1974, which preceded the CTT legislation introduced in the autumn of that year, as we have already noted, was changed in one major respect, the treatment of lifetime gifts, by amendment during the passage of the Act. A Green Paper, inviting representations (which the White Paper did not) might have enabled the Government to have reached a firm decision in advance of the CTT Finance Bill and saved parliamentary time; but the Bill would almost certainly have had to be brought in somewhat later.

Some conclusions and problems

Informal consultations between the revenue departments and trade associations and other representative bodies, whether or not a Green Paper is issued, can considerably improve the form of new taxes. As Dorothy Johnstone records on VAT:

The amounts of education, advice and assistance we received from representative bodies were immense . . . we were in no doubt whatever about their usefulness in total to us as tax administrators. (1975)

VAT, as a major departure from anything hitherto attempted by Customs and Excise, was perhaps exceptional. Even so, Inland Revenue or Customs and Excise cannot be expected to have detailed knowledge of the commercial practices of thousands of traders and professions to enable them to get right, by themselves, the operational details of new taxes.

However, there are a number of difficulties associated with the consultation process, as Mrs Johnstone has shown from the discussions on VAT (Johnstone, 1975).

Table 7.1 *Analysis of Green Papers on taxation*

Date	Green Paper	Degree of commitment	Main departmental source	Changes resulting from discussion	General comment
April 1967	A proposal for a Regional Employment Premium.	The wording of the GP nominally left the whole issue open: but the tone suggested a fairly strongly held intention to introduce. Precise details.	Treasury and Department of Economic Affairs	No major changes.	Not a command paper. Previously sent as a memorandum to NEDC and Regional Planning Councils.
March 1971	Reform of Corporation Tax. Cmnd 4630	Firm commitment to 'remove the discrimination against distributed profits'.	Inland Revenue	Government had favoured split rate system. As a result of consultation the imputation system was chosen instead.	The abandonment of the classical system was not open to discussion. Significant contribution of Select Committee.
March 1971	Value Added Tax. Cmnd 4621	Firm decision to introduce VAT to replace SET and purchase tax. Details illustrative and indicative.	Customs and Excise	Many of the details determined as a result of consultation. Late changes on scope of zero rating as a result of press and other pressure.	Much of the GP was taken up in explaining how a VAT worked.
July 1971	The Future Shape of Local Government Finance. Cmnd 4741	None. No clear proposals.	Treasury	n.a.	Very vague GP reviewing possible alternative sources of local government finance and displaying the

Date	Title	Recommendations	Origin	Government response	Remarks
October 1972	Proposals for a Tax Credit Scheme. Cmnd 5116	Nominally the decision of principle was left open but the government 'commended the proposals.' Fairly precise in administrative details. Some important issues specifically left open (e.g. to whom child credits should be paid).	Interdepartmental Group (Arthur Cockfield author of the proposals)	Government accepted important changes of detail as a result of recommendation of Select Committee.	Costed options included. Estimates of administrative savings. Figures of benefits illustrative.
March 1972	Taxation of Capital on Death: a possible Inheritance Tax in place of Estate Duty. Cmnd 4930	None. But some fairly detailed alternative proposals included.	Inland Revenue	n.a.	
August 1974	Wealth Tax Cmnd 5704	To the principle of a wealth tax, but little else. Various degrees of 'hardness' amongst other suggestions.	Inland Revenue	n.a.	No majority report of Select Committee but considerable common ground amongst main reports differing in important ways from emphasis of GP.

1. Doubts arose about the status of the consultation documents issued by Customs and Excise to trade associations. There was a tendency on the part of the trading public to assume that the contents were 'harder' than was in fact so, and therefore a demand arose for a much wider circulation than was intended. Not only would this have been expensive in resources (requests were received for fifty or a hundred copies of a lengthy document) but, more seriously, it would have spread misleading impressions.

2. Problems of communication were apparent not only between Customs and Excise and trade associations but also within the trade associations. Permanent officials or committee Members do not necessarily accurately reflect the views of ordinary Members. Unless sufficient time is allowed for associations to consult their own membership the views presented to Customs and Excise may be idiosyncratic or reflect, say, only the larger organisations.

3. It is particularly difficult to find a place in the consultative process for the 'small man', who typically does not belong to a trade association but who has to operate a tax such as VAT.

4. Complications arose as a result of Budget secrecy. Traders wished to know whether their accounting system, say, should provide for one rate of tax or two – but this was a Budget decision.

5. Difficulties arose on the interface between the consultations and the responsibility of the executive for presenting its proposed courses of action to Parliament. Members of Parliament sought copies of consultation documents which, had they been provided, might have led to misleading conclusions. This difficulty is less likely to arise when the process of consultation takes place through the medium of a select committee of the House.

Some of these difficulties that became apparent with VAT might be expected to resolve themselves once both revenue departments and the interested public became more accustomed to the consultative process; but this is unlikely to happen with them all. In particular, unless some deliberate effort is made, Green Papers are unlikely to elicit the view of the 'small man' or the general public. The 'corporate view' is likely to predominate. Tax is a technical subject. Response to a Green Paper may need to be properly researched and presented. Only 'corporate' bodies have the access to such expertise. Other problems arise in relation to practice with respect to Green Papers. As we have seen, they may or may not be issued in respect of a new tax. A starting-point for improvement would be a commitment by government to undertake to issue a Green Paper as a matter of invariable practice whenever a new tax was being seriously considered. But, in the light of experience, the form and content of Green Papers also need to be more carefully considered if they are to serve their purpose effectively. Whilst they need not all follow the same pattern, some guidelines on composition would be useful. The following conclusions may be drawn from the experience of tax Green Papers to 1976.

1. If a Green Paper is to generate useful discussion, it probably must contain either some degree of commitment by government, or at least some proposals which are sufficiently serious and precise for people to get their teeth into (even though they need not be 'hard').

2. The objectives of a Green Paper need to be clarified and the contents related to the objectives. Dorothy Johnstone (1975) suggests that the VAT Green Paper fell somewhat between the stools of a document 'for general public discussion' and a consultative document for trade associations.

3. Where a government commits itself to the principle of a new tax, but leaves open almost everything else (as with WT) a Green Paper needs to meet certain criteria if it is to lead to the most meaningful discussion. These criteria might be summarised as follows:

(a) Clear objectives so that the details may be considered in the light of the purposes.
(b) An adequate perspective on the new tax (e.g. the new tax needs to be presented in the context of related taxes, and possibly of foreign experience).
(c) Analysis of economic and social consequences. (At least the possibilities need to be indicated.)
(d) Costed options so that a realistic choice can be made between alternative features or procedures.
(e) An estimate not only of revenue yield, but of the likely compliance and administrative costs.
(f) An indication of transitional provisions (where appropriate).

The WT Green Paper signally failed to meet these criteria.

It may be that these criteria are not met for political reasons, e.g. that a government does not wish to include possible economic consequences in a Green Paper, like the one on WT, because they may appear damaging to the idea of having such a tax at all and therefore cast doubt on the wisdom of a commitment already entered into.

This raises the question of how far a Green Paper is a party political document; how far is it presenting the options objectively, how far making a case? Some forms of Green Paper might be better produced, at government request and expense, by a body that is politically neutral rather than by officials in the name of government Ministers.

It is clear that although in the period we are studying we had seven Green Papers on new taxes, the ideal form and coverage has still to be found. Ironically, many observers thought the seventh was 'the greenest yet'.

It may be that there is a case for two kinds of Green Paper. One would be a document that sets the scene for a general discussion on a possible tax reform. The government might commission the study, rather than undertake it itself, but it would be published by the government which would provide the facilities for discussion. This document would endeavour, in as impartial a way as possible, to meet all the criteria listed above.

Secondly, there could be a Green Paper (which could follow the first kind) where the government committed itself to a tax, with objectives clearly spelt out so that much of the consequential detail would necessarily follow. Important issues would, however, be left open to be determined in the light of discussion.

Consultation via extra-parliamentary committees and commissions

Apart from committees within the political parties, and those within the internal structure of government, such as departmental or inter-departmental committees whose membership is confined to civil servants and Ministers, committees or commissions may be set up as part of the consultative machinery in the widest sense – concerned, at least in part, to receive and consider the views of a wider public. These committees are called into being by and largely controlled by the government itself. They vary from the relatively informal to the formal, from the *ad hoc* to the continuing, from the relatively humble to the grand, from the small to the large. They may be concerned only to receive, in confidence, the professional opinions of tax specialists or they may wish to tap as wide a range of views as possible.

During the period of our study there were no Royal Commissions on taxation; the previous Royal Commission had been set up by the Labour Party in 1951 and issued its Final Report in 1955. The Layfield Committee, an External Departmental Committee, not differing significantly from a Royal Commission except in being less grand, sat and reported during this period on Local Government Finance (including the future of rates and the possibilities of a local income tax). No action resulted from its recommendations. It did not cover the areas of our particular interest in this study.

The committees that were established and were at least peripherally concerned with the taxes on our agenda were *ad hoc* working parties of revenue officials and representatives of professional bodies, the so-called Tax Reform Committee, the Richardson Committee on VAT and the TUC/Labour Party Working Party on a Wealth Tax (considered in the next section on organised pressure groups).

The *ad hoc* working parties are examples of department sponsored consultation in which the government itself invites opinion from experts and interested parties. The meetings that the revenue officials may hold with the representatives of a major trade association or a professional body in the kind of consultations on a new tax outlined in the previous section have distinct similarities to these working parties. *Ad hoc* working parties of revenue officials, representatives of professional bodies, in particular the accountancy bodies and the CBI, are often set up. In the early 1970s there were four or five of these groups in existence at any one time, concerned with the practical working out of tax legislation. They related to new taxes in the sense that they examined how a particular section of the legislation was working, e.g. they examined the roll-over provision and retirement reliefs of CGT, to see if there were anomalies.

The Tax Reform Committee, in principle if not in origin, might be regarded as a further extension of the working party concept. The Committee was set up in response to the widespread demand amongst professional organisations in the later 1960s for tax simplification (p. 14). In 1969 the President of the Institute of Chartered Accountants in England and Wales led a deputation to see the Chancellor, Mr Jenkins, about the need for simplification of the tax system. The Institute apparently hoped for the establishment of a standing committee of the House of Commons to look at tax reform. The outcome was the setting up of the so-called Tax Reform Committee under the auspices of the Inland Revenue.

Whilst the activities of the Committee were never publicised and its deliberations were strictly confidential its existence was made known through a written parliamentary question and answer:

Tax System (Simplification)
Mr Sheldon asked the Chancellor of the Exchequer what steps he is now taking to meet representations which have been made to him for the simplification of the tax system.
Mr Roy Jenkins The Board of Inland Revenue and a group of people professionally concerned from a tax-payer's point of view are already holding informal consultations about these problems. It is likely that the consultations will take some time as the problems are difficult and complex
(HC Debates, 15 December 1969, WA col. 237)

Besides revenue officials the Committee consisted of several accountants, tax lawyers and two members of the CBI. Although nominated by the respective institutions in the first instance, membership was essentially on an individual basis. There was no reporting back to institutions.

The Committee spent considerable time initially on the issue of tax simplification and some half dozen papers were submitted to the Chancellor. Thereafter the Reform Committee* settled for a more generally advisory role. It did not, as a matter of course, study each new tax proposal. Its purposes were seen to be mainly two: to act as a sounding board for ideas of the Inland Revenue and of the government in advance of publication and to think ahead about tax issues and discuss some of them in detail. Items discussed included the taxation of benefits in kind, possible changes in the law on foreign employments, and, with respect to new taxes, reform of death duties, a reform which ultimately emerged as a capital transfer tax.

Both the *ad hoc* working parties and the Tax Reform Committee are a recognition of the need to associate the practitioner with details of possible legislation before the Finance Bill stage. The methods are not wholly satisfactory. *Ad hoc* working parties lack continuity whilst the Tax Reform Committee was the subject of a number of criticisms from its non-Revenue members. One critic complained that the Committee was too much controlled by the Inland Revenue. The chairmanship, secretariat and agenda were all Revenue controlled and nearly all the papers discussed came from the Revenue. However this criticism had only limited substance, for it was agreed that only lethargy prevented other members from presenting papers themselves. Others complained that the fruits of the Committee's work were rarely visible to members from outside the Inland Revenue. Some felt that the Committee was simply used by the revenue as convenient to them. It was not clear that anything agreed would actually be adopted in the Finance Bill. Some, at any rate, of the non-revenue members found the constraints imposed by the process of amending tax legislation difficult to accept.

Another criticism was that the membership became inappropriate with the passage of time and there was no easy means of changing it. When set up the membership was suitable, but because members were on the Committee as individuals there was no formal provision for change (although in fact some changes did take place). Some members lost enthusiasm; more importantly however, all were very busy leading members of their profession and the practitioners among them, in the course of time, had acquired senior administrative responsibilities in their own firms and were no longer personally responsible for clients; as a result they were no longer the best people to consider the details of fiscal provisions.

Despite these comments, when, in 1972, the Chairman of the Board of Inland Revenue wrote to the members to ask if they would like the

*Its name was subsequently changed by Sir Geoffrey Howe to Tax Consultative Committee

Committee disbanded, the response was a unanimous 'no'. The Inland Revenue members, more used to the slow pace of legislative change, were in no doubt as to the Committee's usefulness.

Besides these criticisms of its working, membership of the Committee raised a problem for some practitioners. Knowledge that such and such a matter was under discussion could embarrass them in advising a client. Whilst accepting the reality of this problem one Member indicated that over the eight years of the Committee's existence he could only recall three such instances affecting him, and he had had no difficulty in passing the client to another partner on these matters. He did not consider it a major difficulty. On the other hand, if suitability of membership meant frequent client contacts, the most suitable Members would face the most problems.

One view expressed was that with the right Members and a rotating chairmanship (not necessarily solely Inland Revenue) it could be made to work satisfactorily as a tax consultative committee. But this would still leave a vacuum on the matter of tax structure.

The Tax Reform Committee is an interesting attempt to achieve a desirable objective, but it must be questioned if a semi-clandestine body of this kind is the optimum way of doing so, although it may have been the only immediate way open to those who inaugurated it.

The Richardson Committee was set up by the Chancellor of the Exchequer, Reginald Maudling in April 1963 'To inquire into the practical effects of a form of turnover tax . . .' We have already pointed out (p. 34) that the Committee advised against the adoption of VAT either as a replacement for purchase tax or for corporation tax and, clearly, its recommendations had no long-term effect. Here our interest centres on the Committee as a method of consultation. It received thirty-six written submissions from organisations, and representatives of a further nineteen organisations gave oral evidence. Eleven invited papers were received by the Commission, mainly from academics, most of whom also gave oral evidence; nineteen other individuals submitted written evidence. The Committee had discussions with the Chairman Mr K. le M. Carter and one of the members of the Royal Commission on Taxation in Canada. It also visited Paris and met French officials, businessmen and taxation specialists.

The Committee consisted of only three members: the Chairman, Mr Gordon Richardson, at that time Vice-Chairman of Lloyds Bank and later to become Governor of the Bank of England; Sir Henry Benson an eminent accountant; and Sir Donald MacDougall, then Economic Director of NEDC. The Committee reported within a year, so that Mr Maudling, who announced his intention to set it up in one Budget speech, was able to indicate its findings in his succeeding Budget speech. Its small size doubtless explains why it was able to report so quickly despite the weight of evidence it had to digest. But the precedent is not wholly encouraging; its size may also partly explain why its recommendations, though unanimous, were so soon discarded.

Consultation and the role of organised pressure groups

Hitherto in this chapter we have considered the opportunities for consultation from the point of view of government or Departments which, broadly speaking, have themselves desired the consultations. We now examine how external organisations have used those opportunities to influence government, what other means they have sought to that end, and how effective they have been.

By using the experience of half a dozen organised pressure groups differing in resources and in the nature of their interest in tax, we hope to show the part they play in tax policy-making and the variety of approaches they have adopted to meet their various objectives. Even though, in practice, the distinction is by no means always clear-cut, it is helpful to recognise two rather different aspects of tax policy: on the one hand, there are issues of policy, large and small, which often involve matters of political principle; on the other hand, there are technical points of a relatively uncontroversial kind. Some groups are entirely (or almost entirely) concerned only with either one of those categories; others are concerned with both.

The groups selected for study were chosen on the basis of importance, representativeness and variety. The TUC and CBI were obviously of particular importance; they are 'Peak Associations' concerned with broad policy issues, but the CBI also makes technical submissions. The Institute of Chartered Accountants in England and Wales (ICA) is the leading partner in the Consultative Committee of Accounting Bodies (CCAB) and illustrates the approach of the professional associations, such as the Law Society, concerned almost wholly with technical issues. The Country Landowners Association (CLA) has somewhat narrower interests, an especial concern with capital taxes, and is notable for its territorial base. The Child Poverty Action Group (CPAG) is a pressure group of a very different kind with a highly specific objective: besides a continuing interest in child allowances and income tax thresholds, of the new taxes it was active on the scope of VAT and very much concerned with the TC scheme. Tables 7.2 and 7.3 compare, in summary form, methods of these five interest groups in approaching Ministers and Departments on the one hand, and parties, individual MPs and Parliament on the other. In the brief accounts of each we concentrate on the distinctive features.

Besides these five organisations some comments on the 'heritage lobby' are made in Chapter 6 as a result of its vigorous activity in presenting evidence to the Wealth Tax Select Committee. The reader should be warned that the description of the interest groups that follows related to the period of our study and, to the belief of the authors, is accurate to 1977. However, changes may have taken place since that date which do not appear in the text.

TUC

The TUC has an Economics Department with a staff which, in 1977, consisted of twelve persons. The Department was divided into three sections: economic, including tax; industrial; and collective bargaining. One person was particularly responsible for tax but there was considerable interaction between sections. The trade union research unit (TURU) at Ruskin College, Oxford, headed by John Hughes, which is partly financed by the TUC, might occasionally undertake work for the TUC on tax as on other economic issues;* otherwise there was no commissioning of work.

The staff only rarely consider technical details of taxation, but have in recent years been increasingly concerned with some of the broader policy issues of tax, partly because of the effects of inflation on tax thresholds. There is no TUC tax committee as such; any tax matter would normally be dealt with on the TUC Economic Committee. The limited staff resources on tax are not supplemented by tax expertise amongst the Committee Members in general, although there is an individual exception where an official from a union of revenue workers (e.g. the General Secretary of the Inland Revenue Staff Federation) is a member of the TUC General Council and Economic Committee.

The pronouncements of the TUC on tax are principally contained in an annual economic survey which began as a pre-Budget memorandum but from 1968 has been a full-scale Economic Review. The proposals are mainly of the broad policy type, of a fairly predictable kind, advocating heavier taxes on the better off and reductions on the less well off. For example, the TUC opposed VAT, but once it was operating campaigned for a higher rate of VAT on 'luxury' goods. A particular favourite of the TUC has been the introduction of an annual wealth tax. In its first major economic review in 1968 the TUC called for a wealth tax to raise £1000m. Since then it has persistently pressed for a wealth tax of varying degrees of severity, culminating in the attempt to revive

*An interesting piece of tax work by the TURU was its revelation of how the scrip dividend option, contained in the 1973 Finance Act, could be used to reduce tax payments by rich shareholders. Although this discovery was pointed out to the TUC Economic Secretary, the evidence leading to the closing of the loophole was prepared as part of the work of the TURU for the Transport and General Workers' Union (TGWU) (for details see *Inequality*, Evidence of the TGWU to the Royal Commission on the Distribution of Income and Wealth 1976, Spokesman Books, Nottingham, pp. 48–52).

Table 7.2 *Approach of selected pressure groups to Ministers and Departments*

	Submissions to Chancellor of the Exchequer or revenue departments	Meetings with Treasury Ministers	Meetings with officials from revenue departments	Meetings with other Ministers and officials
TUC	Pre-budget submission largely of policy type.	Regular pre and post-Budget meetings especially with Labour Governments.	Hardly ever.	Occasional meeting with PM. Special relationship with Labour Governments. TUC/Labour Party Working Party on Wealth Tax.
CBI	Two pre-Budget submissions: (1) policy; (2) anomalies. Also often comments on Finance Bill.	Regular pre-Budget meeting with Chancellor. Occasional meetings with other Treasury Ministers.	Regular meetings on pre-Budget technical submission. Post Finance Bill meetings. *Ad hoc* meetings; participate in working parties; regular exchange of views on double taxation.	Occasional meeting with PM. Meetings with other departments (e.g. Trade and Industry) in which tax might be on agenda.
ICA and CCAB	Two annual technical submissions to Revenue Departments: (1) anomalies paper (2) Finance Bill paper. An occasional paper to Chancellor.	Very occasionally (e.g. 1969 on tax simplification).	Very frequent on regular and *ad hoc* basis – as CBI but even more so.	Virtually nil.

CLA	Annual pre-Budget letter to Chancellor.	Very occasionally.	No regular pre or post-Budget meetings but fairly frequent *ad hoc* meetings.	Regular meetings with officials of Ministry of Agriculture; occasional meetings with Ministers for Agriculture and Environment.
CPAG	Annual pre-Budget submission. Occasionally at other times.	Frank Field had regular meeting with Chancellor.	Virtually nil.	Occasional meetings with PM and other Ministers, especially DHSS.

Table 7.3 *Approach of selected pressure groups to parties, individual MPs and Parliament*

	Approach to parties	Approach to individual MPs	Evidence to select committees	Promotion of draft amendments Finance Bill	Petitions to Parliament and PQs
TUC	Special relationship with Labour Party.	No. Individual unions have sponsored MPs in Labour Party, but not TUC as such.	Tax Credit Wealth Tax	No (individual unions might).	No.
CBI	No. Approach to Governments rather than parties.	No. Individual trade associations may have special links with individual MPs.	Corporation Tax Tax Credit Wealth Tax	Yes. Amendments circulated to Opposition MPs.	No petitions. Very rarely a PQ.

Table 7·3 *(contd.)*

	Approach to parties	Approach to individual MPs	Evidence to select committees	Promotion of draft amendments Finance Bill	Petitions to Parliament and PQs
ICA and CCAB	Parties offered a discussion on Finance Bill Paper. Always taken up by Conservatives in Opposition, rarely in Government. Labour Party in Opposition took up offer in 1973.	'Anomalies' paper sent to accountant MPs. Finance Bill paper sent to all MPs.	Corporation Tax Tax Credit Wealth Tax	Not normally.	No.
CLA	Continuing relationship; meetings with parliamentary Committees, Shadow Ministers and sympathetic backbench MPs	Liberal and Conservative MPs are CLA members and on CLA	Wealth Tax	Regularly. Usually relies on individual to present but may circulate draft amendment with explanatory brief to sympathetic MPs on Finance Bill Committee.	No petitions. Occasional PQs for inaccessible information.
CPAG	Fringe meetings organised at annual conferences of all parties. General contact maintained with Shadow Ministers.	CPAG members in all parties.	Tax Credit	Regularly. Briefs and draft amendments circulated to all MPs on Finance Bill Committee except Ministers and Whips.	Petition organised on TC scheme. PQs used extensively.

the tax when Mr Healey's enthusiasm for it flagged.

Apart from the power given to trade unions under the Labour Party constitution the TUC, as distinct from individual unions, has a special relationship with the Labour Party. By a reciprocal arrangement, the Economic Secretary of the TUC attends meetings of the Home Policy Committee of the NEC and the Finance and Economic Affairs Sub-Committee, whilst a representative of the NEC is on the Economic Committee of the TUC. From 1972 a TUC/Labour Party Liaison Committee has also existed, consisting of representatives of the PLP, NEC and TUC, which has met regularly both when the Labour Party was in Opposition and in office.

The Labour Government elected in 1974 proceeded with a programme of tax changes very much in line with the tax proposals of the TUC Economic Reviews. But it would be wrong to take this as a simple example of a pressure group dictating to a Government, for Labour's own *Programme* 1972, approved by the annual conference of the Party, contained much the same proposals (Hatfield, 1978, Appendix). On the other hand, the willingness of a Labour Government to implement the proposals of a conference with a political centre of gravity to the left of the PLP was undoubtedly increased by the TUC's stance; and tax changes were part of the 'Social Contract' between the Labour Party and the TUC, by which the promise of wage restraint was bought with a package of economic and industrial measures.

The history of the WT proposals 1974–9 illustrates both the strength and the limitations of the TUC's influence over a Labour Government.

In his first Budget, just a few weeks after entering office, Mr Healey, as Chancellor, promised to introduce a WT, but after the issue of a Green Paper and its consideration by a select committee. The Wealth Tax Select Committee reported in November 1975. In answer to a written parliamentary question from its Chairman, Mr Healey announced on 18 December 1975, that, in consequence of the delay of the Select Committee in producing its report, 'which took a good deal longer . . . than the Government had hoped' and because of 'the many issued involved', he would not be bringing forward proposals for a WT in his 1976 Budget. However, the Inland Revenue would continue its preparatory work and he might publish some draft clauses for public discussion during 1976. No draft clauses were published; there was no mention of a WT in the Queen's speech, 1976. Not long afterwards the Chancellor announced that he was not proposing to introduce a WT in 'the present Parliament'.

This was too much for Mr Jack Jones, Secretary of the powerful TGWU and a leading member of the TUC. In the words of *The Times*, 7 December 1976, the TUC 'wrung from Cabinet Ministers a joint initiative to revive the Left's cherished idea of a tax on wealth'. The

TUC/Labour Party Liaison Committee agreed to set up a working party consisting of two Government Ministers, two trade unionists, two members of the NEC and two of the PLP, in the infelicitous words of Mr Len Murray, 'to look at ways in which we can find a practical way of getting a wealth tax in, hopefully within the lifetime of this present Government'.

The first fruits of the Working Party's deliberations were made public in a document, *The Next Three Years and Into the Eighties*, drawn up by the TUC/Labour Party Liaison Committee and approved by the TUC General Council and the NEC of the Labour Party on 27 July 1977. This agreement recorded (para. 32).

The Government should press on and publish detailed proposals for a wealth tax in the next parliamentary session. The option which the Liaison Committee are considering in detail would entail a threshold of £100,000 at present values with rates rising progressively from 1 per cent of net assets to 5 per cent for fortunes over £5 million.

In fact no such proposals were published by the Government and no wealth tax was brought in. The TUC had put the wealth tax back on Labour's agenda, where it remains, but did not succeed in getting it implemented during Labour's period in office 1974–9. There are a number of possible reasons for the Labour Government's failure to implement a WT (see, for example pp. 50 and 106). During its later stages in office Labour's dependence on the support of other parties would have made it difficult to bring in a controversial piece of legislation. At the end of 1975, however, when Mr Healey first decided to shelve the tax, he may have felt able to do so because of the TUC's failure to deliver its side of the bargain in the 'Social Contract'.

One final comment might be made. The Labour Government's agreement to the Working Party on Wealth Tax was something of a sop to keep the TUC happy and the Chancellor may not have intended to take much notice of the outcome. Yet it is disturbing that not one member of the Working Party, nor indeed, of the TUC/Labour Party Liaison Committee had served on the Parliamentary Select Committee on Wealth Tax, thus no personal experience from the Select Committee's work could be brought to bear. It is highly unlikely that any member of the Working Party could match the detailed knowledge of the subject acquired by many Labour Members who served on the Select Committee. It is more understandable, given the TUC's ideological stance and the purpose for which it sought a WT (redistribution), that the option that the Working Party chose to consider in detail was that which had been rejected by all but one of the Minority Reports of the Select Committee; and that one was the (Jeremy Bray) report which obtained the least support (p. 178).

CBI

Since 1973 the economic staff of the CBI has been significantly increased and in 1977 the economic directorate stood at 24, about twice the size of that of the TUC. Of these, five were in a tax department in comparison with four before 1973. The tax department contains relatively senior people with practical knowledge of tax but with a policy focus. As with the TUC there is considerable 'cross-fertilisation' with other parts of the directorate.

Unlike the TUC, the CBI has specialist tax committees which contain a wide variety of tax experts, mainly from industry and private practice. In 1977 the CBI had a Tax Committee, which met six times per year and comprised some forty persons, mainly from firms that are CBI members. A Tax Panel of about fifteen members met more frequently and acted as a steering group for the Tax Committee. (More recently the Tax Panel has been abolished and the Tax Committee meets more often.) Working parties are set up on specific issues. Thus there was a working party on the tax credit scheme (drawn from the Tax Committee and the Industrial Relations Committee), one on wealth tax and one on the Layfield Report (drawn from the Tax Committee and the Rating Valuation Committee). There is also an elaborate VAT consultative group working mainly as a corresponding group providing information for a VAT panel.

The CBI is very much concerned with both the technical details of tax and more general issues of tax policy of concern to business. These two aspects are kept as distinct as possible by two separate pre-Budget submissions: one is an anomalies paper, and the second is a general review of the economy which contains the CBI's tax recommendations. The CBI is also likely to produce a paper commenting on the Finance Bill provisions. The CBI not only has fairly frequent meetings with Ministers, but, unlike the TUC, has regular meetings with the revenue departments and its members serve on working parties with revenue officials.

In its actions the CBI has not wished to appear in a lobbyist role; rather it has sought, by informal methods, to create a climate of opinion amongst influential people. The Economic Director briefs industrialists for discussions with Ministers, both for formal occasions, such as NEDC meetings, and informal chats. Regular 'tea parties' are also held with the Permanent Secretary to the Treasury, the Accountancy Division of the Department of Industry and with leaders of the accountancy profession.

However, the CBI has become more publicity conscious in recent years. The CBI's annual pre-Budget review is always published and some of the reports of its working parties (for example that on wealth tax). But, until 1976, the approach was rather to accept 'normal' publicity but not to seek it, with the emphasis on briefing CBI members rather than informing the general public. After 1976, under the late John Methven's leadership as Director General, the CBI was more inclined to court publicity, e.g. to launch its major economic reviews with a splash and to hold annual conferences which have been fully reported in the press.

There is no doubt that the technical expertise of CBI members is much respected by the revenue departments and the CBI thus exercises considerable influence over tax details. The general CBI philosophy on tax is more in accord with that of the Conservative than the Labour Party and, as Labour Governments incline to the TUC, Conservative Chancellors naturally tend to act in ways of which the CBI often approves. For example, the easing of CTT under the Conservatives since 1979 has been very much in line with proposals put forward by the CBI as their contribution to Lord Cockfield's review of capital taxes (p. 80). But there are not the same formal links between the CBI and Conservative Party that there are between the TUC and the Labour Party. Trade or industrial associations do not figure in the Conservative constitution as trade unions do in Labour's; there is no reciprocal membership of CBI committees and Conservative Party committees; and nothing comparable to the TUC/Labour Party Liaison Committee. A Conservative Government will always consider the CBI's views sympathetically, not least because, just as Labour gets most of its funds from the trade unions, the predominant source of Conservative funds is big business; but there is no question of the Conservatives being 'contracted' to the CBI.

Moreover the CBI influence may occasionally be weakened, with a Government of any complexion, because of the differing views of its members, who consist of publicly and privately-owned firms, large organisations and small, and firms whose interests are predominantly overseas as well as firms largely or wholly trading in the domestic market. Sometimes it is hard for the CBI to speak with one voice.

ICA and CCAB

The Institute of Chartered Accountants in England and Wales (ICA), with a membership more than six times that of any of the others, is the largest of the six professional accountancy associations that comprise the Consultative Committee of Accountancy Bodies (CCAB). The CCAB was formed to coordinate some of the public activities of the accountancy bodies after proposals for a merger had foundered. The inaugural meeting of the CCAB was held in May 1974, and it came into being as an official entity 1 January 1975. Since then the six accountancy bodies have worked together through the CCAB in making their tax submissions. Before that, for a couple of years, there had been some attempt to cooperate in the field of parliament and law; previously the various bodies acted independently.

The ICA has the major representation on all CCAB sub-committees which are chaired by ICA members. The ICA also provides the secretarial back-up. In the technical field the CCAB committees can act without referring to the CCAB Council.

The resources of the ICA (and to a lesser extent of the other bodies) consist of the expertise of their members with good technical secretarial back-up from headquarters. The method of the ICA, as part of the CCAB, in preparing two regular submissions each year, illustrates the point.

Each autumn the Technical Advisory Committees of the ICA in each region are invited to send in a list of tax 'anomalies' by a specific date. These consist of detailed comments on points in the Finance Acts that do not make sense in practice: the object is to rectify anomalies which members have found in dealing with their clients. These proposals are put into some sort of order and related to the relevant Finance Acts by the Secretariat and then considered for one or two days by the Taxation Sub-Committee of the Parliamentary and Law Committee. (The Taxation Sub-Committee, with a membership of about twenty-four, is very broadly based with about 65 per cent of its membership drawn from the provinces.) Under the CCAB arrangements other accountancy bodies are invited to send representatives to the Sub-Committee meetings. The document for consideration by the Taxation Sub-Committee might contain sixty points, with possibly two or three comments drawing attention to general problems rather than suggesting solutions, and might consist of from ten to fifteen pages.

The Taxation Sub-Committee prepares a draft which goes to the Tax Steering Committee (with three ICA members and one from each of the other Accountancy bodies). The Steering Committee check the technical content and ensure that the document is in line with ICA and CCAB politics; then, as approved, it goes from the Chairman (a Council member) to the revenue departments. A similar procedure is followed with the second annual document on the Finance Bill.

The ICA and CCAB do not seek to promote broad policy measures which might be construed as of a party political kind. Exceptionally, however, they may make some sort of stand on a general issue, such as, in 1969, the urgent need to simplify the tax system (p. 14).

The ICA works even more closely with the Inland Revenue than the CBI and its influence on the technicalities of the tax system is considerable. It can be argued, however, that this close link between revenue officials and accountants is not entirely healthy. The Inland Revenue may be too easily dissuaded from a proposed course of action, such as a particular method of taxing 'perks', because the accountancy profession maintains that it will be too difficult or time consuming to operate. It has also been suggested that there is, in effect, collusion between the Revenue and accountancy bodies about the maintenance of the system: if the accountants argue that the profession has not the capacity to cope with some new proposal, the Revenue accepts this as a strong reason to drop it.

CLA

The Country Landowners Association has a Tax Department which, in 1977, was headed on a part-time basis by a barrister well-known for his writings on taxation. The Department included another lawyer and two former senior principal inspectors of taxes. An Economics Department (of two qualified staff) may also consider some tax issues, such as the effect of tax policy on land ownership; and lawyers in other departments of the CLA may also occasionally be concerned with tax matters. The CLA has occasionally commissioned research studies, for example a study of the effect of CGT on land ownership by Alan Harrison of Reading University.

The Tax Department works in conjunction with the Taxation Sub-Committee of the Executive Committee and includes various MPs who are members of the CLA. The Economics Sub-Committee also includes past and present MPs as members. The policy-making body of the CLA is the Executive Committee to which the Sub-Committees report.

The strength of the CLA comes not only from its 40,000–50,000 members who are landowners (including many owner-occupiers) but also from a professional membership of some 500, consisting of land agents, surveyors, solicitors, etc. Technical material is sent out to them as a flow of circulars, and they in turn send back queries. A regional infrastructure is also very important. Each region has its own chairman and secretary. The Tax Department deals with a flow of queries from the regions which in turn provide headquarters with information about the region. This strong regional basis makes the organisation very suitable for influencing individual MPs in territorial constituencies. The CLA has a conscious policy of education and CLA members have been encouraged to have open days for the general public, schools and so on.

Another particular feature of the CLA is its close links with the Department of Agriculture. One medium of influence on the Ministry of Agriculture and the Chancellor is through the Economic Development Committee (EDC) on Agriculture on which CLA members sit. The Agricultural EDC has a series of study groups, including one on finance, with a tax study group attached to it which has published a report on the impact of taxation on agriculture. The CLA are usually brought into consultation with the Inland Revenue on any proposed legislation affecting their interests – sometimes at their own request, sometimes at the Revenue's. As so often, one cannot be certain about the influence of a particular group, but the reliefs to agriculture (including woodlands) which successive governments have granted under estate duty and then CTT (pp. 41–2) would seem, on the face of things, to indicate effective pressure.

CPAG

Whilst the pressure groups we have so far examined would all disclaim the description of lobbyist organisations, the Child Poverty Action Group would unashamedly embrace that title. Its essential intent is to influence governments in one fairly narrow direction and to use all legitimate means of education, persuasion and pressure to that end.

Until his election to Parliament in 1979, the CPAG's Director was Mr Frank Field. In 1977 the CPAG had a staff of nine, of whom about half were secretaries and none of whom had any specialist knowledge in tax matters. It might commission a small piece of research or hire a research assistant for a particular project, e.g. Mrs Molly Meacher prepared its evidence for the Select Committee on Tax Credit. It has members from all political parties who are a source of information and strength.

The CPAG uses publicity to the maximum, and is the only one of the five pressure groups we have examined to promote petitions. A unique feature of CPAG is its use of parliamentary questions; it has thereby effectively converted civil servants into its temporary research assistants and provided itself with information for use in its campaign which it can rightly claim to come from an impeccable official source.

By his own qualities and successful press publicity, Frank Field won himself a standing which secured, from 1970, a regular annual meeting and an occasional additional meeting with the Chancellor of the Exchequer. More than most of the other organisations CPAG has also kept in close touch with Opposition shadows. It has also been prepared to work with and through other pressure groups when this would increase its effectiveness, e.g. trade union support was secured to ensure that the Labour Government enacted the child benefit scheme.

In relation to the taxes of our particular study, the CPAG was on the winning side in getting children's clothes and footwear zero-rated for VAT against the Chancellor's better judgement. It has also helped to ensure that, if the TC scheme were to be implemented, child credit would be paid to the mother through the Post Office rather than the cheaper method of payment to the father by the employers. However, this was not an issue on which the Chancellor's conviction clearly differed from that of the CPAG, and given the other pressures, had the CPAG not existed the outcome on this issue would doubtless have been the same. The outcome, without the CPAG, in extending the zero-rating of VAT is more debatable. Much of the success of the CPAG as a pressure group in the 1970's rested on the integrity, sincerity and operational flair of its Director, Frank Field.

Individuals and the press

Individual experts

The role of the unpaid expert is considerable at every stage of the tax policy-making process. They participate in the party policy-making committees from which some have moved into government as special advisers to the Chancellor or a revenue department. They give evidence as individual experts to select committees. They may act as advisers and unpaid research officers to individual MPs serving on select committees and in this capacity largely write a minority report: the three select committees on tax produced between them eight reports (or nine if the Report of the Chairman of the Wealth Tax Select Committee is counted in both its unamended and amended forms) of which at least two were very largely written by academics. Unpaid specialists, tax practitioners with accountancy and legal expertise, give valuable assistance to the Opposition on the Finance Bill, explaining implications and drafting amendments. Moreover the writings of academics, partly channelled in the policy-making direction by the Institute for Fiscal Studies set up for this purpose in 1969, also exert an influence, if not a precisely definable one, on tax policy-making.

Undoubtedly the most influential contributions are those of experts who are politically active and attach themselves to a particular party, of whom, of course, the outstanding examples are Nicholas Kaldor and Arthur Cockfield.

There are, however, unsatisfactory features in relation to the contributions of individual specialists. Some of these features we have already touched on at the party stage (p. 85), but it is useful to remind ourselves. The party's choice of a specialist to advise on a particular topic is often on a haphazard basis, which cannot be relied on to produce the best man. Moreover the most politically active in a party sense are not necessarily the best-equipped to advise. Whilst the parties may consider what academics or practitioners have published, they do not use academics to undertake research of a long-term nature, where academics ought to excel. Further, the Labour Party, both at the policy-making stage and in opposing the detail of Finance Bills, lacks the advice of tax practitioners which has been of considerable help to the Conservatives.

Academics have also come in for particular criticism from civil servants. Inland Revenue officials considered that insufficient of the work of academics was relevant to their needs whilst Treasury officials held that more empirical work should be undertaken by academics and especially that there was a need for more work on the effects of taxes. As one senior economic adviser put it: 'There is too much thinking about ways of taxing people and too little about the effects of the tax system on the efficiency of the economy.'

The view that research on taxation was inadequate was endorsed by the Expenditure Committee of the House of Commons (1975):

We conclude that research into the impact of taxation is haphazard . . . both Ministers and Parliament could be better informed by the results of modern research methods . . . we therefore recommend that the Treasury, in conjunction with the revenue departments and the Social Science Research Council should review their arrangements for taxation research.

The Financing of Public Expenditure HC 69-I

The press

The influence of the press on tax policy-making has some obvious similarities to that of academics and other specialists through their published works. Indeed, in so far as academics publish in the press, which they often do in the quality daily and Sunday papers, and in weekly or monthly journals, the two are identical: the press is the medium of the specialist's views.

Press influence, however, may mean much more than simply presenting individuals views as feature articles. Tax and economic correspondents have their own views which they may persistently pursue in a paper, thus exercising a continuing influence on the climate of opinion. Or, irrespective of the views of specialists, a paper may take up a particular tax issue as highly newsworthy and conduct a major campaign on it – with all the paraphernalia of leading articles, features, photographs, case studies and the like.

To attempt to assess the influence of the press on tax policy-making over a decade and a half would be a major study in its own right and well beyond the scope of this book. Rather we hope to give the flavour of the press contribution mainly by a couple of specific illustrations.

First, it can be said that in the process of consultation, particularly the discussion of Green Papers, the press plays a vital part. It indicates the content of a Green Paper and makes known the Government's willingness to receive comments; and comment on discussion documents by the serious press is an important part of that consultation.

Secondly, the press is a pervasive influence. Its effect is not confined to the direct impact of press comment on Ministers and officials, important though that may sometimes be. The views of newspapers and journals affect party members, members of pressure groups and MPs and thus have a secondary reaction on policy.

The influence of the serious press on tax policy-making is well illustrated by reference to the reports carried in the *Financial Times* during the passage of the Finance Bill on CTT in the early months of 1975. The tax correspondent, Mr John Chown, in a series of articles, was a persistent and telling critic of CTT. One interesting outcome was that the Chief Secretary to the Treasury, Mr Joel Barnett, who was responsible for piloting the Bill through the House of Commons, considered it necessary, or at least desirable, to respond personally to the criticisms in a lengthy article which the paper published on 12 March 1975: 'Why the Capital Transfer Tax Critics are Wrong'. The subsequent easements to the tax, in particular the concession of a lower rate of tax on gifts, introduced during the passage of the Act, may owe something to the paper's comments. Certainly, they helped to create a climate of opinion favourable to such changes.

Perhaps the best example of the influence of the popular press is the campaign to secure the zero-rating of children's clothes and footwear for VAT. This issue was taken up by the popular press as well as being supported by the CPAG. The Chancellor, Mr Barber, although unconvinced of the validity of the case, conceded the relief in the 1973 Finance Act. Under the influence of the press MPs had become worked up about the issue, and he was particularly concerned that VAT, which was associated with the Common Market, should not be too unpopular.

Conclusions

There have been considerable changes in the scope and range of consultation since the introduction of Green Papers. Government has tended to be more 'open' and groups have become accustomed to preparing 'responses' to Government discussion documents. But Green Papers, if they are to help Government gain *acceptance* of legislation *and* provide it with technical information, must be more carefully designed. It is doubtful, too, whether the current arrangements for working parties of revenue officials and tax specialists, and the confidential and semi-secret Tax Reform Committee, are satisfactory. They provide a very limited and somewhat clandestine means of bringing the outside expert into the process of tax policy-making.

We see evidence in the current methods of consultation of the 'distributive' mode of policy-making – of concessions and reliefs granted to particular sectors of the community in response to pressure. These tax expenditures are often a departure from strict rationality and indicate a degree of real power in the hands of interest groups – a power to secure advantages for their members or their clients.

A special relationship exists between the Labour Government and TUC, which is an example of the political bargaining process at work. The idea of capital taxes in exchange for incomes policies recurs throughout the period of our study, but it reached a peak of formality in the Social Contract.

Thus it is clear that an outstanding feature of the period we have studied is the change in the process of consultation; since 1963 consultation on tax policy has widened and taken on new forms. The long-established forms of relatively informal consultation by departments and Ministers before and during the drafting of legislation have been extended and more fully utilised (outstandingly with VAT) and officials have taken a more open and less anonymous part in public conferences and public debate. Over the same period Green Papers on tax matters have been introduced (from April 1967); an unpublicised 'Tax Reform Committee' has been established (1969); and as we saw in Chapter 6, the use of *ad hoc* select committees of the House of Commons for the consideration of new taxes has been revived (from 1971). The contrast is sharply revealed by comparing how SET was introduced in 1966 and VAT in 1973: the former, introduced without warning in a Budget, to be incorporated in the immediately forthcoming Finance Bill; the latter the subject of two years of consultation before final legislation. One result of these procedural changes has been an increase in the volume and variety of submissions from interested parties.

The trend to increasing consultation has not been wholly uniform, however. Of the new taxes we have been studying the latest to reach the statute book, CTT, benefited from neither Green Paper nor select committee. And Sir Geoffrey Howe, for all his protestations of the virtues of consultation (Howe, 1977), made use of neither method in reviewing CTT and making far-reaching changes in it (pp. 41–2) though he has subsequently published very general Green Papers on *The Taxation of Husband and Wife* (Cmnd 8093, 1980) *Alternatives to Domestic Rates* (Cmnd 8449, 1981) and *Corporation Tax* (Cmnd 8456, 1982).

The new methods themselves are not free from difficulty and unresolved problems. The effect of changing procedures for consultation may have been to alter, in a subtle way, the nature of the policy-making process in Britain, shifting it somewhat from party government to a more pluralistic mode in which the opportunity for group influence is enhanced.

8 Conclusions

How is tax policy made? Does the process ensure that objectives are fulfilled?

In this book we set out to answer two questions. The first was why so many new taxes had been created in the period from 1964 to 1975. We found that the need for new revenue, although pressing, was not the main reason that governments introduced *new* taxes. In the main they found the necessary extra revenue they required to support expanding public expenditure from other sources. The two predominant concerns behind the introduction of new taxes were the need to encourage economic growth (and consequentially to boost tax revenues) and the desire for greater equity in the tax structure, which was primarily prompted by an underlying desire to reduce inequalities of income and wealth.

We then went on to ask 'How is tax policy made?' and the follow-up question 'How effective is the process?' We suggested in Chapter 1 that there is not necessarily only one model of effective tax policy-making, and that in particular the models appropriate where economic goals are sought might be different from those appropriate where taxes are intended to serve political objectives. Where the primary goals are political we might expect to find political models of decision-making more in evidence than the model of economic rational choice and its variants. How far have these expectations been borne out by the evidence from the introduction of eight new taxes? What modes of policy-making do governments choose and are these the most appropriate and effective routes through the policy-making machinery to ensure that objectives are attained?

There can be no doubt that the process of making tax policy is complex and that there are many interwoven strands in the progress of any one tax from its conception in the mind of academic or politician to its actual operation in the economic and social systems. As each of the new taxes has flowed, to a greater or lesser extent, through an issue machine we can summarise the institutions and stages of policy-making in Figure 8.1. Each tax was the subject of somewhat different treatment as it passed through the institutions of the political system and so the eight cases provide interesting material for comparison and offer some striking contrasts. Their progress through the machine reveals the relevance of different models of decision-making to the different types of policy goals, and thus we can draw some conclusions about the

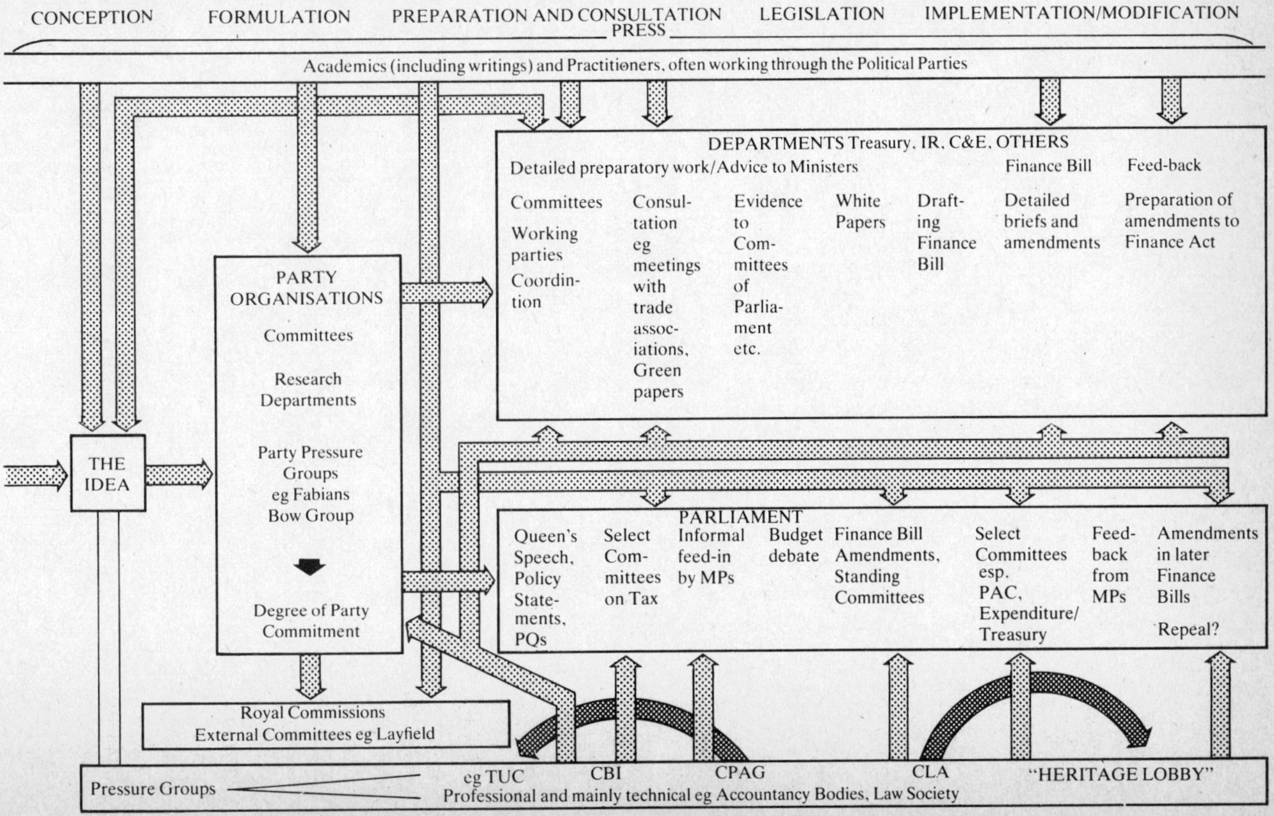

Academics (including writings) and Practitioners, often working through the Political Parties

DEPARTMENTS Treasury, IR, C&E, OTHERS

Detailed preparatory work/Advice to Ministers

Committees	Consul-	White	Draft-	Finance Bill	Feed-back
Working	tation	Papers	ing		
parties	eg		Finance	Detailed	Preparation of
Coordina-	meetings		Bill	briefs and	amendments to
tion	with			amendments	Finance Act
	trade				
	assoc-				
	iations,				
	Green				
	papers				

PARLIAMENT

Queen's	Select	Informal	Budget	Finance Bill	Select	Feed-	Amendments
Speech,	Com-	feed-in	debate	Amendments,	Committees	back	in later
Policy	mittees	by MPs		Standing	esp.	from	Finance
State-	on Tax			Committees	PAC,	MPs	Bills
ments,					Expenditure/		
PQs					Treasury		Repeal?

PARTY ORGANISATIONS

Committees

Research Departments

Party Pressure Groups eg Fabians Bow Group

Degree of Party Commitment

Royal Commisions External Committees eg Layfield

THE IDEA

Pressure Groups

eg TUC   CBI   CPAG   CLA   "HERITAGE LOBBY"

Professional and mainly technical eg Accountancy Bodies, Law Society

Figure 8.1   Tax policy in the UK: new taxes

effectiveness of the machinery for the processing of those policies that primarily have economic objectives and those that, by contrast, have primarily political objectives.

The first stage in the creation of any new tax is the determination of objectives and goals. It is clear from the eight taxes of our study that the key stage in the determination and emergence of policy goals has been the party stage. It is at this point that objectives and goals are established and clarified. Here, therefore, we should expect to see the operation of political rationality. With only one exception, SET, and with possibly a further partial exception in the TC scheme, the principle of the new taxes evolved in the party stage and thus they afford suitable evidence of the extent to which political rationality operates in British parties. How are objectives chosen? Are goals selected because they fit in with a clearly thought out party ideology, or form part of a systematic approach to politics? Are they adopted because of the existence of power blocs within the party and are required to ensure their support? Or are they chosen to attract votes at the next election?

The new taxes we have studied almost all became official party policy because they fitted in with the party's general ideological stance. CT (classical style), CGT, CTT and WT were all the product of the Labour Party's concern to reduce inequalities of income and wealth and to make sure that the wealthy paid their full share of taxation. Perhaps the commitment of some members of the Labour Party to the principles of equality was not total. But they had enough attachment to the idea to be willing to trade a commitment to reduce inequality for the incomes policy necessary to fulfil the practical requirements of successful government and to win elections. The goal of equality was thus determined both by ideology and by the necessity of retaining trade union support for government policy.

For their part the Conservatives, too, chose to promote taxes that stemmed from their fundamental ideological predispositions. Their ideological commitment to business enterprise was reflected in their adherence to CT (imputation), although this tax, like VAT, also reflected their concern with the efficiency of taxation. The general desire of the Conservatives for fewer and more simple forms of government is reflected in their desire for simplification of the tax structure.

Even the two exceptions to the general rule of ideological origins, SET and the TC scheme, to some extent reflected party ideology. SET, with its emphasis on productive industry and its discouragement of service industry, fitted well with Labour Party views on the economy in general, and with the location of its supporters within industry. TC, with its emphasis on cash benefits freely available to the individual to do with as he liked, in place of specific, means-tested social benefits, reflected the Conservative ideology of self-help and self-reliance. It promised less government and more efficient government as well as greater freedom to the individual social security beneficiary. Thus it is clear that each one of these taxes was selected as an instrument for the realisation of general party objectives – objectives derived from each party's view of the world and of what they would like it to become.

Thus there is evidence from our study of the exercise of some forms of political rationality in the selection of goals consistent with a party's general ideological position and likely to attract its traditional supporters. As far as new taxes are concerned, however, we do not find much evidence of political rationality in terms of the selection of goals most likely to appeal to the mass electorate (Downs, 1957, 1960; Brittan, 1975). The decision to include new taxes in party manifestos is explained more in terms of ideology and internal power relations than in terms of the 'political trade cycle',* though proposals to abolish a tax may have electoral advantage more directly in mind, as with the Conservative commitment on SET.

Our study also reveals that the parties showed only limited capacity for rational consideration of their chosen objectives. They did not examine them in sufficient detail, nor did they fully explore the consequences of their chosen actions. For successful policy-making it is not enough for parties simply to state broad and general aims. They need to examine them in some depth and consider how they might best be achieved before they set off on the long journey through the policy-making machine. If objectives are insufficiently considered and clarified by the party proposing the tax, the policies are more open to influence from the bureaucracy and from affected interest groups. Analysis of Labour Party speeches and documentation reveals how far they failed to develop a clear, coherent philosophy of what they sought in advocating a reduction in the inequality of wealth. For example, what levels of wealth holding needed to be the target if inequality was to be reduced significantly? Did they wish to reduce inequality irrespective of how the wealth was acquired? Was it more important to tax inherited wealth than personal savings? Was it relevant how individuals used their wealth, and so on? (Sandford, 1979). Why were these questions never addressed before the party announced its commitment to WT? The lack of political rationality of this sort in the selection of WT as an instrument for the reduction of inequality can be explained in part through the history of how it became party policy. Long advocated in general terms, it finally emerged as a manifesto commitment following party conference votes and the bargain struck with the trade unions. It

*For an analysis of electoral attitudes towards a WT, see Alan Lewis, Cedric Sandford and Carole Fleming, *A Survey of Attitudes Toward Wealth, the Wealthy and the Proposed Annual Wealth Tax*, Occasional Paper No 1, Bath University Centre for Fiscal Studies, 1979.

did not become a firm commitment as a result of rigorous theoretical and ideological analysis within the party's policy-making machinery.

The failure of the Labour Party to clarify and refine its objective of redistribution lies at the heart of the failure of the taxes that it introduced to meet that objective. It is clear from events that within the Labour Party only limited consideration was given to CTT and WT. CTT was changed in major ways from the first White Paper; the WT Green Paper was characterised by exceptional vagueness and the tax itself eventually indefinitely postponed. Recent statements from Labour Party supporters recognise that the attempts at redistribution through the enactment of CTT and CGT failed. Loopholes were replaced by generous exemptions says an article in *New Society*, and revenue from CTT (plus the residue from Estate Duty) continues to fall in real terms. CGT is more of a tax avoidance device than a tax (*New Society*, 17 September 1981). The authors of *Manifesto* (1981) also recognise the failure of Labour's attempts at redistribution of income and wealth through the devices of capital taxation. They argue for more radical methods of achieving the goals of redistribution, and base their suggestions on a more radical view of what is to be redistributed – in their case it is all wealth regardless of origin. But they, too, are vague about targets as well as the instruments that would best achieve their objective of eliminating maldistribution of wealth. Thus they write:

We must therefore envisage on the one side periodic wealth levies taking major proportions of concentration of personal wealth into common ownership, and on the other side the development of institutions of social ownership capable of managing effectively the personal wealth that is taken over.

(Cripps *et al.*, *Manifesto*, 1981, p. 196)

Two further examples can be given from Labour tax policy-making which suggest a reversal of the rational order of policy-making – which should be first determine and refine your goals and then find the best means to achieve them. My Roy Jenkins, as Chancellor of the Exchequer, imposed a substantial increase in SET at the same time as announcing that he had commissioned Professor W.B. Reddaway to undertake a comprehensive study of the effects of SET. With revenue demands pressing it is perhaps understandable that he should not have felt able to wait for the Reddaway Report before increasing SET rates. Less excusable was the procedure of the Labour Government in 1974, which announced a commitment to CTT and WT a few months before setting up the Commission on the Distribution of Income and Wealth whose brief was to discover the facts in this field. The capital tax legislation was passed and the Select Committee on Wealth Tax had completed taking evidence on the particular *instruments* before the Royal Commission had issued its first report on the background of wealth ownership. Even if the need for new taxes on the distribution of wealth could be taken for granted in the light of existing evidence on wealth distribution, the data that the Commission compiled would have been useful in considering the most appropriate form and rate structure for both of these taxes. If the Commission was not to be used in this way it is difficult to see what role it was designed to play in the tax policy-making process.

The biggest charge of political irrationality which can be levied against the Conservative Party rests on their penchant for giving undertakings to abolish particular taxes before they had made any realistic studies of what to put in their place. This happened with SET and CTT. It also happened with domestic rates. In the case of SET there had, it is true, been some general debate for years on widening the tax base, and VAT was a possibility. But the commitment to abolish SET was a simple response to a generally unpopular tax, not a result of rational political choice of objectives. With CTT and rates the commitment to abolish appeared to falter and weaken once the Conservatives attained office. CTT has not been abolished but has been so amended that it now resembles the tax it replaced. Rates remain because no acceptable alternative as a source of local revenue has yet been identified.

We have suggested that the identification and clarification of goals takes place at the party stage, and that some form of political rationality (fitting in with an ideological pattern, or mobilising support) is required to ensure that the objectives are fully worked out and understood within the party before any further steps are taken. Our evidence suggests that this does not always happen and that policy-making sometimes takes place in reverse order or in the absence of clearly set out goals.

The next important step in policy-making, once the goals have been selected, is the design and choice of instruments. Whether or not this function can be performed by political parties, or is best left to the administration, is debatable. Traditional theories of the political system suggest that politicians select goals and bureaucrats determine the optimum means of achieving them. This view of the political process assumes that a distinction can be made between ends and means, and it also assumes that politicians are capable of putting forward clearly defined goals for the bureaucrats to work on. British politicians have largely accepted this view of how policy is made, and as a result they have not felt an urgent need to develop sophisticated party machines, fuelled by large sums of money, which are capable of taking the stages of policy-making beyond the general idea into the formulation of alternative means or instruments. The Labour Party in particular remains poorly staffed, poorly funded and thus incapable of in-depth policy analysis. Nor can the parties draw upon great independent research institutes such as Brookings or the American Enterprise Institute. They are haphazard in their use of academic advice. As a result there is something of a policy vacuum between the articulation of broad and general goals by parties and the establishment of well worked out schemes by which those goals can be attained. In some cases the policy vacuum is filled by a 'great man' who works out tax schemes for the party. Lords Kaldor and Cockfield have been able to carve out their niches as policy-makers precisely because there was a lack of other machinery for doing, in Britain, what scores of academic and independent researchers do in the USA.

Once goals have been chosen by the parties through the exercise of political choice, then the policy-making process moves from the various models of political rationality to the model of economic rational choice and its variants. This is true whatever the nature of the goals sought, whether they are primarily economic or political, whether they are derived from a reasoned consideration of the practical requirements of a modern mixed economy, or whether they flow from deeply held beliefs about the most desirable form of society. Whatever the nature of an objective those who hold it want to see it fulfilled. Thus they must, logically, try to select the most likely means of achieving it. This requires two sets of decisions to be made. They must identify the optimum policy instruments through the exercise of rational economic choice, and they must make a 'judgement' about the most appropriate route to take through the policy process to ensure that the instrument is adopted and the objective achieved. Two kinds of decision model are therefore involved: rational choice and political 'judgement'. There is little point in any political party wanting to promote economic growth or to reduce inequality of income and wealth if it allows policy instruments to be selected that cannot do the job, or if, once having selected its instruments, permits them to go through the process or policy-making in such a way that they are weakened and their purpose subverted. Whether or not it is reasonable to expect that political parties could carry out studies of alternative tax forms and offer to their civil servants a list of worked out alternatives to choose from, or whether the politicians leave the task of selecting alternatives to the civil service, someone has to perform this task. To what extent have parties examined alternatives before taking office, and to what extent in the absence of such a step have their instructions to the civil service explicitly requested them to perform the task?

The evidence that we have collected provides examples of failure to explore alternatives fully before a party makes a commitment to tax reform. The experience of CT is instructive in this respect. The differences between the parties over CT emerge as primarily ideological.

The Labour Party argued for CT (classical system) on the grounds that it would promote retention and re-investment of profits and that it would tax the recipients of dividends more heavily. The Conservatives, for their part, contended that CT (classical) was unfair double taxation of dividends; that the tax did not necessarily mean more retention, and if it did, it did not necessarily mean more investment. More significantly, the Conservatives argued that the quality of investment would be lower and that it was better for dividends to be distributed and the funds reinvested through the market.

Professor Geoffrey Whittington (1974), after reviewing the evidence about the effects of CT, concluded that fiscal discrimination against dividends 'probably' increased the savings available for reinvestment by companies and 'possibly' involved a worse allocation than if the funds were allocated through the capital market.

However, the empirical evidence offers no grounds for strongly held views on the subject of differential dividend taxation; the issue involves qualitative margins which are too narrow for our present data and techniques to deal with. Nevertheless, strongly held views on the subject will persist because it arouses prejudices arising from fundamental value judgements concerning the virtues or evils of a free market system.

In other words, there was little to choose between either method of CT in terms of its capacity to encourage economic growth. If there is so little difference between the effects of the two tax instruments, why go to all the time, trouble and expense to change from one to the other? Attachment to a particular view of the way in which the world should work, rather than an exploration of the best means of encouraging economic growth, is the primary explanation for the see-saw changes in tax policy between the two systems of corporation tax. But the Conservatives also felt the need to placate their supporters among the business community who preferred the imputation to the classical system.

With their other two new taxes, VAT and the TC scheme, the Conservatives appeared to take greater care over the exploration of different approaches and alternatives. If the Green Paper is to be taken as a guide, in proposing VAT the Conservatives had at least considered other general sales taxes which might have met the same objectives. And the whole history of VAT's adoption as party policy is one of slow appreciation of its merits as an alternative. Certainly there was no great enthusiasm for it at the start (p. 112). At least, with VAT, the Conservatives cannot be accused of inadequate preparation and their manifesto commitment was a conditional one (p. 74). Similarly with the TC scheme. Given the complexity of the task, it was not surprising that they did not enter office with a fully worked out scheme for a

negative income tax; but they had not made a hard manifesto commitment to introduce such a scheme.

It might be argued that details of alternative schemes ought to be left,
and indeed necessarily have to be left, to the civil service. That then
raises the question, 'Do governments ask the civil service to do this
kind of examination before committing themselves to a policy instrument?' Our evidence shows that this is not always the case. The WT
affords a clear illustration. There is a revealing exchange in the Wealth
Tax Select Committee between Mr John Pardoe MP and Mr W.H.V.
Johnson, a Commissioner of Inland Revenue giving evidence to the
Committee. Mr Pardoe indicated some of the alternative ways of
reducing inequality in the distribution of wealth and then put the
question to Mr Johnson.

Mr Pardoe   Have the Board of Inland Revenue ever done a study to
show which of these methods would achieve the fairer distribution of
wealth that is apparently desired?
Mr Johnson   Not a study in that sense. These are questions that are
always under examination, of course. You cannot study the effect of a
particular tax until you have it.

Mr Pardoe repeated the question with a particular reference to the
alternative effects of a donor and a donee-based death duty and put the
specific question:

Mr Pardoe   Have you actually been asked for this study?
Mr Johnson   Not a formal study, no.

(Minutes of Evidence, p. 11)

Our study suggests that, like the parties, the departments (at least
those concerned with the making of tax policy) lack adequate machinery for designing new tax instruments. Apart from lack of research
facilities, there is an explanation why the revenue departments depart
from the requirements of strict rational choice. The main function of
the revenue departments is to administer and collect existing taxes.
They have a direct function to perform, unlike some of the other central
government departments, such as DES and to some extent Environment and the DHSS (with respect at least to its Health Service functions) which are organisations for the coordination of the work of
de-centralised agencies. Such coordinating departments generally have
some policy development and research machinery which is a natural
consequence of the nature of their work.

Because they have an operating function the revenue departments
can monitor the effects of current tax policy and can provide Ministers

with some 'feedback' on problems encountered in the administration of taxes as a by-product of their primary task. But they do not have a detailed research capacity. It is therefore not surprising to find that the revenue departments, being largely operational departments, have, by and large, exhibited an incremental approach to tax policy-making. Given the constraints of their primary functions they can only build on what they already know and have directly experienced. Our study does not reveal that there is either great enthusiasm, or powerful machinery, in the revenue departments for turning them over to a new function of tax designer. Members of revenue departments concerned with aspects of tax policy are much more interested in the practical details of collection. And the Treasury, too, eschews the role of tax designer. The exchange in the Wealth Tax Select Committee quoted above is not only a reflection of the failure of a new government to seek from the departments the information required for a more rational approach to the choice of policy instruments, but also, almost certainly, an indication of the limited capacity of the departments to supply that sort of information.

Thus an incremental approach to the search for new tax instruments is perhaps inevitable if the task of constructing new taxes is left largely to the departments. Their prime task is to keep the system going and the revenue flowing in. Their job is to apply the policies that Ministers have brought into office with them, and their views of what can be done is, of necessity, somewhat confined to what they have done successfully in the past. It is this feature which creates the pressure towards incrementalism in the revenue departments, not some natural inborn and indefinable conservatism of the bureaucrat. Thus, in the reform of death duties the Inland Revenue undoubtedly favoured continuing a donor-based death duty on the lines of the previous estate duty. Similarly with wealth tax: in their evidence to the Select Committee the Inland Revenue were clearly battling very hard for a WT with a high threshold administered along with CTT and in very much the same kind of way that CTT and estate duty had been administered in the past. This administrative practice is in marked contrast to the wealth taxes on the continent of Europe, which have much lower thresholds and are administered along with income tax rather than with death duty. This is no unimportant detail, and shows the effect of past and current practice on the capacity of the administrative machine to respond to new demands put upon it by politicians.

We see therefore, in the stages between choice of objective and design of instrument, a departure from the requirements of pure rational choice of means because alternatives are not fully explored and, in the case of taxes at least, the functions of the departments create attitudes among their members inimicable to the full exploration of all possible alternatives. Unless, therefore, the party takes the initiative in selecting optimum instruments incrementalism must remain an inevitable feature of tax policy-making.

As we showed in Chapter 1 there are other more 'political' ways in which policy-making may depart from the requirements of pure rational choice. The effects of the intervention of interest groups and the likelihood of bargaining between governments and powerful groups outside the political institutions, or between groups of politicians vying for power within political institutions, can all push a policy away from its optimal path. What does our study of tax policy-making reveal of the operation of such political forces?

As we have shown, interest groups enter the tax policy-making process at all of its stages, but especially after the policy goal has been determined by the political party. They may enter when a government has decided in principle to legislate, but wants first some wider consultation, perhaps when a Green Paper is issued, or if a select committee is appointed, and they also play a considerable part during the consideration of legislation by Parliament. The number of groups active at every stage of the tax policy-making process has increased over the period we have studied and many of the better organised among them have developed well-oiled machinery for responding to governments' tax proposals. How far can we say that our study shows evidence of group politics at work determining the form of taxation in Britain?

Whilst it has helped to improve the rationality of policy-making by increasing the flow of information, the effect of the more 'open' approach to tax policy-making adopted in the later part of this period has been to encourage pressure group activity. It drew groups closer into the policy-making process, and it brought their claims under the light of publicity. Before the move to more 'open' policy-making the mysteries of tax policy development remained shrouded in budget secrecy. Now that more channels of communication have been opened up groups have taken advantage of their opportunities.

The new routes by which groups have been able to press their claims over this period, as well as the extension of consultation with Departments and Ministers, include the changes made in the procedure of the House of Commons, and the use made of select committees and standing committees to consider taxation. Until the mid-1960s the successive changes to House of Commons procedure ensured a steady progression of governmental power. Procedure was altered bit by bit from about the middle of the nineteenth century to the end of the 1950s to produce a finely tuned legislative instrument for processing government inspired legislation while permitting the minimum number of changes to its provisions. The pace of procedural change in this direction reached its peak in the 1945–50 Government. For a number of reasons (some associated with general dissatisfaction with the by then lowly position of the ordinary member – see Robinson, 1978) the new taxes introduced in the 1960s put a great strain upon the Finance Bill procedure. Ill-designed and too hastily introduced legislation had to be heavily amended by the Government itself. The new taxes were more and more complex, contained more of significance to particular interest groups, and were less easy for members or Ministers to understand. Parliament was no longer willing to accept any and all legislation the Government put before it.

From the mid-1960s procedural reform through the greater use of committees (pp. 187 and 217) drew interest groups more into the Parliamentary arena than before; the nature of the legislation was in any case more likely to attract their attention (indeed, at least one interest group owed its existence to the proposed wealth tax); and as well as seeing some advantage for themselves by entering the parliamentary arena the interest groups with their specialist knowledge of the details of taxation were able to assist Members by the provision of information. All these factors together, therefore, combined to increase the impact of interest groups on the new tax legislation over the ten-year period. Thus by 1974 the picture is rather different from that described by Surrey (1957) who asserted that (in the 1950s) British governments could expect their tax legislation to emerge from the House of Commons pretty much as it went in. He noted a sharp contrast between the capacity of interest groups to determine tax policy outcomes in the USA and their relative lack of power in Britain. That judgement may still be broadly true as a relative statement, but the absolute description of the influence of pressure groups must be amended. From our study there is definite evidence of the operation of group politics, and of political bargaining. Even the 'redistributive' taxes, such as wealth tax, were considered not under the pre-1960 procedures designed for effective party government, but under procedures of policy-making more appropriate to the making of 'distributive' policies. Our study shows that where a government sets out to achieve a redistributive policy then it would do best to stick to the traditional British machinery of government if it wants to achieve its objective. On the other hand the procedures followed showed up the difficulties and deficiencies in the proposals.

The experience with CTT and WT provides some support for the views of some Labour Party supporters of the 1930s that socialism is unlikely to come by parliamentary means.

The parliamentary machine is certainly an admirable instrument for the preservation of capitalism. The capitalist class, having got into power, has very naturally devised a system of government designed to make fundamental changes difficult, if not impossible, by purely constitutional means . . . It is based on the assumption that a government, in the course of its tenure of office, will have just a few major measures to bring forward . . . But if we set out to introduce socialism we shall need to make . . . changes affecting the entire social system. This is utterly impossible within the traditional limits of parliamentary procedure.

(Sir Stafford Cripps, *Can Socialism Come by Constitutional Means?* Socialist League, 1935)

G.D.H. Cole and Harold Laski, both writing in the 1930s, took the same view. If a party wants to introduce socialism then it is not likely to do so if it embarks upon an open policy-making process by which the ruling class and its interest groups can water down all socialist proposals. Our analysis of the Labour Party's attempts at redistributive policies shows that failure may certainly have been in part due to lack of clear objectives, but that it was also due to the routes they took through the policy-making process.

Apart from the outstanding example of interest group influence afforded by the bargain struck with the trades unions over wealth tax (which failed to materialise) we can find a number of instances where pressure from interest groups or the media led to important changes in the details of taxation. The zero-rating of children's clothes for VAT is one such. Another is the agricultural concessions made to CTT in the years following its introduction. A further good illustration of the effect of pressure groups is to be found in the substantial modifications that the majority of the members of the Select Committee on Wealth Tax made to the proposals in the Green Paper and in particular the much more generous treatment which all the main reports of the Select Committee proposed should be accorded to heritage objects. And the effect of pressure group politics on the fate of the TC scheme should not be underestimated either. There was therefore evidence of an increase in the capacity of groups to influence the outcomes in tax policy-making. The role of the TUC in obtaining WT as part of a political bargain is the outstanding example, but the significant position of farming, forestry and business interests in the economy enabled them to obtain advantages. The effect might suggest the operation of a pluralist model in British tax policy-making. It could also, bearing in mind the nature of concessions gained, be suggestive of a 'ruling class' at work. But on the other hand groups with no apparent power beyond that of the ballot box, like the CPAG, have also been able to affect the details of tax legislation through the opportunities afforded to groups.

Concessions to pressure groups, whilst they may show political wisdom or good judgement (for the non-socialist at least!) are almost always contrary to rational policy-making. Thus the zero-rating of children's clothes created anomalies; large children fail to benefit and small adults can benefit. If the object had been to give more support to parents, the rational choice would have been to increase child allowances rather than to complicate VAT with this additional zero-rating and awkward borderline. Similarly, the concessions under CTT for farmers are of doubtful benefit to the industry. Such tax concessions tend to become capitalised. In other words, the market reacts to them by equalising the post-tax rate of return, which implies that as a result of the concession land prices rise still further. This gives a once and for all benefit to existing owners of land, makes it more difficult for farm managers to acquire their own farms, and, by virtue of the higher value, partly offsets the tax concessions by putting the farm into a higher CTT bracket.

Such tax reliefs for particular parties are all in the nature of tax expenditures (or 'distributive' policies, see pp. 17–18). In their costs to the Exchequer they are the equivalent of outright subsidies, and the benefits frequently go to the better off. They complicate taxes and create anomalies, and make further reform more remote by introducing 'losers' (Willis and Hardwick, 1978).

Our analysis of the tax policy-making process has revealed a number of departures from the conditions of rational choice. It also suggests that incrementalism and pluralism are the most significant models in explaining such departures. Firstly, it is clear that there is not always political rationality in the selection of goals and objectives. Secondly there is something of a policy vacuum in the design of optimum instruments because alternatives are not fully explored. Thirdly there is evidence of incrementalism in the departments. And finally there is evidence of the growing influence of groups. These last three encourage deviations from the model of rational economic choice of instruments. There is also some suggestion of lack of political judgement where goverments have taken inappropriate procedures for their objectives. While it may be appropriate to have a more 'open' policy-making process and to bring in more groups for consultation when an economic objective (such as regulation) is sought, it may hinder the realisation of political objectives, especially those intended to have a redistributive effect. The picture of tax policy-making is summed up well in the words of C.E. Lindblom as 'an untidy mixture of social interaction and limited analysis' (1977, p. 323).

Where does this leave us? How effective has this untidy and imperfectly rational tax policy-making process been in practice? What is the fate of the eight new taxes? Is there any evidence that they did, in spite of the way they were made, achieve their objectives?

Of the eight, two, CT (classical version) and SET, have been repealed and two others, the TC scheme and the WT, have never made the statute book. Whatever criticisms can be made of the TC scheme, and they are substantial ones, there can be little doubt that had it been implemented in 1977 as the Conservatives planned, the muddle and overlap between the social security and the income tax provisions would have been less than they were in 1982. Moreover, and it is a salutory thought that may even give the CPAG cause to pause, the 1982 levels of child benefit were actually below the revenue-neutral levels of the TC Green Paper of 1973.*

What of the four taxes that remain on the statute book? CT (imputation version) remains much in the form in which it was introduced, except that stock relief has bitten into the revenue to be derived from it. However, there is much dissatisfaction with the tax, mainly as a result of the high levels of inflation; and a new very general Green Paper was published early in 1982 about the possible reform of CT. Whilst CGT, too, remains on the statute book, some important changes have been made since 1966 in the principle of the tax, one of the most significant being the abandonment of the deemed realisation rule for property transferred at death. This change has accentuated the locking-in effect of the tax and means that if assets are held for a sufficient time, CGT is avoided altogether. Again, as with CT, CGT remained an unsatisfactory and much criticised levy, mainly because of the effect of high rates of inflation. Successive Chancellors considered indexation and tapering as possible remedies, but resorted simply to short-term expedients until in 1982 Sir Geoffrey Howe provided for indexation against further inflation. The effect is to favour large property holders in contrast to the small man holding his assets in building society or savings bank accounts. As for CTT – partly at the hands of Mr Healey himself, but still more at the hands of Sir Geoffrey Howe and Lord Cockfield – it has been transformed from the intention announced by Mr Healey of a severe tax on the rich not subject to avoidance to a much lighter tax which, now that cumulation has been restricted to ten years, is not so very different in terms of its avoidability from the old estate duty with its seven year *inter vivos* provision. With death duties we have come full circle.

Only VAT remains with something like its old structure and probably increasing in acceptability with age. But even VAT was subject, under the Labour Government, to a change of principle through the introduction of the higher rate, which in turn was abolished by the Conservatives on their return to power; and there is continual concern about the high compliance costs for small businesses. We are left with a pretty pitiful result from two decades of enthusiastic tax reform.

*TC remains on the political agenda, however. It is favoured by the SDP/Liberal Alliance and the Conservatives have not wholly abandoned it. WT, also, is almost certain to feature in the next Labour Party manifesto and might be in the SDP/Liberal Alliance programme as well.

And no one could claim that these taxes met their stated objectives. Apart from SET and (since 1979) VAT, they raised little, if any, new revenue. Indeed, they were not expected to do so; but they were intended either to promote economic growth or to redistribute income and wealth. There has been no discernible economic growth as a result of SET, or CT in either of its forms. And there are few signs of redistribution of income and wealth as a consequence of CGT and CTT. Indeed, those who have the funds and the wit can probably protect themselves at least as successfully from the need to pay taxes as they could before the reforms of capital taxation were mooted.

Although the tax policy-making process cannot be said to have been effective in restructuring the British tax system over the past fifteen years the cost of the process has been incalculable in total. It would be possible to put a figure on some of the costs. For example, offices were acquired in anticipation of the WT but then disposed of again. Perhaps, more significant in the long term, the computerisation of income tax was postponed because of the expected introduction of the TC scheme and is only now going ahead. But beyond these specific costs, there is the whole party political and administrative effort in designing the new taxes. It would be impossible to calculate the man and woman hours involved in party meetings, research departments, publication of pamphlets, departmental planning committees and so on. The cost in parliamentary time too has been immense, many extra days allotted to Finance Bills and three long select committee inquiries. Then there is the effect of the chopping and changing of tax policy upon industry and commerce and individuals, especially accountants and solicitors, who need to expend considerable intellectual effort to master the complex practical details of a new tax and whose intellectual capital is rendered obsolete by its repeal. All this amounts to an immense waste of time and effort and detracts from the ability of those concerned to engage in productive work. It also generates many inequities for tax-payers, e.g. between the heirs of those who die just before or just after some new CTT or CGT concession.

Can such waste of time and effort be avoided in the future? Could the tax policy-making process be improved?

Some recommendations for better tax policy-making

There have been many recommendations for reform over the years and our study has emphasised some of these and highlighted some previously unnoted deficiencies. Because the party stage is so crucial with new taxes it is desirable that there should be changes in the parties to improve political rationality in the selection of objectives. This is a matter for the parties themselves. They could pay more attention to the internal logic of their ideological positions and refine and clarify their objectives. Then, to assist parties in the difficult bridging exercise between objectives and instruments there needs to be an increase in the quality, quantity and range of inputs to party policy-making machines. The possibilities that have been put forward include the provision of state money to political parties or as general support for Opposition and backbench MPs, secondment of academics to party organisations for longer-term research, increased contacts between Opposition parties and the revenue departments, increased use and a more systematic circulation of Opposition Green Papers, increased assistance for back-bench MPs which would both enable them to play a further part in select committees on taxation and parliamentary debates on the sub-ject, and would also make them more resistant to exaggerated claims from pressure groups. It is not only pressure groups which make exaggerated claims. One senior official in the revenue services held that part of the blame for the imbalance between effort and outcome with respect to tax reform lay with academics, over enthusiastic in their advocacy of new taxes. Our study in part supports this contention. The remedy lies, as we have suggested, in securing practical as well as academic inputs to the parties, so that they are more discriminating in their commitments. It would also help if academics who press for tax changes devoted more time to mastering tax details as well as tax principles and if there were increased contact between academics and government departments. The injection of 'political advisers' into the departments (already to some extent in operation) could be extended to smooth the links between party objectives and design of tools.

At the departmental stage when the taxes must be designed in detail so that they can be successfully administered and collected, the biggest need is probably for a committee on the tax side corresponding to PESC on the expenditure side; a committee of civil servants drawn mainly, but not exclusively, from the two revenue departments and the Treasury. This committee would be in a position to look ahead in the light of anticipated revenue needs and to place proposals for new taxes into the context of the present and likely future tax system. Treasury concern hitherto has been predominantly with tax as an instrument of demand management, and although the revenue departments each have divisions concerned with broader issues and take a forward look at the tax system, each is restricted to its own sphere of taxation. The fiscal policy division of the Treasury might form the nucleus of the proposed committee, but would require considerable strengthening. Such a committee should also be responsible for drawing up a tax expenditure budget as in the USA and Canada. In the case of some new taxes, such as the TC scheme and capital taxes, there are considerable effects upon other departments, and thus there is a greater need for coordination with those Departments (DHSS and Industry) whose area of concern is affected by proposed changes in the tax structure. The existence of an 'outer circle', those who need to be brought into the tax policy-making process, needs more explicit recognition.

Probably the most useful single reform of the legislative process would be either to introduce new taxes in a separate Bill as an invariable rule,* or alternatively to take much of the detail out of the annual Finance Bills by providing for a second Finance Bill each year which would deal largely with technical details and have been the subject of extensive prior discussion with tax specialists. Such a Bill might go through more or less on the nod. This kind of proposal is by no means novel and has received the backing of the present Chancellor, Sir Geoffrey Howe, when Shadow Chancellor. It is not likely, however, to appeal to any party that wants to ensure firm adherence to ideological principles throughout the legislative process, and would be regarded as weakening the government's control over legislation.

Further measures are required to improve the process of discussion of new taxes before they reach the legislative stage. A number of proposals for reform have been put forward that are relevant to this issue. Firstly (and this would affect policy-making both in the Departments and Parliament) it has been suggested that a unified Budget would better enable both Government and Parliament to get to grips with the effects and relationships between taxation and expenditure. At present the expenditure side is planned over five years in PESC, but taxation is simply altered in response to spending needs. The unified budget would be one step towards recognition of the overall structural effects of taxation and would also relate tax expenditures to both taxation and explicit spending programmes. Secondly, it has been suggested that there should be more regular procedures for a pre-legislative stage of consultation and discussion in Parliament. A Green Paper before a new tax could become an invariable rule and the contents of the Green Paper could be such as to ensure that the significant questions were answered (p. 197). Publication of the Green Paper could be followed by consideration either in *ad hoc* select committees, or preferably, in a permanent select committee of the House of Commons specialising in taxation. This committee would concentrate on the structure of taxation and develop an expertise among its members. Such a committee would parallel on the MPs' side the tax committee that we have proposed on the civil service side. If this proposal is not acceptable – and it has been rejected on several previous occasions – the experiment in the 1980–82 parliamentary session of sending Bills to

---

*For the origin of the practice of including all taxes for the year in a single Finance Bill, see footnote on p. 108.

standing committee *before* they appear on the floor of the House could be extended to cover new tax legislation.

Then there are the suggestions for more open government. There may well be a good argument for budget secrecy with respect to changes in tax rates to prevent forestalling: the determination of some tax rates are matters which the Chancellor may need to leave until the last minute for purposes of demand management. That apart, the arguments for budget secrecy, especially in the case of new taxes for which a commitment has already appeared in a manifesto, and an announcement may have already been made in the House itself, seem to be, at best, shallow. If government is open and information is available to all, then there is no fear that some may obtain financial advantage from inside knowledge. One suspects that one of the reasons why Chancellors like Budget secrecy is for the dramatic effect they can have on Budget day in pulling their surprises out of the red box; but the price to be paid may be too high when these surprises include ill-designed legislation of a long-term nature. In any case, the element of Budget secrecy with respect to tax changes has been severely eroded in practice over the past few years through the operation of the cabinet leak.

Finally, some have suggested that the besetting evil of British policy-making (including economic policy-making) lies in the operation of adversary politics (Finer, 1975) and that the remedy is electoral reform. We have found some evidence of the costs of adversary politics in our study of tax policy-making. Governments have undone much of what previous incumbents have established. The costs are great and the benefits are few. But, ultimately, the reform of the electoral system alone cannot make for better policy-making if parties cannot decide exactly what they want and take appropriate steps to make sure that they get it. Even if electoral reform were to encourage the development of consensus about what to do, its effects might be defeated unless policy makers are armed to overcome incrementalism from the bureaucratic machine and the influence of well-organised interest groups.

References

Books and articles

Allison, Graham T. (1969), 'Conceptual Models', *American Political Science Review* **63**, September, 689–718.

Allison, Graham T. (1971), *Essence of Decision: Explaining the Cuban Missile Crisis*, Boston, Little Brown.

Atkinson, A.B. (1972), *Unequal Shares: Wealth in Britain*, London, Allen Lane, The Penguin Press.

Atkinson, A.B. (1973), *The Tax Credit Scheme and the Redistribution of Income*, London, IFS.

Bach, G.L. (1971), *Making Monetary and Fiscal Policy*, Washington, Brookings.

Bachrach, P. and Baratz, M.S. (1962) 'Two Faces of Power', *Amercian Political Science Review* **56**, December, 947–952.

Barber, A. Lord. (1975), *Great Britain's Tax Credit Income Supplement*, New York, Institute for Socio-Economic Studies.

Barker, A. and Rush, M. (1970), *The Member of Parliament and his Information* London, Allen and Unwin.

Bauer, Raymond A. and Gergen, K.J. (1968), *The Study of Policy Formation*, New York, Free Press, Macmillan.

Bentley, Arthur F. (1949), *The Process of Government*, Evanston, Principia Press (Chicago, University of Chicago Press, 1908).

Braybrooke, David (1974), *Traffic Congestion goes through the Issue Machine*, London, Routledge.

Break, George F. and Pechman, Joseph A. (1975), *Federal Tax Reform: The Impossible Dream?* Washington, Brookings.

Breton, Albert (1974), *An Economic Theory of Representative Government* London, Macmillan.

Brittan, S. (1971), *Steering the Economy*, revised edition, Harmondsworth, Penguin Books.

Brittan, S. (1975), 'The Economic Contradictions of Democracy', *British Journal of Political Science* **5**, April, 129–159.

Brown, C.V. February (1968), 'Misconceptions about Income Tax and Incentives', *Scottish Journal of Political Economy* XV, 1–21.

Brown, C.V. and Jackson, P.M. (1978), *Public Sector Economics* Oxford, Martin Robertson.

Buchanan, James M. and Tullock, G. (1962), *The Calculus of Consent*, Ann Arbor, University of Michigan Press.

Butler, D. and Rose, R. (1960), *The British General Election of 1959*, London, Macmillan.

Clarke, Sir Richard (1973), 'The Long-term Planning of Taxation', in *Taxation Policy* (eds. B. Crick and W. Robson), London, Penguin.

Clayton, G. and Houghton, R.W. (1973), 'Reform of the British Income Tax System', in *Taxation Policy* (eds. B. Crick and W. Robson), London, Penguin.

Coombes, David (1966), *The Member of Parliament and the Administration*, London, Allen and Unwin.

Coombes, David *et al.* (1976), *The Power of the Purse: The Role of European Parliaments in Budgetary Decisions*, London, Allen and Unwin/PEP.

Crick, B. and Robson, W. (eds.) (1973), *Taxation Policy*, London, Penguin.

Cripps, Francis *et al.* (1981), *Manifesto: A Radical Strategy for Britain's Future*, London, Pan Books.

Cripps, Sir Stafford (1935), *Can Socialism come by Constitutional Means?* Socialist League.

Crosland, A. (1964), *The Future of Socialism*, revised edition. First published 1956, London, Cape.

Crossman, Richard (1977), *The Diaries of a Cabinet Minister*, vol. III, London, Hamish Hamilton and Jonathan Cape.

Curry, R.L. and Wade, L.L. (1968), *A Theory of Political Exchange: Economic Reasoning in Political Analysis*, Englewood Cliffs, N.J., Prentice Hall.

Cyert, Richard M. and March, James G. (1964), *A Behavioural Theory of the Firm*, Englewood Cliffs, N.J., Prentice Hall.

Dahl, R.A. (1971), *Polyarchy*, New Haven, Yale University Press.

Dalton, H. (1923), *The Capital Levy Explained*, Labour Publishing Co.

Dalton, H. (1955), 'Taxation and Social Justice', *New Statesman and Nation*, July.

Dean, Peter N. (1971), 'Do you Pay too much Tax?', *The Technical Journal*, March.

Downs, Anthony (1957), *An Economic Theory of Democracy*, New York, Harper and Row.

Downs, A. (1960), 'Why the Budget is too Small in a Democracy', *World Politics* xii, 54–63.

Downs, A. (1967), *Inside Bureaucracy*, Boston, Little Brown.

Dror, Yeziekiel (1968), *Public Policy-Making Re-examined*, San Francisco, Chandler.

Else P.K. and Marshall G.P. (1979), *The Management of Public Expenditure*, London, Policy Studies Institute.

Finer, S.E. (ed.) (1975), *Adversary Politics and Electoral Reform*, London, Anthony Wigram.

Fisher, N. (1973), *Iain Macleod*, London, Andre Deutsch.

Friedman, Milton (1962), *Capitalism and Freedom*, Chicago, University of Chicago Press.

Hatfield, M. (1978), *The House the Left Built: Inside Labour Policy-making 1970–76*, London, Victor Gollancz.

Hayhoe, B. (1968), *Must the Children Suffer?*, Conservative Political Centre.

Heclo, Hugh and Wildavsky, Aaron (1975), *The Private Government of Public Money*, London, Macmillan.

Heidenheimer, Arnold J., Heclo, Hugh and Teich-Adams, Carolyn (1976), *Comparative Public Policy: The Politics of Social Choice in Europe and America*, London, Macmillan.

Howe, Sir Geoffrey (1977), 'The Reform of Tax Machinery', *British Tax Review*, No. 2.

Ilersic, A.R. (1962), *The Taxation of Capital Gains*, London, Staples Press.

Johnson, Nevil (1966), *Parliament and Administration: The Estimates Committee 1945–65*, London, Allen and Unwin.

Johnstone, Dorothy (1975), *A Tax Shall be Charged*, London, HMSO.

Jordan, Grant (1977), 'Grey Papers', *Political Quarterly*, **48**, no. 1.

Kaldor, N. (1955), *An Expenditure Tax*, London, Allen and Unwin.

Kaldor, N. (1956), *Indian Tax Reform*, New Delhi, Ministry of Finance, Government of India.

Kaldor, N. (1958), 'Reform of Personal Taxation', *The Accountant*, April.

Kaldor, N. (1966), *Causes of the Slow Rate of Economic Growth of the United Kingdom*, Cambridge, Cambridge University Press.

Keegan, William and R. Pennant-Rea (1979), *Who Runs the Economy? Control and Influence in British Economic Policy*, London, Temple Smith.

King, A. (1972), 'How the Conservatives Evolve Policies', *New Society*, July 20.

Lasswell, Harold (1951), *Politics: Who Gets What, Where, How?*, Glencoe, Ill., Free Press.

Lees, Dennis, (1967), 'Poor Families and Fiscal Reform', *Lloyd's Bank Review*, October.

Lewis, Alan, Pleming, Carole, and Sandford, Cedric (1979), *A Survey of Attitudes Towards Wealth, The Wealthy and the Proposed Wealth Tax*, Occasional Paper, no.1, Bath University, Centre for Fiscal Studies.

Lindblom, Charles, E. (1955), *Bargaining: The Hidden Hand in Government*, Santa Monica, California, Rand Corp.

Lindblom, Charles E. (1959), 'The Science of Muddling Through', *Public Administration Review* **19**, 79–88.

Lindblom, Charles E. (1977), *Politics and Markets*, New York, Basic Books Inc.

Lindberg, Leon (1977), 'Energy Policy and the Politics of Economic Development', *Comparative Political Studies* **10**, October, 355–383.

Lowi, T. (1964), 'American Business, Public Policy, Case-Studies and Political Theory', *World Politics* **16** July, 677–715.

Mackintosh, J.P. (1968), *The British Cabinet*, second edition, London, Stevens.

Mackintosh, J.P. (1973), 'The House of Commons and Taxation', in *Taxation Policy* (eds. B. Crick and W. Robson), London, Penguin.

Meade, J.E. (1964), *Efficiency, Equality and the Ownership of Property*, London, Allen and Unwin.

Meade, J.E. (1972), 'Poverty in the Welfare State', *Oxford Economic Papers* **24**.

Miliband, Ralph (1969), *The State in Capitalist Society*, London, Weidenfield and Nicolson.

Millar, David (1976), 'Parliamentary Control of Taxation in Britain', in *The Power of the Purse: The Role of European Parliament in Budgetary Decisions* (ed. David Coombes), London PEP/Allen and Unwin, 198–214.

Mills, C.W. (1956), *The Power Elite*, New York, Oxford University Press.

Morley, Lord (1903), *Life of Gladstone*, London, Macmillan, New Edition 1905, 2 vols.

Mosley, P. (1981), 'The Treasury Committee and the Making of Economic Policy' *Political Quarterly* **52**, July, 348–355.

Musgrave, Richard A. and Peacock, Alan T. (eds.) (1958), *Classics in the Theory of Public Finance*, London, Macmillan.

Niskanen, William (1974), *Bureaucracy: Servant or Master?*, London, Hobart Paperback, IEA.

O'Connor, James (1973), *The Fiscal Crisis of the State*, New York, St. Martin's Press.

Olson, M. (1965), *The Logic of Collective Action: Public Goods and the Theory of*

Groups, Cambridge, Massachussets, Harvard University Press.

Patten, C. (1980), 'Policy-making in Opposition', in *Conservative Party Politics* (ed. Henry Zig-Layton), London, Macmillan.

Pechman, Joseph, A. (1977), *Federal Tax Policy*, third edition, Washington, Brookings.

Pemberton, J.E. (1969), 'Government Green Papers', *Literary World* LXXI, no. 830, August.

Pliatzky, Leo (1982), *Getting and Spending*, Oxford, Basil Blackwell.

Polsby, N. (1960), 'How to Study Community Power: The Pluralist Altern-ative', *Journal of Politics* 22, August, 174–84.

Prest, A.R. (1967), *Public Finance*, third edition, London, Weidenfeld and Nicolson.

Ramsden, J. (1980), *The Making of Conservative Party Policy: The Conservative Research Department since 1929*, London, Longman.

Reddaway, W.B. (1970), *The Effects of Selective Employment Tax: First Report, The Distributive Trades*, London, HMSO.

Reddaway, W.B. (1973), *The Effects of Selective Employment Tax: Final Report* Cambridge, Cambridge University Press.

Redlich, Josef (1908), *The Procedure of the House of Commons*, London.

Reid, G. (1966), *The Politics of Financial Control*, London, Hutchinson.

Revell, J.S. (1969), 'Changes in the Social Distribution of Property in Britain during the Twentieth Century', *Department of Applied Economics Reprint Series*, no. 295.

Rhys Williams, B. (1967), *The New Social Contract*, London, Conservative Political Centre.

Rhys Williams, Lady J. (1943), *Something to Look Forward To*, London, McDonald.

Riker, William H. (1962), *The Theory of Political Coalitions*, New Haven, Yale University Press.

Robinson, A. and Ysander, B.C. (1981), *Flexibility in Budget Policy: The Changing Problems and Requirements of Public Budgeting*, Stockholm, Work-ing Paper no. 50, The Industrial Institute for Economic and Social Research.

Robinson, Ann (1978), *Parliament and Public Spending*, London, Heinemann Educational Books.

Rose, Richard (1974), *The Problem of Party Government*, London, Macmillan.

Ryle, Michael (1967), 'Parliamentary Control of Expenditure and Taxation', *Political Quarterly* 37, 435–446.

Sandford, C.T. (1971), *Taxing Personal Wealth*, London, Allen and Unwin.

Sandford, C.T. (1979), 'The Wealth Tax Debate', in *The Wealth Report* (ed. Frank Field), London, Routledge and Kegan Paul.

Sandford, C.T., Godwin, M.R., Hardwick, P.J.W. and Butterworth, M.I. (1981), *Costs and Benefits of VAT*, London, Heinemann Educational Books.

Sandford, C.T., Pond, C. and Walker, R. (eds.) (1981), *Taxation and Social Policy*, London, Heinemann Educational Books.

Sandford, C.T., Willis, R. and Ironside, D.J. (1973), *An Accessions Tax*, London, IFS.

Sandford, C.T., Willis, R.M., and Ironside, D.J. (1975), *An Annual Wealth Tax*, London, IFS.

Schultze, Charles L. (1968), *The Politics and Economics of Public Spending*, Washington, Brookings.

Sewill, Hilary (1966), *Automatic Unit of National Taxation and Insurance*, London, Conservative Political Centre.

Sharkansky, Ira (1969), *The Politics of Taxing and Spending*, Indianapolis, Bobbs-Merrill.

Simon, H.C. (1957), *Administrative Behaviour, A Study of Decision-making Processes in Administrative Organisations*, second edition, Glencoe, Ill., Free Press.

Stewart, Michael (1977), *The Jekyll and Hyde Years: Policies and Economic Policy since 1964*, London, J.M. Dent.

Stutchbury, O. (1968), *The Case for Capital Taxes*, Fabian Tract, 388.

Stutchbury, O. (1977), *Too Much Government?* Ipswich, The Boydell Press.

Surrey, Stanley, S. (1957), 'The Congress and the Tax Lobbyist: How Special Tax Provisions Get Enacted', *Harvard Law Review* 70, May, 1145–1182.

Surrey, Stanley, S. (1973), *Pathways to Tax Reform*, Cambridge, Mass., Harvard University Press.

Truman, D. (1951), *The Governmental Process*, New York, Knopf.

Vickers, Sir Geoffrey (1965), *The Art of Judgment*, New York, Chapman and Hall, Basic Books.

Walkland, S.A. (1968), *The Legislative Process in Great Britain*, London, Allen and Unwin.

Wallace, Theo and Wakeman, John, (1968), *The Case Against a Wealth Tax*, London, Bow Group.

Weber, Max. (1947), *The Theory of Social and Economic Organisation*, trans. by A.N. Henderson and Talcott Parsons, New York, Free Press.

Wheare, Kenneth (1955), *Government by Committee*, Oxford, Oxford University Press.

Wheatcroft, G.S.A. (ed.) (1965), *Estate and Gift Taxation – A Comparative Study*, London, Sweet and Maxwell.

Whittington, G. (1974), *Company Taxation and Dividends*, London, IFS, Lecture Series no.1.

Willis, J.R.M. and Hardwick, P.J.W. (1978), *Tax Expenditures in the United Kingdom*, London, IFS.

Wildavsky, A. (1975), *Budgeting: A Comparative Theory of Budgetary Processes*, Boston, Little Brown.

Wilson, H. (1971), *The Labour Government 1964–70*, London, Michael Joseph.

Wootton, Graham (1970), *Interest Groups*, Englewood Cliffs, N.J., Prentice Hall.

Publications by political parties
Party manifestos and campaign guides for each election, and Annual Conference reports for each party.

Labour party
See also Stutchbury (1968).

Signposts for the 60s, 1961 Conference Paper.
Into the Seventies, 1969.
Agenda for a Generation, 1969.
Labour's Economic Strategy, 1969.
Labour's Programme, 1973.

Conservative Party
See also Hayhoe (1968), Rhys Williams (1967), Sewill (1966) and Wallace and Wakeman (1969).

Report of the VAT Task Force, Conservative Central Office, 1977.

Liberal Party
Ownership for All, 1938.

Public documents and reports

White Papers
Corporation Tax, Cmnd 2646, 1965.
Taxation of Capital Gains, Cmnd 2645, 1965.
Selective Employment Tax, Cmnd 2986, 1966.
Reform of Personal Direct Taxation, Cmnd 4653, 1971.
Value Added Tax, Cmnd 4929, 1972.
Reform of Corporation Tax, Cmnd 4955, 1972.
Capital Transfer Tax, Cmnd 5705, 1974.

Green Papers
The Development Areas: A Proposal for a Regional Employment Premium, 1967.
Value Added Tax, Cmnd 4621, 1971.
Reform of Corporation Tax, Cmnd 4630, 1971.
The Future Shape of Local Government Finance, Cmnd 4741, 1971.
Taxation of Capital on Death: A Possible Inheritance Tax in Place of Estate Duty, Cmnd 4930, 1972.
Proposals for a Tax Credit System, Cmnd 5116, 1972.
Wealth Tax, Cmnd 5704, 1974
The Taxation of Husband and Wife, Cmnd 8093, 1980.
Alternatives to Domestic Rates, Cmnd 8449, 1981.
Corporation Tax, Cmnd 8456, 1982.

Other
Royal Commission on the Income Tax, 1920, Cmd 615, London, HMSO.
Committee on the National Debt and Taxation, 1927, Cmd 2800, London, HMSO.
Royal Commission on the Taxation of Profits and Income, 1955, *Final Report*, Cmd 9474, London, HMSO.
Control of Public Expenditure (the Plowden Report), 1961, Cmnd 1432, London, HMSO.
NEDC, *Conditions Favourable to Faster Growth*, 1963, London, HMSO.
NEDC, *Value Added Tax*, 1969, second edition, 1971, London, HMSO.
Report of the Committee on Turnover Taxation (the Richardson Report), 1964, Cmnd 2300, London, HMSO.
Report of the Fiscal and Financial Committee (Neumark Report on Tax Harmonisation), 1963, EEC, Brussels.
Report of the Royal Commission on Taxation (the Carter Report), 1966, Ottawa, Queen's Printer,
Negative Income Tax, 1974, Paris, OECD.

Report of the Committee on Financial Aid to Political Parties (The Houghton Report), 1976, Cmnd 6601, HMSO.

The Structure and Reform of Direct Taxation (The Meade Report), 1978, London, Institute of Fiscal Studies, 1978.

The Taxation of Net Wealth, Capital Transfers and Capital Gains of Individuals, 1979, Paris, OECD.

Budgetary Reform in the U.K. (The Armstrong Report), 1980, Oxford University Press for the IFS, London.

Annual financial statements and budget reports. Trades Union Congress, *Economic Review* (annually from 1967).

Select Committees on Taxation

Select committees on taxation matters in the twentieth century
(1) Select Committee on Income Tax 1906 (365) ix.659.
(2) Select Committee on Luxury Duty 1918 (101) iv.43.
(3) Select Committee on Land Values 1919.
(4) Select Committee on Increase of Wealth (War) (1920) (102) vii.33.
(5) Report of the Joint Select Committee on the Income Tax Bill 1918 (95) iv.1.
(6) Select Committee on Betting Duty 1923 (139) v.I.
(7) Select Committee (1) Excise Duties
       (2) Medical Stamp Acts 1936.
(8) Select Committee on Corporation Tax 1970/71, HC 622.
(9) Select Committee on Tax Credit 1972/3, HC 341.
(10) Select Committee on Wealth Tax 1974/5, HC 696.
       Vol. I Report and Proceedings on the Committee, Vols. II and III Minutes of Evidence, vol. IV Appendices to Minutes of Evidence.

Other select committees that have looked at tax-related matters; the 'elastic terms of reference' examples

Estimates Committee
Third Report 1945/6, PAYE, HC 171.
Fourth Report 1956/7, Customs and Excise Collection, HC 128.
Seventh Report 1960/1, Schedule A, HC 245.
1968/9, Cost of Collection, HC 474.

Expenditure Committee, General Sub-Committee
Ninth Report, 1974, Public Expenditure, Inflation and the Balance of payments, HC 328.
First Report, 1975/6, The Financing of Public Expenditure, HC 69–1.
Fourth Report, 1975–76, The White Paper 'Public Expenditure to 1979/80 (Cmnd 6393)', HC 299.
Eleventh Report, 1976/7, The Civil Service, HC 535.

Committee of Public Accounts
Fifth Report, 1975/6, HC 556 (Cost of Administering the Tax System).
Tenth Report, 1976/7, HC 536 (Cost of Administering the Tax System).
Sixth Report, 1977/8, HC 574 (Taxation of Directors' Remuneration, Taxation of Partnerships, VAT, Computerisation of Tax Work).

Select Committee on Procedure
First Report 1958/9, HC 92
Expediting the Finance Bill 1962/3, HC 190

Expediting the Finance Bill 1964/5, HC 276
Financial Procedure 1965/6, HC 122
The Finance Bill 1966/7, HC 382
Dates of the Session – the Financial Year 1967/8, HC 356
Scrutiny of Public Expenditure and Administration 1968/9, HC 410
Expediting the Finance Bill 1969/70, HC 302
First Report 1970/71, HC 276

Index